Remembering the Holocaust and the Impact on Societies Today

Remembering the Holocaust and the Impact on Societies Today

Simon Bell

PEN & SWORD
HISTORY

First published in Great Britain in 2021 by
Pen & Sword History
An imprint of
Pen & Sword Books Ltd
Yorkshire – Philadelphia

ISBN 978 1 39901 209 6

Printed and bound in the UK by CPI Group (UK) Ltd,
Croydon, CR0 4YY.

Pen & Sword Books Limited incorporates the imprints of Atlas,
Archaeology, Aviation, Discovery, Family History, Fiction, History,
Maritime, Military, Military Classics, Politics, Select, Transport,
True Crime, Air World, Frontline Publishing, Leo Cooper, Remember
When, Seaforth Publishing, The Praetorian Press, Wharncliffe
Local History, Wharncliffe Transport, Wharncliffe True Crime
and White Owl.

For a complete list of Pen & Sword titles please contact

PEN & SWORD BOOKS LIMITED
47 Church Street, Barnsley, South Yorkshire, S70 2AS, England
E-mail: enquiries@pen-and-sword.co.uk
Website: www.pen-and-sword.co.uk

Or

PEN AND SWORD BOOKS
1950 Lawrence Rd, Havertown, PA 19083, USA
E-mail: Uspen-and-sword@casematepublishers.com
Website: www.penandswordbooks.com

*To my wife Bev, my sons Josh and Ben, my sister Jane,
and to other family members for always being there.*

Contents

About the Author

Simon Bell is a former mental health nurse with over thirty-seven years of National Health Service experience in England. The first fifteen years of his career were spent working in hospitals, and included – in old asylum care – looking after severely damaged, elderly survivors of the war in Europe and of the Holocaust. That instilled a long-held interest not just in the Holocaust but in the consequences of all hatred and discrimination. He has dealt with survivors of other genocides and also liberators who bear the emotional scars of the horrors that they witnessed. For some twenty-two years he worked with mentally disordered offenders, and has dealt with most types of criminal behaviour, witnessed the consequences of crime, and dealt with those who have experienced the extremes of personal trauma. Aside from a clinical role, he also helped to deliver training to a range of mental health, social care and criminal justice workers in helping them to understand and deal with people who have experienced childhood and adult sexual abuse. In the summer of 2016 Simon retired from health care. He has an MA in Second World War Studies: Conflict, Societies, Holocaust. Simon prides himself on not having any formal allegiance to political parties or groups. He is however, dedicated to challenging intolerance and hatred in all of its forms, and seeking to ensure that those who might be targeted or oppressed are supported and cared for. He has been fortunate to have visited Auschwitz-Birkenau on a number of occasions, as well as other sites in Poland that are associated with the Holocaust. He has spent time meeting and exchanging correspondence with survivors and scholars, historians and others who share his interest.

Acknowledgements

Acknowledgements are offered to the academic staff at the University of Wolverhampton, most notably Professor Dieter Steinert, Professor John Buckley, Professor Stephen Badsey and Evelyn Price. Further acknowledgements are offered to visiting lecturers, the Holocaust Educational Trust, and, most importantly, to survivors of the Holocaust and descendants from that period who have offered so much inspiration and encouragement.

Introduction

The impetus for this book was the decision by the Polish government, in early 2018, to criminalize any suggestion of Polish citizens being involved in the crimes of the Holocaust during the period of the German occupation and subjugation of that territory.

To learn from the past, it is necessary to understand it. Verifiable facts are not disputable, but the interpretation of history is ever changing as new knowledge and information comes to light. This book is not intended as a hostile criticism of any nation. Its intent is to explore the nature of national memory, particularly in nations that experienced the Holocaust first-hand, and how that memory can be sculpted to fit a narrative which sits more comfortably in the psyche of those who are descendants of both perpetrator and victim. Poland is a country I hold with great affection. I am fortunate to have Polish friends and to have visited sites in that land where the dedication to history is robust, respectful and diligent. However, part of this book will address the role of some Poles during the Holocaust when that country was occupied and subjugated by the regime of Nazi Germany. Recent legislation in Poland has sought to criminalize language and writings that suggest any participation by Poles in the Holocaust during the period of German occupation. Some of the background to this legislation stems from understandable frustration with the continued reference to camps such as Auschwitz as 'Polish camps' rather than the more factually correct 'German Nazi camps'. Poles are concerned that the deliberate or inadvertent reference to the camps in this way misrepresents their nation and implies Polish responsibility not just for the function of the camps, but also for other crimes against Jews during the Nazi occupation of the country. Supporters of the legislation correctly observe that, from the commencement of the occupation in 1939, until the liberation in 1945, the Polish state ceased to exist. As such, it cannot be held accountable for the crimes committed by Germany in that territory. Opponents of the legislation raise concerns that a law that criminalizes discussion about the role of Poles in the Holocaust is, in effect, a legislative means of denying accepted historical facts. There are points of debate in both of these perspectives. Antisemitism existed in Poland before the German occupation, it continued during the war, it was on occasion demonstrated by violence, hostility and even murder, and was apparent not just in the immediate post-war period, but has continued to manifest itself since.

Of course, as will be shown, the finger of criticism has been pointed at many nations that were occupied by the Nazi regime, and nations that did not experience that trauma directly. It was not just the violent acts that led to the suffering and death of millions, it was the refusal to help, the willingness to support German forces, the entrenched antisemitism that also manifested in the United States and Great Britain, the lack of interest, the indifference, the antipathy and hostility. These factors empowered and enabled the Nazi regime as much as collusion, collaboration and participation in the crimes.

The Polish Holocaust law has been referred to as *ius Grossii* in reference to Jan T. Gross, the Polish-born historian who has written extensively about the Jedwabne massacre and the pogrom at Kielce.[1] The historian Jan Grabowski argues that the law will seek to repress any scholarship perceived as being inconvenient to the Polish state and that it will repress popular and academic debate.[2] Grabowski asserts that the law will also revive the debate about Polish culpability for the pogroms at Jedwabne and Kielce, whilst concurrently allowing Poland to use the moral shield it is offered through the number of citizens deemed to be Righteous Among Nations.[3] Furthermore, by excluding Poles from acts of violence and criminality during the Holocaust, there is a justifiable assertion that this constitutes distortion or even denial of history.[4] Deniers are said to 'distort, falsify, and pervert the historical record'.[5] Deniers such as David Irving refer to 'revisionism', whereas historians such as Robert Jan van Pelt refer to 'negationism'.[6]

The historian Tony Judt observed that Eastern Europe after 1945 had more to remember and also more to forget than Western Europe. Most Jews were killed in the East and local populations participated in the murders. The authorities in the post-war east of the continent appear to have taken care to erase aspects of wartime history – including the Holocaust – and in the official rhetoric and textbooks Jews are not part of the story.[7]

This book will argue that the Holocaust law in Poland is flawed. It is a misguided piece of legislation that seeks to criminalize the reference to Polish camps whilst also criminalizing any suggestion in speech or writing that implies complicity, collusion, collaboration or participation by Polish citizens in the crimes of the Holocaust. Such legislation risks denying historical fact and stifling honest research and discussion. The integrity of scholarly and historical investigation and debate requires that accepted and enforced narratives must be open to challenge and examination. Legal restrictions are unnecessary. A more constructive approach could be taken by the Polish government in encouraging education. Of course, erroneous reference to Polish camps is wrong, but this can be addressed more effectively by consistent use of more appropriate language and an acceptance that occasionally people make mistakes without malice. Additionally, there is required an open acknowledgement that in Poland, as elsewhere in occupied Europe, citizens were involved in the crimes of the Holocaust. This does not deny the Poles (or others) their status as victims of occupation and conquest. It does not deny that many Poles (and others) assisted Jews at great personal risk. It does accept that consistent interpretation of historical truth – based on multiple primary and secondary sources – is needed to show the entirety of the wartime experience and the relationship of occupied nations with their Jewish communities.

It can be asserted that the Polish Holocaust law relates to the Polish state which clearly ceased to function as an independent and autonomous country during the years of occupation. However, it is also asserted that elements of the state were maintained, such as the police, fire service, and civic offices. Whilst these may have been strictly under the control of the occupying forces, with risk of punishment or death for failing to cooperate, it will be shown that there was collaboration and collusion at many levels of Polish society. Furthermore, some of the harm against Jews was initiated by Poles independently of German influence or control. Civilians and Polish agents of the occupied state were involved in anti-Jewish crimes. It is accepted that whilst the state of Poland was occupied, elements of the nationhood of Poland – its culture, religion and people – were contributing factors in some of the crimes of the Holocaust. Some people, in the territory that was pre-war and wartime Poland, also identified as Germanic through heritage and the areas where they lived.

Antisemitism, hostility, violence and pogroms in Poland existed before and after the war. The murders peaked during the occupation, and the period in its immediate aftermath, but they are part of a continuum in Polish history. The hostility towards Jews is demonstrated in acts committed at all levels of Polish society, and forms part of a much greater picture. It becomes difficult to exonerate and exculpate an entire nation state when the evidence against some of its citizens is so clear. This is of relevance to the broader issue being discussed and is why, on balance, the Holocaust law, and any similar attempt to legislate honest research or discussion, is flawed.

In contemplating the value and validity of the primary and secondary research material used, it has been essential to consider a number of factors. As identified in the body of this book there are debates on survivor and other witness testimonies. These debates relate to when the testimony was recorded, who documented the testimony, whether there were linguistic or cultural factors that impacted upon the quality of witness testimony recording, issues linked to polyphony (literally multiple voices), the motivation of the witness and the person or organization taking the testimony, plus, of course, the quality of memory. This does not seek to invalidate witness testimonies, which are an invaluable resource to historians in understanding personal observations and experiences. There may be discrepancies in recollections of specific details, but the general nature of similar accounts adds to their validity and usefulness. As Viktor Frankl stated in *Man's Search for Meaning*: 'This book does not claim to be an account of facts and events but of personal experiences, experiences which millions of prisoners have suffered time and time again.'[8]

The literature referred to herein has identified elements of criminality by Poles and other citizens of Europe prior to, during and following the German occupation. The criminality during the period of occupation is essential to the arguments being put forward about the Polish Holocaust law. It shows that even in subjugated and occupied Poland, there was still a sense of nationhood and of 'being Polish' amongst many of the population. Whilst some Poles who cooperated with Germans in the persecution of Jews may have done so due to fear, threats, danger and inducements, there were also Poles – civilians and those in positions of authority – who cooperated, colluded and collaborated enthusiastically with – and at times acted independently of – the Germans in causing harm to the Jewish population.

This book will question whether, despite being subjugated societies occupied by a brutal regime, some citizens participated in the crimes of the Holocaust. As the evidence suggests there was Polish participation, then the Holocaust law, as it is phrased, may be seen as a legal effort to exculpate wrongdoers and control debate, when a more honest ownership of the past would better serve the truth of history and the potential to learn about the past with healthy research, investigation and integrity.

The aims of the sections on Poland are to assess and consider available historical evidence and to view how this, in the context of the Holocaust law, would suggest that alternatives to punitive legislation would be a more constructive approach. Furthermore, this book will consider other nations (but not all of those occupied by Nazi Germany) and how their governments and citizens were involved, unwittingly or not, in the Holocaust. Similarly, although the United States was not occupied, and mainland Britain remained free; these two nations are also worthy of discussion. Both, as victors in the Second World War, have assumed the moral high ground (often justifiably so), but have erased from popular history the criticisms that they may deserve. This book will also look at the issue of negationism, or Holocaust denial, its origins and notable protagonists, and how laws are used to address this issue whilst also maintaining the liberty of free speech and expression. Additionally, other chapters will seek to address aspects of the Holocaust in France, the Netherlands, Ukraine and Hungary.

This book is not just about Poland, although, because of the Holocaust law, Poland has merited extensive discussion. It is also about the bigger picture of the Holocaust involving occupied and unoccupied countries. Efforts have therefore been made to seek out a range of balanced and credible sources. Where possible, multiple sources have been used to address individual issues. In considering this information, the analysis will seek to understand not just the Holocaust law of Poland, but also the sometimes-selective perspective on history and national memory demonstrated by many nations.

This book will firstly consider the law as it was introduced by the Polish government earlier in 2018. It will examine the responses to the law from a range of organizations and individuals. The concept of Holocaust denial or negationism will be discussed, along with how legislation seeks to protect free speech and those who may be harmed by it. It will consider the United States and Great Britain, neither of which had their mainland territories occupied, but which, through acts or omissions may have facilitated or enabled some of the crimes of Nazi Germany. France, the Netherlands, Ukraine and Hungary are discussed to consider how they responded as territories that were subjugated and may also have cooperated with the Nazi regime. The evidence of Polish crimes during the period of German occupation will be examined, particularly regarding notable pogroms and the actions of civilians, the police, the fire service, civic officials and the Catholic Church. Post-war crimes and pogroms in Poland will be looked at up to the political unrest of 1968. The attitudes of Poles and the citizens of other nations towards Jews historically, including established antisemitism with religious, cultural, social and political influences will be examined. Ultimately there will be consideration of antisemitism in Poland and elsewhere today and whether all of this, as a whole, demonstrates a continuum of hatred that has at times manifested in hostility, violence and murder. This book will consider and discuss how the integrity and legitimacy of historical research and debate should allow for criticism of nation states and the citizens therein. It may at times be necessary to invoke legal sanctions to protect historical truth, but education and information are more useful tools. It must be accepted that widely acknowledged historical truths are fluid, rather than being universally static. They are open to review and reinterpretation as new sources of information become available. Legal sanctions hinder honest research and discussion. Finally, the book will consider what, if any, lessons have been learned from actions and inactions of various nations during the Nazi period, and whether there are warnings and alarm bells that should be ringing due to the rise of populist and ethno-nationalism today.

It will be apparent that there is only limited discussion on the specific crimes of Nazi Germany against Jews, other minorities, and citizens of the occupied territories. There is no intention to avoid or diminish German culpability. Those crimes are well researched and documented in thousands of books. The varying levels of culpability of other nations are less frequently addressed, and that is what this book seeks to do.

The Holocaust, and the German antisemitism that enabled it, was undoubtedly a complex series of events, ultimately stretched over much of the twelve-year duration of Nazi rule in Germany and the hostile invasions of many sovereign nations. The responsibility for the Holocaust rests primarily and absolutely with Germany, the German people of that time and the Nazis. That is accepted in these pages and will not be addressed at any great length. The motivations for the brutal antisemitic policies, the dehumanizing and slaughter of the Jews of Europe, the murder of others due to racial heritage, religion, sexuality, political beliefs, gender, age and physical or mental ability have been addressed and explored in many other works.

The Holocaust did not begin with the ghettos, execution pits, gas chambers and Jew hunts; it began with words and attitudes. Nazi hostility towards Jews was not restricted to Europe and found receptive and enthusiastic supporters across many occupied and unoccupied territories. There was also indifference towards Jews, a lack of concern about their plight, plus opportunism and willing exploitation demonstrated by thousands and possibly millions of others. Of course, there was resistance, and the undoubted courage of many who tried to help and save their Jewish friends, neighbours, colleagues and family members. There was also the harmfulness of the bystanders, and of those who either failed to recognize what was happening, or did not act when the evidence of extreme harm was clear. That will be the subject of the following pages. It is intended to look at the response – and the culpability – of some of the nations involved in that period, some of which were occupied territories, some of which were not. Learning from the history of genocide requires not just an examination of the obvious criminals and wrongdoers, it also requires an examination of those who enabled, empowered, facilitated, encouraged, supported, participated and permitted the crimes to occur. A picture emerges of wider guilt and responsibility.

The Jews of Europe were transported to the Nazi concentration and death camps in Poland, and as such, the reality is that much of the carnage took place on occupied Polish territory. Of course, many Poles assisted Jews, but, as will be shown, some were involved in the criminality against that population. The same can be said to be true of other countries that were occupied. It is accepted that citizens of occupied territories were victims of the Nazis – because they were – but it needs to be said that some were involved in the crimes that the Nazis committed against Jews.

History rightly perceives the Allied forces as liberators. They are the countries that held the moral high ground against the Axis powers, and held them to account after the war. The United States was not occupied, but questions have been asked whether it could have done more to save lives after details of the plight of Jews became known, whether it could have done more to accept refugees, whether some of its citizens and businesses profited from and supported Nazi Germany, and whether the United States turned a blind eye to some of the crimes of former Nazis when they were seen as being potentially useful in the post-war years. The mainland of Great Britain was not occupied, but the Channel Islands (Crown Dependencies) – geographically proximate to the British mainland – were. Those isolated islands experienced some of the harshness of German occupation. The facility to resist may have been limited due to the isolation of island life, but there was also collusion and cooperation. The British government has continued to receive criticism for policies of appeasement in the 1930s, when the dangers Germany posed were becoming apparent. The British were also aware of the existence of Nazi concentration and death camps, long before Allied forces began to liberate them in 1944 and 1945. It is questioned whether more could have been done to stop or hinder the mass murder of Jews. Some British activists supported the Nazi regime. These issues will be addressed. France, the Netherlands, Ukraine, Hungary and Poland are cited as former occupied countries that experienced the full force of Nazi-led brutality and genocide. There was resistance here too, help was offered to Jews, and many gave their lives trying to save others. But there was also collusion, cooperation, enablement, participation and active involvement in the denouncement, exploitation and murder of Jews. For those who were not actively participating or resisting, there was the willingness and the ability to just stand by, which helped seal the fate of so many innocent lives. The people of those nations bear no guilt today for the crimes that took place over seventy-five years ago. But lessons need to be learned, and that requires an honest acceptance of the wrongdoings of the past.

Chapter 1

Legislation: The Polish Holocaust Law

The controversy over the flawed, false and wholly inaccurate description of Auschwitz and other camps as 'Polish death camps' has existed for a long time. It came to a head somewhat in May 2012 following a speech at the White House in Washington by President Obama. In a ceremony during which the president was posthumously awarding the Medal of Freedom to Jan Karski, he referred to Karski as having

> served as a courier for the Polish resistance during the darkest days of World War II. Before one trip across enemy lines, resistance fighters told him that Jews were being murdered on a massive scale and smuggled him into the Warsaw Ghetto and a Polish death camp to see for himself. Jan took that information to President Franklin Roosevelt, giving one of the first accounts of the Holocaust and imploring to the world to take action.[1]

Radek Sikorski, the Polish foreign minister, referred to this as being indicative of ignorance and incompetence.[2] There was condemnation from Poles who insisted that Obama should have referred to a 'German death camp in Nazi-occupied Poland'.[3] The White House quickly tried to repair the damage of any offence caused, with Tommy Vietor, the National Security Council spokesman, stating that Obama had 'misspoke' and that he was actually referring to Nazi death camps in Poland.[4] The White House claim that Obama had mistakenly used the phrase that caused offence seems plausible, but the reaction is an indicator of Polish sensitivity around this subject.

Of course, Polish sensitivity predates the speech by President Obama. Writing a postscript to a conference held at Princeton University in 2010, Benjamin Frommer described a letter that was read on behalf of the consul general, Ewa Junczyk-Ziomecka. The letter, and the theme it introduced, was scathing of any suggestion of Polish culpability during the Holocaust.[5]

On 6 February 2018, Poland's president, Andrzej Duda, signed what has been referred to as the Holocaust bill into law. The law introduced the potential for courts to issue fines or up to three years' imprisonment for those who describe Nazi camps in Poland as 'Polish death camps' or for suggesting 'against the facts' that the nation or state of Poland was complicit in the genocide committed by Nazi Germany during the Second World War. The Polish government asserted that the law was necessary to protect the reputation of the people and state of Poland as victims of the Nazis.[6] The deputy prime minister of Poland, Beata Szyldo, defended the bill by stating: 'We, the Poles, were victims, as were the Jews. It is the duty of every Pole to defend the good name of Poland.'[7] The ruling Law and Justice Party government appears to have introduced the law as part of a series of attempts to assert legal control over the media.[8]

Article 55 a. 1 of the law states:

> Whoever publicly and against the facts ascribes to the Polish Nation, or to the Polish State, the responsibility or complicity for Nazi crimes committed by the III German Reich as defined by article 6 of the International Military Tribunal attached to the international agreement concerning the prosecution and the punishment of the leading war criminals of the Axis powers, signed in London on August 8, 1945, or other crimes that constitute crimes against peace, humanity, or war crimes, or [whoever] otherwise greatly diminishes the responsibility of the real perpetrators of these crimes, shall be subject to fine or three years of imprisonment. The sentence shall be made public. It will be, of course, the police and the prosecutors who will, henceforth, establish the facts and what can be said and written.[9]

The reference to 'publicly and against the facts ascribes to the Polish nation' is the key point of the law that part of this book is concerned about. Whilst, in legal terms, the Polish state autonomy ceased during the years of occupation, with the government in exile and the military decimated, Poland, as a self-defining entity of nationhood and as a land inhabited by those who considered themselves to be Poles, continued to exist. Some of those Poles, whether coerced, forced, threatened, induced, or acting independently, were involved in the crimes of the Holocaust. Polish Justice Minister Zbigniew Ziobro opined that the law was a means of defending the good name of Poland wherever an act of slander or falsification occurred. Furthermore, he suggested that this applied to the generations of Poles who had suffered most at the hands of the Nazi Germans who were 'accused of complicity, and sometimes – however incredible it may sound – even of agency in the perpetration of the Holocaust, which was committed on the occupied soil of Poland by the Germans'.[10]

It is accepted that the population of Poland suffered greatly under German occupation. It is further accepted that many Poles assisted Jews, and that Poland has more people recognized by Yad Vashem as Righteous Among Nations than any other country, with 6,863 individuals cited out of the 26,973 honoured up to 1 January 2018.[11] However, there were Poles who assisted the German occupiers in a range of ways, and who committed acts that directly led to harm and death of oppressed Jews. This will be addressed further, but it is of importance that the law as introduced by the Polish government may seek to exculpate en masse all Poles, rather than accepting as historical fact that some Poles were responsible for criminality linked to the Holocaust. It is also worth noting the observation by Jan Grabowski that some in Polish society may actually trade on the 'righteous' label bestowed on so many, and that being seen as a nation of sacrifice and compassion during a time of suffering has national and international benefits. Based on the evidence that Poles were involved in crimes against the Jews, this may be seen as what Grabowski describes as 'a pernicious historical fallacy'.[12]

The international response to the Holocaust Law was notable for the collective condemnation of the proposal and for the wide range of voices offering opinions. Somewhat surprising was the tone used by some in seeking to defend the law. As *The Times of Israel* reported on 21 March 2018, some of Poland's more conservative lawmakers accused American and Israeli Jews of using objections to the law as a pretext for getting money off the Polish state for Jewish property that had been seized during the era of communist rule.[13] Jerzy Czerwinski, a Polish senator, said on state radio on 19 March 2018 that he saw the opposition to the law as having a 'hidden agenda' and suggested that 'we know that Jewish circles, including American, but mostly the state of Israel, are trying to get restitution of property or at least compensation'.[14]

Senator Orrin Hatch, a Republican in the United States Senate, who is also on the board of directors of the U.S. Holocaust Memorial Museum issued a statement via a press release on 19 February 2018, in which he said:

> As a member of the United States Holocaust Memorial Council and a strong supporter of Israel, I urge President Duda and Prime Minister Morawiecki to reject this terrible affront to the Jewish people. This bill, which was drafted as the world commemorated International Holocaust Remembrance Day, would be severely detrimental to those in Poland who want to learn from the dark lessons of the past and work towards a brighter future.[15]

Yad Vashem issued a number of statements on the issue. On 27 January 2018, a press release stated that Yad Vashem opposed the legislation which if felt would potentially blur the historical truth of assistance the Germans received from Poles during the Holocaust.[16] The statement accepted that the term 'Polish death camps' was a misrepresentation, but asserted that restrictions on statements by scholars regarding any Polish complicity are a serious distortion.[17] On 1 February 2018, Yad Vashem offered a response to the law after it was passed the previous day by the Polish Senate. The statement reiterated the opinion that the law would blur historical truths due to the limitations it placed on suggestions that there was any complicity by segments of the Polish population in crimes against Jews during the Holocaust.[18] It further added that the correct way to combat the use of the term 'Polish death camps' was by educational activities rather than criminalizing such statements.[19] Additionally, it was suggested that the law passed by the Polish Senate could potentially jeopardize open discussion about any role the Polish people played in the persecution of Jews during the Holocaust.[20] On 6 February 2018, President Duda ratified the law, which drew a further response from Yad Vashem. The statement issued by Yad Vashem on that day warned once again that the wording of the law was likely to result in history being distorted because of the limitations it would place on public expressions about the collaboration of some parts of the Polish population.[21] Concern was expressed that the law would jeopardize free and open discussion about the role of Poles in the murder and persecution of Jews during the

Holocaust, and that there could be implications in the areas of Holocaust research, remembrance and education.[22]

Criticism of the law came from other notable Holocaust education and remembrance organizations, suggesting a general consensus of opinion. Karen Pollock, on behalf of the Holocaust Educational Trust in the United Kingdom, issued a statement accepting the importance of accurate language when discussing the Holocaust, but noted that the law 'has the potential to inhibit objective research, discussion and education about the history of the Holocaust and could open the door to revisionism and denial'.[23] The United States Holocaust Memorial Museum (USHMM) suggested that 'the law would chill a free and open dialogue addressing Poland's history during the Holocaust, including in Polish schools and universities as well as the media'.[24] The USHMM acknowledged that many Poles had helped and saved Jews but stated that some Poles were complicit in crimes against Jews, including identifying, denouncing, hunting down, blackmailing and plundering Jewish property.[25] Furthermore, as will be addressed later, in July 1941, Poles in Jedwabne participated in the murder of hundreds of their Jewish neighbours.[26]

Stephen Smith of the USC Shoah Foundation was equally vociferous in his observations. He suggested that the new law showed weakness and insecurity, adding that facing historical facts did not need to come at the expense of national pride.[27] Furthermore, he observed that the reputation of Germany had been enhanced by taking responsibility for crimes during the Holocaust and that Poland would do well to follow its example.[28]

In a similar vein, the Wiener Library in London accepted Polish objections to the phrase 'Polish death camps', but noted that 'the historical evidence that some Polish people committed or were complicit in large scale robbery, violence and murder of Jewish men, women and children is incontestable. The work of reputable scholars leaves us in no doubt about this. Any law that discourages the scholarly investigation of historical events is a bad law'.[29]

In a further criticism offered by a high-profile Holocaust remembrance organization, the International Holocaust Remembrance Alliance (IHRA) also stepped into the fray. As with the aforementioned statements there was acceptance that the phrase 'Polish death camps' is incorrect, with Poland being justified in demanding that it stop being used. The IHRA offered support for this stance.[30] There was acceptance too that the Polish state ceased to exist during the period of German occupation, but also suspicion was raised about any law which seeks to protect national honour.[31] It noted that some of the Poles who protected Jews from Germans also had to protect them from fellow Poles.[32] Concern was rightly raised that the legislation could hinder honest research, particularly in Poland.[33] The statement proposed a demand that the law should be annulled in preference for free inquiry, research and publication, as well as the right to err.[34]

The strength of feeling about the law is such that Efraim Zuroff, the Eastern Europe director of the Simon Wiesenthal Centre, observed: 'Everybody knows that many, many thousands of Poles killed or betrayed their Jewish neighbours to the Germans, causing them to be murdered.'[35] Some concern has been expressed that external pressure on the Polish government could have a negative impact. Piotr Buras, of the European Council on Foreign Relations Warsaw office, suggested that the criticism could 'push the government further into the position of a besieged fortress, strengthening both the nationalistic rhetoric ... and the nationalistic mood of the country'.[36]

The defensiveness of the Polish government is understandable when it comes to the erroneous use of the phrase 'Polish death camps'. However, it is wrong to deny any complicity or collaboration by Poles in the harm caused to Jews during the Nazi period of occupation. The massacre at Jedwabne in 1941 is a key example of Poles killing their neighbours.[37] As the *Financial Times* observed, open debate about facts and causes, is necessary in developing understanding and reconciliation.[38] Failure to accept the historical evidence of the past promotes risks of being accused of revisionism – an allegation directed at the governments of Hungary, China, Russia and Turkey, each of which is accused of manipulating history for political purposes – and also of curtailing free speech and criminalizing criticism.[39]

The law appears to be an attempt to exculpate the entirety of the Polish nation and to claim that there was no involvement of Poles in the crimes of the Holocaust. Konstanty Gebert, a Polish journalist, challenged the authorities to prosecute him by stating that 'numerous members of the Polish nation are co-responsible for certain Nazi crimes committed by the Third Reich'.[40] Jedwabne has already been mentioned as a key example of Polish culpability and will be discussed in more detail later. The Polish-born historian Jan Grabowski estimates that Poles were responsible for some 200,000 Jewish deaths during the Nazi occupation.[41] He also found multiple examples of Jews who had fled the ghettos only to be betrayed to the Germans by Poles for small rewards of food or money.[42]

The objective of the law – essentially making it illegal to suggest that there was any Polish complicity in the crimes of the Holocaust – is, according to President Duda, intended to guarantee the 'dignity and historical truth' for Poland.[43] However, as Jan T. Gross eloquently argues, the reality is that the law is intended to falsify history. If the issue was the erroneous and offensive use of the phrase 'Polish death camps', then legislation could quite simply have dealt with that; but by broadening the area of concern to include any implication of Polish complicity and collusion, the legislators have potentially stifled research, opinion and discussion about the factual evidence of history.[44] Additionally, the focus of the law has caused offence to survivors and families of those who were harmed by Poles during the period of Nazi occupation.[45] It has been observed that the new law is 'not only unwise and unjust: it is unnecessary'.[46] Furthermore, it was observed in 2010, after the consul general's letter was read to a conference at Princeton University, that the good name of Poland and its people would be better served by confronting the tragedy of history.[47]

The response of Holocaust remembrance organizations, historians, politicians and the press, appears to have been universal in condemning the introduction of the Holocaust law. There is broad and correct acceptance that the use of the phrase 'Polish death camps' is wrong. Clearly these camps existed in the annexed and General Government territories of German-occupied Poland. They were the creation of the Nazi regime and were run by and on behalf of that regime. The function of the camps – slave labour and extermination – was established by the Nazis. That the camps happened to be in territory that was traditionally Polish was not at the behest of the Poles.

It is true that Poland was a victim of brutal conquest and occupation. It is true that millions of Poles suffered and died. It is also true that many Poles helped Jews and that this is acknowledged by the numbers seen as Righteous Among Nations. This alone does not exculpate the people of Poland. Mention has been made to the massacre in Jedwabne when Poles murdered their Jewish neighbours. That this event occurred is not disputed (although some may question the numbers killed and the nationality of the perpetrators). Prosecutions took place after the war and defendants were convicted. This is not open to debate. Other events occurred in which Poles collaborated and colluded with the German regime, or acted independently to cause harm. Denying these realities can be seen as an attempt to deny, revise or negate history. Criminalizing those who speak or write about such events can only stifle the integrity of research and prevent the honest assessment and recording of historical truths.

There is abundant primary and secondary source material that supports the thesis of wrongdoing by some within the Polish community, with evidence of criminality, murder, collaboration and collusion during the attempts to exterminate the Jews in the territory of Poland. Those involved as participants, instigators and supporters included the Catholic Church, community leaders, the police, citizens and neighbours. The section on Poland will explore this in more detail.

Chapter 2

Holocaust Denial

As will be shown, there has been much discussion in many countries, and across abundant legislative bodies, about the concept of free speech, and whether Holocaust denial, or more properly negationism, should be punishable or criminalized. In the United States, free speech, with some exceptions, is protected as absolute under the Constitution. This applies even if the content of the speech causes offence to others. In the countries of Europe that experienced German occupation or control in the Second World War, free speech is also valued, but the history of individual nations, and the ongoing lived experiences of some citizens, have led to legislation being imposed that allows action to be taken against those who not only promote intolerance, but who demonstrate negationism regarding the Holocaust and other genocides. One could argue that the early leaders of the United States saw the protection of free speech as being essential to the new society that they were creating. One could also argue that the United States was not occupied during the Second World War, and as such was somewhat protected from the Holocaust. However, many citizens of the United States fled from Europe during and after the Nazi era, or are descendants of Holocaust victims and survivors. Furthermore, the geographical argument is diminished when consideration is given to Canada where prosecutions have occurred for negationism. Paolo Lobba observed that free speech has been seen as a *conditio sine qua non* for tolerant societies since the earliest days of democracy in ancient Athens. However, he notes that such freedom of speech was not without risks and even Socrates was sentenced to death due to allegedly corrupting younger people.[1]

Negationism differs greatly from healthy debate and discussion among historians. It can be argued that history is neither a science nor an art, but somehow crosses both academic spheres. Artefacts and documents can be proven evidentially using a range of scientific tools and testing methods. Interpretation of facts can be debated and develop over time as more or newer information becomes available. It is accepted that even with the Holocaust – the most researched genocide in history – there will be differences of opinion between historians. The *intentionalists* suggest that Hitler came to power with the intention of murdering the Jews and that his policies were designed and introduced to achieve that aim. However, the *functionalists* suggest that the plan and policies of murdering the Jews evolved primarily from the decisions of Nazi officers in the East when faced with more Jews than they could cope with, and that Hitler only gave approval after the killings had commenced.[2] The negationists, or Holocaust deniers, do not belong to either school of thought. They seek to question the truth of the Holocaust, and will dress their approach under the supposedly legitimate guise of claiming to be revisionists. As a general rule, negationists will use one or more of the following to advance their claims about the Holocaust:

- The Nazis did not use gas chambers to murder millions of Jews.
- Most of those who died in concentration camps lost their lives due to diseases such as typhus, rather than through murder.
- Whilst crimes against the Jews may have been committed, the Nazi leadership was unaware of the nature and extent of such crimes.
- The claims that six million died are a gross exaggeration.
- Claims of atrocities against the Jews are used as a ploy to gain support for the creation of a Jewish homeland and the expropriation of Palestinian land.
- The number of Jews killed pales when compared to the number of dissidents and Christians killed in Soviet gulags.
- Academics are afraid to acknowledge and speak out about the truth for fear of being accused of antisemitism.[3]

It is interesting that those who deny the Holocaust (and other genocidal crimes) claim to be exercising freedom of thought and expression, yet they claim that those who do not share their world view are being hindered by an unprovable fear of accusations of antisemitism. They clearly seek to minimize the harm caused during the Holocaust, and to assert their own unchallengeable interpretation of events and the motives of those who disagree with them. Holocaust denial and antisemitism go hand in hand

– rarely do they occur separately. Similarly, there will be a denial that Hitler and the Nazis were 'far-right' or fascists, even when the weight of historical and political opinion suggests that those labels are appropriate. Claims will be made that the Nazis were obviously 'Socialists' because it is in the party name – Nationalsozialistiche Deutsche Arbeiterpartie (NSDAP) – but the deniers conveniently refuse to acknowledge that socialists, trade unionists and communists (the traditional left of politics) were perceived to be enemies of the Nazis, and suffered heavily during purges throughout the period of the Third Reich. Indeed, when Dachau concentration camp opened in 1933, the first inmates included many such political opponents. As the NSDAP newspaper *Völkischer Beobachter* claimed: 'The main core of the inmates of the concentration camps, are those Communist and Marxist functionaries who, as experience shows, would immediately resume their struggle against the state if set free.'[4] Furthermore, for the deniers there is also a need to defend National Socialism and fascism. The existence of the Holocaust makes National Socialism and fascism indefensible and difficult to promote as a political alternative today.[5]

When negationists and deniers question the total number of Jews killed, they ignore the consensus among most historians that the numbers are between 5 million and possibly as many as 6.5 million European Jews.[6] Robert Jan van Pelt suggests that Raul Hilberg's estimate of the total number of Jewish deaths is the most reliable, and as such he opines that the Holocaust claimed 5.1 million Jewish lives, of which, over 800,000 died due to ghettoization and general privation, 1.3 million were murdered in open-air shootings, and up to 3 million died in the camps. And of the camps, Auschwitz had the highest mortality with 1 million, followed by Treblinka with 750,000 and Belzec with 550,000 Jews.[7] Nikolaus Wachsmann suggests it can be estimated that 2.3 million men, women and children were forced into SS concentration camps (excluding camps solely for extermination) between 1933 and 1945, and of these 1.7 million lost their lives.[8] At Auschwitz, a camp central to the Nazi plan for the extermination of European Jewry, some 200,000 Jews were selected on arrival for slave labour with other prisoners, whilst it is suggested by Wachsmann that 870,000 Jewish men, women and children were selected for immediate death in the gas chambers without ever being registered in the camp.[9] Elements of the far right can seek to deny the totality of the Holocaust, and will refer to the numbers registered in Auschwitz, compared to the estimated deaths. It is a valid observation – and this is supported by most historians – that many of those who died in Auschwitz, were sent straight to their deaths without ever being registered.

The response of nation states to negationism has been varied. In continental Europe, as will be shown, many countries criminalize Holocaust denial. There is an understandable reason for this as most of the crimes of the Holocaust occurred in Europe; during the post-war years the sensitivity to those crimes, and the impact upon survivors and their descendants, dictated that a robust response was required in dealing with anything that appeared to minimize or justify Nazism. The European Union (EU) introduced the EU Framework Decision 2008/913/JHA to try to bring harmony in the criminal legislation available to combat racism and xenophobia.[10] The Decision promoted the banning, punishment and criminalization of denialism or negationism, and also for the justification and trivializing of the Holocaust and other international crimes.[11] By November 2010 the Decision was due to be implemented by member states of the EU, but as of 2014 most of the legal systems in Western Europe had not adopted it. In the countries of the former Soviet bloc the Decision inspired legislation to deal with past atrocities and crimes committed by the former communist regimes.[12] It has been argued that the vagueness of the definition of denialism as a crime is an issue further impacted by concerns about the legality of imposing laws that affect freedom of speech and historical research. It has been suggested that denialism should only be punished when it falls into the remit of existing hate-speech crimes.[13]

The EU Decision has a number of origins. A joint action was agreed by the EU in July 1996, regarding how to combat xenophobia and racism. It was proposed to strengthen cooperation between judicial systems to address denialism more uniformly, including for offences of 'public condoning, for a racist or xenophobic purpose, of crimes against humanity and human rights violations' and 'public denial of the crimes defined in Article 6 of the Charter of the International Military Tribunal of Nuremberg'.[14] Furthermore, there has been concern about speech crimes since international tribunals first applied incitement to genocide as a crime, and some scholars argue that Holocaust denial should be seen as an international crime on its own merits.[15]

The EU Decision stipulates in Article 1 that it makes punishable publicly denying, trivializing or condoning the international crimes of (a) genocide, crimes against humanity and war crimes as defined by the International Criminal Court and (b) crimes as defined in Article 6 of the Charter of the Nuremberg Trial. This broadened the scope of the Decision beyond the Holocaust. However, it has been observed that many states expressed concerns about restrictions of free speech, which resulted in multiple additional clauses needing to be added.[16]

There are limits to the Decision too, in that it addresses denial regarding genocide, war crimes and crimes against humanity, but only when the crimes relate to 'a group of persons or a member of such a group defined by reference to race, colour, religion, descent or national or ethnic origin'. It was also designed to cover conduct that 'is carried out in a manner likely to incite to violence or hatred against such a group or member of such a group' as defined in Article 6 of the Charter of the International Military Tribunal appended to the London Agreement of 8 August 1945.[17] This omitted to deal with victims targeted because of political beliefs.[18] Furthermore, although the intention of the Framework Decision appears to be noble, it has been met with difficulties for member states and courts in balancing freedom of speech and denial of genocide.[19] Additional clarity is offered in Article 1(2) where it states that 'Member States may choose to punish only conduct which is either carried out in a manner likely to disturb public order or which is threatening, abusive, or insulting.'[20] However, in recognition of the need to protect free speech, Article 7(1) states that the 'Framework Decision shall not have the effect of modifying the obligation to respect fundamental rights and fundamental legal principles, including freedom of expression and association.'[21]

Negation of genocidal crimes, it has been argued, potentially allows for them to be repeated.[22] It is quite reasonably suggested by some historians, that in states where genocide occurred or that saw the rise of perpetrators, the imposition of laws to punish negationism not only renounces the past, it also demonstrates solidarity with those who were harmed.[23]

Whether criminalizing negationism is the correct approach is open to debate. There is a common misunderstanding that one of the most high-profile court cases involving Holocaust denial was a criminal case, when in fact it was a civil court proceeding initiated by the denier, the British writer David Irving. In 2000, he brought a case against Deborah

Lipstadt, a U.S. academic, and her publishers, after she had described him as a Holocaust denier in her book *Denying the Holocaust: The Growing Assault on Truth and Memory*.[24] Irving attempted to obtain compensation for libel. He failed in his quest and lost the case. The judge described him as racist and antisemitic, and observed that it was incontrovertible that Irving qualified as a Holocaust denier.[25] The judge, Mr Justice Gray, in summing up the case against Irving noted:

> The nature and extent of the misrepresentations of the evidence together with Irving's explanation or excuses for them ... Irving's conduct and attitudes outwith the immediate context of his work as a professional historian, including the evidence of his political or ideological beliefs as derived from his speeches, his diaries and his associates.[26]

Furthermore, Gray observed that Irving's distortion of history was intentional:

> I have seen no instance where Irving has misinterpreted the evidence or misstated the facts in a manner which is detrimental to Hitler. Irving appears to take every opportunity to exculpate Hitler ... If indeed they were genuine errors or mistakes, one would not expect to find this consistency ... [T]here are occasions where Irving's treatment of the historical evidence is so perverse and egregious that it is difficult to accept that it is inadvertence on his part. Mistakes and misconceptions such as these appear to me by their nature unlikely to have been innocent. They are more consistent with a willingness on Irving's part knowingly to misrepresent or manipulate or put a 'spin' on the evidence so as to make it conform with his own preconceptions. In my judgment the nature of these misstatements and misjudgements by Irving is a further pointer towards the conclusion that he has deliberately skewed the evidence to bring it into line with his political beliefs.[27]

In a twist to the relationship between Irving and Lipstadt, in 2006 Irving appeared as a defendant in criminal proceedings in Austria. He was charged with Holocaust denial, which is a criminal offence in Austria.

Whilst Irving was in custody awaiting trial, Lipstadt called for him to be released. She sought to protect his freedom of speech even though his actions in 2000 had attempted to curtail her own rights to free expression. Irving was sentenced to three years' imprisonment.[28]

Irving had long acquired a reputation as a historian of Germany during the war, with a particular aptitude for locating hitherto unavailable primary sources. However, it was becoming increasingly apparent that he appeared to have a bias in favour of Germany and was critical of the Allies. The historian Hugh Trevor-Roper wrote in critical tones:

> When a historian relies mainly on primary sources, which we cannot easily check, he challenges our confidence and forces us to ask critical questions. How reliable is his historical method? How sound is his judgement? We ask these questions particularly of any man who, like Mr Irving, makes a virtue – almost a profession – of using arcane sources to affront established opinions.[29]

Trevor-Roper was further critical of Irving's methodology and judgement, stating: 'He may read the manuscript diaries correctly. But we can never be quite sure, and when he is most original, we are likely to be least sure,' adding that the work of Irving had a 'consistent bias'.[30]

David Irving is one among many negationists. He is part of a continuum that has existed since the end of the Second World War. It is primarily a problem among the far-right, but has found sympathetic ears on the far-left too. As Lipstadt observes, Holocaust denial has found an acceptance among neo-Nazis in both Europe and North America. They have moved from claiming that the Holocaust was justified, to now claiming that it is a hoax.[31] Additionally, Lipstadt notes that 'Extremist nationalist groups in those Central and Eastern Europe countries with a tradition of populist antisemitism have a particular attraction to Holocaust denial'.[32] Furthermore, some of these populist movements are historically linked to those who collaborated with the Nazis and as such, if they can aim to show that the Holocaust did not occur, then cooperation with the Nazis becomes less outrageous.[33]

In France, the most vocal high-profile negationist through the 1980s and 1990s was Robert Faurisson. He has argued that the massacres and the deaths in gas chambers are part of a Zionist lie that allows Israel to benefit financially. Additionally, Faurisson asserted that the gas chambers in Auschwitz and other camps never existed.[34] In Germany, Wilhelm Staeglich's book *Der Auschwitz-Mythos: Legende oder Wirklichkeit* (*The Auschwitz Myth: Legend or Reality*) was published in 1979 and tried to introduce an academic form to Holocaust denial.[35] These negationists were preceded by others. Frenchman Paul Rassinier was one of the earliest to deny reports from survivors of the camps and questioned whether there had been gas chambers.[36] In the 1960s Rassinier published *The Drama of European Jews*. Ironically, Rassinier had been a respected historian who had been detained in Buchenwald due to being a socialist. He maintained that the Holocaust was a creation of the Allies, the Soviets and Zionists.[37] It has been suggested that Rassinier mainly used unsupported assertions and dubious evidence to back up his argument, but his work provided inspiration for the next phase of Holocaust denial literature, including Irving's *Hitler's War* and the writings of Arthur Butz.[38]

In 1973, in the United States, Austin J. App wrote *The Six Million Swindle* and claimed that the total number of Jewish victims was 300,000. He went further by claiming that at least 500,000 Jewish victims of the Holocaust had actually gone to Israel.[39] Another American, professor of engineering Arthur R. Butz published *The Hoax of the Twentieth Century* (1976) which endeavoured to add academic legitimacy to Holocaust denial. It argued that more people had been killed in the Allied bombing of Dresden than in the camps, that Zyklon-B was merely used as an insecticide, that deaths were caused by typhus and that no gassings occurred in Auschwitz.[40]

A part of the denial story that has achieved notoriety was the 1988 trial of German-Canadian Ernst Zündel, in which the defence called 'expert' witnesses including David Irving and Fred Leuchter. *The Leuchter Report* was commissioned by the French negationist Robert Faurisson.[41] Fred Leuchter had cast himself as an expert on gas chambers due to his role in building execution chambers in the United States. He had illicitly obtained samples from various sites in Majdanek and the Auschwitz complex and had formed an opinion that the concentrations of hydrogen cyanide were not compatible with the levels that would be required for mass killings. His report, *The Leuchter Report: An Engineering Report on the Alleged Execution Gas Chambers at Auschwitz, Birkenau and Majdanek*, contested that the idea that six million victims had passed through the Nazi camps was a myth and that execution chambers were non-existent.[42]

Subsequent assessments of the report eviscerated it, and suggested that it was totally flawed and unreliable with absolutely no scientific value.[43] Furthermore, Leuchter's credibility and qualifications as an expert witness were cast into serious doubt. As Richard J. Evans observes (writing about the Irving–Lipstadt case): 'The Leuchter Report had long since been exposed as an incompetent and thoroughly unscientific document compiled by an unqualified person; it was completely discredited, along with its author, at the second Zündel trial in 1988.'[44]

Much of the focus of negationists has been on Auschwitz and other camps. Their efforts have been to find fault in one element of the Holocaust history, in order to cast doubt on the entirety of the accepted knowledge of the genocide. In essence, they pursue the legal maxim of *falsus in uno, falsus in omnibus*: if one part of the evidence can be shown to be false, then all of the evidence becomes unreliable. For this reason, negationists such as Irving, Faurisson, Zündel, Leuchter and others have put so much effort into trying to prove that there were no gas chambers at Auschwitz.

Negationism is not confined to the few so far cited. The *Journal of Historical Review* (JHR) is published by the Institute for Historical Review (IHR) which was founded in 1979. The IHR has sought to give legitimacy to Holocaust denial by the publication of pseudo-academic articles and essays.[45] It is dedicated to challenging the 'myth' of the Holocaust.[46] It claims not to deny the Holocaust but aims to provide a forum for revisionist history in which accepted accounts can be challenged. It adopts a stance consistent with most other negationists in this assertion of what it means by revisionist history:

> There is no dispute over the fact that large numbers of Jews were deported to concentration camps and ghettos, or that many Jews died or were killed during World War II. Revisionist scholars have presented evidence ... showing that there was no German program to exterminate Europe's Jews, and that the estimate of six million Jewish wartime dead is an irresponsible exaggeration. The Holocaust – the alleged extermination of some six million Jews (most of them by gassing) – is a hoax and should be recognized as such by Christians and all informed, honest and truthful men everywhere.[47]

David Duke, former Imperial Wizard of the Ku Klux Klan and still a prominent political force, is a Holocaust denier and continues to voice antisemitic opinions.[48] Jean-Marie Le Pen, founder of the French far-right political party Front National dismissed the gas chambers as a 'mere detail in history' and claimed that historians doubted their existence.[49] In 2018, Arthur Jones stood unopposed as a nominee for the Republican Party in the Chicago area, despite being verbal and open about his Holocaust denial, antisemitism and racism. The Illinois Republican Party denounced him, and the National Republican Congressional Committee stated that he would not be endorsed.[50]

A simple search on Google will reveal over 200,000 entries (many may be repeats) merely from typing the search word 'Holohoax'.[51] It can be asserted that the internet has been a force for good in furthering the reach of information and educational material about the Holocaust and other genocides. Conversely, the internet also allows harmful information and ideas to be accessed and shared unchallenged, and often beyond the reach of law-enforcement agencies and current, ever-developing legislation.

Holocaust denial is criminalized in some countries and tolerated as a right under free speech laws in others. In the countries of continental Europe that experienced the full murderous horror of the Nazi regime, the wounds are still raw and the sensitivity to any denial of events is strong. There is also sensitivity about the participation of citizens of once-occupied or Nazi-ruled nation states in the actions of the Holocaust. The legislation varies, but will be briefly looked at here.

Freedom of expression is protected in the European Union under Article 10 of the European Convention of Human Rights (ECHR).[52] Paragraph 1 of Article 10 states that

> Everyone has the right to freedom of expression. This right shall include freedom to hold opinions and to receive and impart information and ideas without interference by public authority and regardless of frontiers.

The ECHR accepts the right to freedom of expression, but it also acknowledges that in some contexts such freedom may require qualification. There are therefore exceptions to freedom of expression as clarified in Paragraph 2 or Article 10 where it states that it may be subject to such formalities, conditions, restrictions or penalties as are prescribed by law and are necessary in a democratic society, in the interests of national security, territorial integrity or public safety, for the prevention of disorder or crime, for the protection of health or morals, for the protection of the reputation or rights of others, for preventing the disclosure of information received in confidence, or for maintaining the authority and impartiality of the judiciary.[53]

Some would argue that legal moralism is the basis for criminalizing negationism. However, as Paul Behrens eloquently asserts, such moralism risks allowing a moral framework of a society to act independently from any international community in which that state is embedded.[54] Furthermore, any state embedded into an international system is expected to adhere to shared values, most notably human rights.[55] Criminal law, by contrast, works on the premise that perpetrators of harm need to be punished. Criminalizing negationism assumes that harm is caused – psychological and physical – particularly to survivor communities, and that denial, or minimizing suffering, attacks dignity and causes damage.[56] It has been asserted regarding the provisions on denialism held within the previously mentioned EU Framework Decision on racism and xenophobia, that dignity comes from beyond the reach of law, and that human dignity requires the state to recognize the right of individuals to speak.[57] Behrens also suggests that potential criticisms of this viewpoint are that 'just as a State granting unbridled liberty ends up promoting not its weakest citizens, but its greatest bullies, a State granting unbridled freedom of speech ends up supporting not those who speak the truth, but those who shout the loudest'.[58] He adds further that there are reasonable concerns that criminalizing negationism may impact upon human rights.[59]

There are varied approaches to Holocaust denial and negationism. In the United States there is generally strong opposition to restricting freedom of speech, with the hope that discussion and an exchange of opinions will expose the racism and mendacity of genocide deniers, the objective being that harmful opinions will be overcome with alternative opinions.[60] In the European Union Holocaust denial and denial of other genocides is seen as being harmful to survivors and their descendants. It is criminalized in Austria, Belgium, the Czech Republic, France, Germany, Hungary, Poland, Romania, Slovakia, Slovenia and also in Switzerland (which is not in the EU). The potential punishments vary from fines to imprisonment.[61] Some EU member states criminalized genocide and Holocaust denial before the Framework Decision of 2008. In Germany, Holocaust denial has been a criminal offence since 1985.[62]

It is a crime in Germany to belittle, deny, or approve acts committed during the time of the Nazi regime in a manner that could disturb the public peace (which allows for private conversations, but limits public utterances). German law criminalizes Holocaust denial specifically: 'publicly or in a meeting approv[ing] of, den[ying] or downplay[ing] an act committed under the rule of National Socialism ... in a manner capable of disturbing the public peace'.[63] German Basic Law, or *Grundgesetz*, guarantees freedoms to express and disseminate opinions in speech, writing and pictures and to seek information without being hindered, but freedoms can be limited under general laws and the right to personal dignity.[64] German law allows for the criminalizing and punishment of hate speech, with Section 130 of the *Strafgesetzbuch*, or Penal Code, which specifically refers to 'incit[ing] hatred against segments of the population or call[ing] for violent or arbitrary measures against them' or by 'assault[ing] the human dignity of others by insulting, maliciously maligning, or defaming segments of the population'.[65] It is also a crime to approve, deny, or render harmless the violence of Nazi rule in a manner that can assault the human dignity of victims.[66] Furthermore, Sections 84 to 86a of German Basic Law empower the government to declare some political parties as illegal, prohibit the use of their symbols, and ban their propaganda.[67]

The 1990 Gaysott Act in France criminalized Holocaust denial, making it an offence to question the scope and existence of the Holocaust, with punishments of up to a €45,000 fine and five years' imprisonment.[68] In Switzerland, in 1995, Article 261 of the penal code was updated to state:

[W]hoever publicly, by word, writing, image, gesture, acts of violence or any other manner demeans or discriminates against an individual or a group of individuals because of their race, their ethnicity, or their religion in a way which undermines human dignity, or on those bases, denies, coarsely minimizes or seeks to justify a genocide or other crimes against humanity shall be punished by up to three years' imprisonment or a fine.[69]

Before the 2008 Framework Decision similar Holocaust denial laws were passed in Austria, Belgium, the Czech Republic, Luxembourg and Romania, with punishments ranging from fines to imprisonment. Hungary, in 2010, criminalized public Holocaust denial and even questioning the Holocaust in a manner that could hurt the dignity of victims. Slovakia updated its own Holocaust denial law in 2011 to include denial of the Armenian genocide.[70]

In the United Kingdom (specifically England and Wales) there is no offence classified purely in relation to the Holocaust or genocide denial. The Crime and Disorder Act 1998 allows for eleven pre-existing or basic offences to include aggravated factors. They apply to a range of assault, public order offences and harassment offences where racially or religiously aggravated features will result in a higher sentence.[71] Section 28(1) of the Crime and Disorder Act states that an offence becomes aggravated if:

(a)   at the time of committing the offence, or immediately before or after doing so, the offender demonstrated towards the victim of the offence hostility based on the victim's membership (or presumed membership) of a racial or religious group; or

(b)   the offence is motivated (wholly or partly) by hostility towards members of a racial or religious group based on their membership of that group.[72]

The aim of this part of the Act, in tackling xenophobia and race hate crime, is to show that such offences are viewed more seriously and requiring of more severe punishment. It has been observed that hate crimes have the potential to cause greater harm than basic offences, and as such, the culpability of the offender increases. This acknowledges that such crimes are an attack against an individual's sense of identity, as well as their membership of a minority group.[73] The police and the Crown Prosecution Service define hate crime as:

Any criminal offence which is perceived by the victim or any other person, to be motivated by hostility or prejudice, based on a person's disability or perceived disability; race or perceived race; or religion or perceived religion; or sexual orientation or perceived sexual orientation or transgender identity or perceived transgender identity.[74]

The definition allows for the victim of an offence to perceive that the crime was motivated by prejudice or hostility aimed at several potential factors that define that person's sense of self.

The situation in the United States differs from Europe. This is due to the First Amendment of the Constitution of the United States which includes the line, 'Congress shall make no law ... abridging freedom of speech'.[75] This is not an unlimited freedom, as the United States Supreme Court has stated that 'the right of free speech is not absolute at all times and under all circumstances. There are certain well defined and narrowly limited classes of speech, the prevention and punishment of which has never been thought to raise any Constitutional problem'. The Supreme Court included within this clarification 'insulting' or 'fighting' words, 'those which by their very utterance inflict injury or tend to incite an immediate breach of the peace'.[76]

Negationist statements and Holocaust denial that would be prosecuted in Europe – including the situation which led to David Irving being imprisoned in Austria – would be classed as protected speech under United States constitutional law.[77] The general interpretation of the Constitution and rights under the First Amendment is that banning the dissemination of unpleasant or dangerous ideas through censorship or criminalization is likely to be counterproductive. The U.S. stance is that it is better to respond with debate and condemnation.[78] Of course, the situation in Europe in the post-war years was very different from that of the United States. During the period immediately following the war the countries of Europe had to ensure that there was no resurgence of Nazism, particularly in Germany and the territories of its former allies, and in those regions where the Nazi occupation may have been viewed positively by some citizens. Curtailing some freedoms – including prohibiting Nazi propaganda or symbolism – made sense. There was (and is) an understandable need to restrict the proliferation of ideas associated with the Nazi regime.[79]

Negationism needs to be seen for what it is – a blatant attempt to deny or reinterpret history in order to fulfil an agenda. As has been shown, that agenda is often antisemitic and has found a ready and receptive audience amongst neo-Nazis, others of the far-right, and some on the far-left. It is often combined with hostility towards Israel with efforts made to justify it. Negationism can be found in amateurish internet sites, poorly written pamphlets and in pseudo-academic journals. It is voiced by populist-nationalist politicians and by less eloquent political agitators.

As has already been discussed, in the United States, the First Amendment protects free speech even if it causes great offence. When neo-Nazis and white supremacists marched in Charlottesville chanting 'Jews will not defeat us', there was almost universal outrage. But the Constitution defends their right to be offensive. In many European countries, particularly those that experienced the Holocaust first-hand, laws have been imposed to punish Holocaust denial. The EU Framework Decision sought to set universal standards across the European Union, but its objectives have been inconsistently met. The United Kingdom has laws that punish hate speech, but no specific laws linked to Holocaust or genocide denial.

There is a difficult balancing act – defence of free speech and punishment of Holocaust and genocide denial – that national legislative bodies need to address. Words that cause offence and distress to survivor or victim communities must be condemned and there are good reasons to impose punishments. As will be alluded to further in this book, history must be researched, understood and told, if societies are to learn from the mistakes of the past. That requires honesty in accepting and protecting the truth. The search for honesty and integrity in the research and teaching of the Holocaust does not just apply to Nazi Germany and the territories it occupied. The next two chapters will therefore consider the United States and Great Britain.

Chapter 3

The United States

Historical research, certainly up to the 1990s, showed criticism of the administration of Franklin D. Roosevelt for allegedly being passive and indifferent to the persecution and murder of Jews by the Nazi regime.[1] In 1967, Arthur Morse's *While Six Million Died: A Chronicle of American Apathy* was critical of the Roosevelt administration. David Wyman's *The Abandonment of the Jews: America and the Holocaust, 1941–1945* was equally if not more severely critical about the response of the U.S. to the Holocaust.[2]

During the build-up to the Second World War, the United States was still recovering from the Great Depression. Isolationism, nativism and antisemitism had become increasingly apparent. In 1939, this manifested most notably when legal efforts to save Jewish children from Europe were rejected.[3] During the 1930s it was considered to be politically unwise to suggest raising quotas of immigrants, even if that meant rejecting those fleeing oppression. In an alarming parallel to some of the political rhetoric heard today, Senator Lewis Schwellenbach of Washington State said that fighting immigration was 'the best vote getting argument'. He added: 'The politician can beat his breast and proclaim his loyalty to America ... he can tell the unemployed man that he is out of work because some alien has his job.'[4]

The U.S. Immigration Act of 1924 made entry into the United States conditional upon race and used race-based tables of national origins.[5] Attitudes among some U.S. politicians changed somewhat after the German pogrom of 9/10 November 1938 (*Kristallnacht*). They were aware that some Americans would block attempts to increase immigration quotas, so the focus was on German refugee children. In early 1939, Senator Robert Wagner and Representative Edith Rogers introduced a bill that would grant entry to 20,000 German refugee children aged 14 years or younger over the course of two years. This would be outside of the existing quotas.[6] There was a stipulation in the bill that the refugee children would be supported and cared for by individuals and organizations to prevent them from becoming public charges.[7] Up until that time, the 1924 Immigration Act had effectively stopped immigration from Eastern and Southern Europe.[8] Initially the bill was favourably received by politicians from both sides, labour leaders, religious and women's groups, the YMCA and the churches. Many newspapers supported it – 85 papers from 30 states, including 26 southern newspapers. Well-known actors also provided endorsement.[9] The support was short-lived and countered by hostility. In *The Politics of Rescue: The Roosevelt Administration and the Holocaust, 1938–1945*, published in 1970, Henry Feingold suggested that the nation-state system, limiting the responsibility of one country for events occurring in another country, was part of the problem. He also asserted that the Roosevelt administration showed 'indifference and even complicity in the Final Solution' and that the view of the State Department was that 'all one had to do was wait, and refugees clamouring to come to the U.S. would be converted into silent corpses'. Additionally, he also suggested that rescue was not the main concern of American Jews.[10]

There was significant, powerful and vocal opposition to the Wagner-Rogers Bill, including from the American Coalition of Patriotic Societies, the American Legion, the Junior Order of United American Mechanics, the Ladies of the Grand Army of the Republic, the Daughters of the American Revolution and the Patriotic Order Sons of America. John Trevor, leader of the American Coalition of Patriotic Societies, declared that America already had its own 'undernourished, ragged and ill' and that Congress had to 'protect the youth of America from this foreign invasion'.[11] As if this rhetoric was not already too similar to the rhetoric of contemporary populist nationalists, these groups also argued that America should care for its own children before worrying about non-Americans.[12] The American Immigration Conference Board issued a leaflet which stated: 'America's Children are America's Problem! Europe's Children in Europe are Europe's Problem!'[13] It also put forward the argument that America's children should have first claim to America's charity.[14] There appears to have been little or no compassion or attempt to understand the plight of Jewish child refugees fleeing Europe. The belief that the Wagner-Rogers Bill would deprive American children of much needed care and support took hold, even though the head of the United States Children's Bureau issued assurances to the contrary.[15]

By March 1939, a poll of U.S. senators showed that the majority would not offer support for the Wagner-Rogers Bill, and in effect, it was doomed.[16] Arguments against it continued, sometimes with an undercurrent of antisemitism. The bill was seen as being a Jewish bill, with pointed remarks being made that the refugee children were Jewish. The president of the United Daughters of 1812 addressed a conference in Washington D.C. suggesting that as America was a Christian nation it should care for its own before letting in foreigners.[17] Others described the children as 'an invading host' and the first step towards letting in millions. Despite the levels of opposition, in June 1939, the full Senate Immigration Committee voted in favour of a heavily amended Wagner-Rogers Bill, agreeing to the 20,000 children being allowed into the U.S. but only as part of the existing quota permitted from Germany.[18] The bill was grossly dissimilar from that which was originally proposed.

There are further indications that elements of the U.S. government were reluctant to help Europe's Jews. Secretary Morgenthau was presented with a secret memorandum from officials in the Treasury in December 1943. Part of the memorandum stated:

> [O]fficials of this Government were so fearful that this Government might act to save the Jews of Europe if the gruesome facts relating to Hitler's plans to exterminate them became known, that they not only attempted to suppress the facts, but, in addition, they used the powers of their official position to secretly countermand the instructions of the Acting Secretary of State [Welles] ordering such facts to be reported. We leave it for your judgment whether this action made such officials the accomplices of Hitler in this program and whether or not these officials are not war criminals.[19]

On 13 January 1944, Morgenthau received an eighteen-page report titled, *Report to the Secretary on the Acquiescence of this Government in the Murder, of the Jews.* In response, Morgenthau arranged to meet with President Roosevelt, John Pehle and Randolph Paul in order to ask the president to establish a commission aimed at rescuing refugees.[20] The meeting resulted in assurances from Roosevelt that action would be taken. Less than a week later Roosevelt issued Executive Order 9417, which created the War Refugee Board.[21]

Better known than the Wagner-Rogers Bill is the fateful story of the MS *St. Louis*, a ship owned by the Hamburg-Amerikanische Packetfahrt-Actiengesellschaft company. It set sail from Hamburg on 13 May 1939 bound for Cuba, with 937 mainly Jewish passengers on board. They were travelling officially as German tourists to Cuba but most anticipated immigrating to the United States. Of those passengers 909 held tourist landing permits, and 734 of that number were part of the quota numbers for eventual entry to the United States.[22] On 27 May 1939, the ship arrived off Havana but was refused docking rights in the harbour. It remained at anchor until 2 June when it set sail to travel between Cuba and Florida whilst negotiations took place to try to gain permission for the passengers to disembark. Twenty-eight passengers were permitted to disembark in Havana, of which twenty-two were Jews, four were Spaniards and two were Cubans. On 6 June, the captain set course for the return journey to Europe. During that journey, in order to prevent the passengers from returning to Germany, whence they had fled, the governments of Belgium, France, the Netherlands and the United Kingdom agreed to give them with refuge.[23] Ultimately, 907 Jews returned to Europe (one had committed suicide and one died), many of whom would not survive the war.[24] The British, French, Belgian and Dutch governments had only offered *temporary refuge* to the passengers due to being assured that most of them ultimately intended to settle in the U.S. It is often missed that the U.S. had agreed to accept 27,370 permanent German residents per year, and that quota had a bearing on the *St. Louis* passengers. Of the 937 original passengers, approximately 650 did survive the war, and approximately 450 of that number eventually obtained residence in the U.S.[25]

The accepted and often unchallenged narrative about the voyage of the *St Louis* was summed up in a 1997 interview with Michael Fink (previously Michael Barak), a former passenger who had sailed with his parents. He recalled the ship sailing between Cuba and Florida, with the passengers hoping to enter the United States: 'My father, like the other nine hundred passengers on the *St. Louis*, was off the coast of Miami, and he ended up in Auschwitz. How did that happen? I hold the United States responsible for the death of my father.'[26]

Of course, the voyage and the tragedy of the *St. Louis* is not so malignantly simple. Other factors contributed. Some might argue that in May and June 1939, the war had not started and the full peril that the Jews of Europe faced was not known. Such an argument is clearly naïve. Nazi hostility to Jews was well known: the Nuremberg Laws, the Reich Citizenship Laws, and the events of *Kristallnacht* in 1938 had made that clear. Furthermore, there were multiple communiqués and conversations between diplomats as well as newspaper reports.[27]

Many are to blame for the plight of the passengers, including most notably Nazi Germany which wanted Europe to be free of Jews, the U.S. government which would not intervene in the affairs of Cuba, the antisemitism of Cuba, the weakness of the Jewish American community, and the officials of the Hamburg-Amerika shipping line for allowing the passengers to sail in the knowledge that they would not be allowed to disembark in Havana.[28] Many blame the Harvard-educated Jewish American lawyer Lawrence Berenson. He was tasked by the New York-based Joint Distribution Committee (JDC) with arranging the safe disembarkation of the *St. Louis* passengers.[29] Berenson appeared to be a good choice. He had formerly been the president of the Cuban Chamber of Commerce in the U.S. and had previously successfully used his Cuban connections to purchase 1,000 visas for Jews trying to leave Germany. Some would suggest his overconfidence in his negotiating abilities led to his failure.[30] In planning the evacuation from Germany Berenson had been in contact with Manuel Benitez, the Cuban director-general of immigration, with whom he met and handed over $125,000 in cash. Days later, the Cuban embassy in Berlin started issuing visas for the first 1,000 passengers.[31]

Benitez was one of many in Cuba who grew wealthy from the sale of visas and landing permits. However, it was his wealth that caused Cuban President Federico Brú to issue a decree on 5 May 1939, which ended Benitez's power to issue landing permits.[32] From that point on, permits could only be issued by the secretaries of state and of labour with a bond of $500 required from each person arriving. This of course deprived Berenson of his main contact.[33] It is often asserted that Berenson understood that the way to do business in Cuba was to pass the right amount of money to the right politician.[34] It has been reported that once the Cubans agreed to take the passengers, Berenson believed that he could negotiate a reduced price. Berenson had clearly lost the option of working with and through Benitez. Batista (the future Cuban leader) declined to get involved, which meant potentially Berenson would have to deal directly with President Brú, and risk it becoming public knowledge that an American citizen had tried to bribe the president of Cuba.[35] The JDC was also not in favour of paying bribes but was willing to pay the $500 bond for each passenger.[36]

On 4 June, Berenson met with President Brú. The president asked that on top of the $500 bond per passenger, a further $150 per passenger should be deposited to cover living costs, all of which had to be completed within 48 hours. To reinforce the seriousness of the offer, Brú released the details to the press. Berenson made a counter-offer which was refused. The JDC suggested that he pay what was requested but Berenson was convinced he could still negotiate a better price.[37] However, the Cuban president responded by contacting Chase National Bank and ended the negotiations after this offer had been made.[38] The Cubans clearly held all the cards in the negotiations and by going public they had limited the options available to Berenson and the JDC. If Berenson had agreed to Brú's demands it is likely that the *St. Louis* passengers would have disembarked in Havana and would have survived. For Brú, this negotiating stance gave him power. If he allowed the Jews to land in Cuba, he would risk his presidency; if he sent then away, he would become an international pariah. The public offer to Berenson meant that he would be seen as the one at fault.[39] Berenson failed by trying to play bribery politics when the rules had changed. The Cuban government issued an announcement on 6 June 1939 which stated:

> Agreement was reached two days ago with Señor Berenson to land the exiles on the Isle of Pines after he had deposited $500 cash per person with a subsidiary guarantee with regard to food and lodging. He was given 48 hours to meet these requirements. Yesterday Senor Berenson made an alternative proposal offering $443,000 for the *St. Louis* passengers, plus $150 additional for the refugees on the *Orduna* and *Flandre*, the sum to include expenses for food and lodging. The Cuban government could not accept the proposal, and having passed excessively the time allowed, the government terminates the matter.[40]

History has sought to apportion blame for the fate of the *St. Louis* passengers on the U.S. government. Clearly the government could have done more, but it is apparent that the fault lies with the Nazis for creating the refugee conditions, with the Cubans, and with Lawrence Berenson. Others share guilt, but these are the main culprits.

A criticism of the Americans and British is that they could have done more to intervene and help the Jews of Europe. The violence of the Nazis and the suffering of the Jews was known about long before the first concentration and extermination camps were liberated. As mentioned earlier, even the Nazi press was reporting on Dachau in the early months of the regime, although at that time it was housing political opponents. The Nuremberg Laws were reported on, and the horrors of *Kristallnacht* in 1938 got extensive coverage and revealed in detail the dangers Jews in Germany faced. Prior to the war starting, America and Britain maintained a diplomatic presence in Germany, and journalists and tourists were able to move freely around to bear witness to events as they unfolded. In November 1935, *The Times*, a London-based newspaper, reported on the ghettoization of German Jews due to the Nuremberg Laws. It stated: 'The laws are being interpreted as meaning that a Jew, as a second-grade citizen, is not fit to exercise any occupation within the German national community.' It referred to 'savage fanaticism' aimed at 'the total destruction of the whole Jewish community in Germany', and cited the catchphrase *'Juda verrecke'* (May Jewry perish).[41] By 1938, British politicians were speaking in parliament about camps such as Dachau and Sachsenhausen, and by October 1939, the British government produced a publicly available white paper which commented on the treatment German nationals were receiving in Germany.[42] The paper mentioned that some evidence had previously been kept from the public to prevent hindrance of a peaceful settlement with Germany, and a further article in *The Times* stated that the British government did not want to take action which could inspire hatred. The white paper did mention the plight of the Jews, referred to sadistic cruelty, and described Buchenwald as the 'City of Sorrow'.[43] By November 1940, reports from the Polish government in exile spoke of atrocities in its country. Throughout 1940 reference was made to mass executions and deportation to concentration camps in a joint statement by the Polish and Czech governments. Numerous newspaper articles referred to the brutality of the Gestapo and the treatment of Jews. Mention was even made of the murder of over 5,000 people either individually or en masse as part of the policy of removing Jews and Poles to make space for Aryan Germans.[44]

Ignorance of German brutality could not be claimed by the British, and it could not be claimed by the Americans. In February 1940, the Polish courier Jan Karski reached the Polish government in exile in France and advised of the conditions in Poland.[45] In 1996, *The New York Times* obtained the declassified transcripts of intercepted messages revealing that the Germans were massacring Jews in the Soviet Union in the weeks following the start of Operation Barbarossa. The report in *The New York Times* stated:

> One transcript, for instance, from the town of Slonim in Belarus, states, 'In yesterday's cleansing action in Slonim by the police regiment Mitte, 1,153 Jewish looters were shot.' The message on July 18, 1941 – less than a month after the German invasion – was signed by General von dem Bach-Zelewsky, the German commander in Belarus, and transmitted to Heinrich Himmler, the head of the SS, and Commander Daluge of the Order Police. In another message, dated Aug. 7, 1941, General von dem Bach-Zelewsky wrote, with evident self-congratulation: 'The action of the SS cavalry brigade proceeds. By noon today, a further 3,600 were executed, so that the total number [executed] by Calvary Regiment Eastern is 7,819. Thereby, the number of 30,000 in my area has been exceeded.[46]

It has been observed that this shows the British, and therefore presumably the Americans, were aware of atrocities being committed against Jews as early as September 1941, over a year before both countries publicly acknowledged what was happening to Jews in German-occupied Europe.[47]

In November 1942, Karski brought information about the conditions in the Warsaw ghetto and the transportation of Jews to labour camps. That account was also given to British Foreign Secretary Anthony Eden and to President Roosevelt, and included claims that two million Jews had already been killed. Karski brought microfilm with him containing details of the mass murders at Auschwitz.[48] In October 1941, Winston Churchill and President Roosevelt both produced statements denouncing German savagery.[49] In January 1942, representatives of nine occupied countries met in London to condemn the atrocities of the Nazis and commence plans for eventual punishments after the war was over.[50]

There has been extensive research and commentary on the subject of whether or not the Allies could have bombed Auschwitz once they became aware of the atrocities being perpetrated there. Bombing of the camp was first proposed as early as 1941, with several further proposals being made in 1944. Requests were made by the Polish government in exile and by Jewish groups.[51] There were also requests during 1944 from the War Refugee Board and from Jewish groups for the rail lines, rail junctions and marshalling yards to be bombed. The source of the requests included the Czechoslovakian government in exile.[52] The proposed bombing was refused by the Operations Division of the War Department, based partly on the rationale that it would divert much needed military resources and assets which were needed elsewhere in other theatres of war.[53] The last request was submitted to the War Department in August 1944. It included requesting the Mediterranean Allied Air Forces (MAAF) to send a combat command unit capable of destroying rail lines.[54]

On 27 August 1944, Brigadier General Barnwell R. Legge, the American military attaché, sent a message to the War Department. Its contents were unambiguous: 'From Military Attaché, signed Legge. Jews in Hungary appeal through the Polish consul here for aid against daily deportations. 12,000 to extermination camp Auschwitz. Urgently request bombardment rail lines Galanta-Leopoldov and Vrutki-Zilina-Cadca [in Slovakia].' It clearly refers to the Jews being transported to Auschwitz from Budapest.[55] In response, on 28 August 1944, General Clayton Bissell, assistant chief of staff for intelligence at the War Department sent the request from Legge to General Henry M. Wilson, supreme allied commander for the Mediterranean: 'Switzerland reports appeal by Jews in Hungary through Polish Consul Switzerland for aid against deportations and extermination 12,000 Camp Auschwitz. Bombardment rail lines Galanta–Leopoldov and Vrutki–Zilina–Cadca requested urgently. This for information and action deemed necessary.'[56]

The request was sent to MAAF where it was viewed as something that fell outside of normal bombing operations. Lieutenant Colonel W. F. R. Ballard from MAAF Intelligence Analysis Section wrote to Colonel Mills on 30 August, stating:

The bombardment of the railway lines referred to would not prohibit deportations of the political prisoners [sic] from the camp at

Oswiecim, inasmuch as there is a relatively dense railroad net in the area and other lines could be used. It is suggested that this area is at too great a distance to effectively cut and keep cut all of the lines surrounding Oswiecim for an indefinite period, particularly when consideration is given to the other commitments of the Fifteenth Air Force.[57]

Eventually, a cabled message was sent to the War Department that due to the distances and the number of targets involved, it would not be a feasible or a particularly successful mission as damage would be minimal and easily coped with by the Germans on the ground.[58] It is apparent that the railway lines and marshalling yards referred to were not at Auschwitz, but rather, they were in Slovakia or Hungary and were used to transport Jews *to* Auschwitz. Additionally, those targets were clearly within range of Allied bombers as raids by the American Fifteenth Air Force and the RAF had taken place on railway lines in Hungary in late summer and early autumn 1944.[59] It is more probable that the request for bombing raids was denied due to other military commitments and the main operational objective of winning the war.[60] The U.S. Strategic Air Forces Europe had responsibility for prioritizing resources and operations and whilst communications, railways and waterways had always been legitimate military targets, they varied in priority.[61] The operational range of the Fifteenth Air Force was from France to Bulgaria, and the priority with regards to railways had to be those that supplied Axis forces.[62] Additionally, reconnaissance photographs of railways and marshalling yards after bombing raids showed that some lines were back in use within twenty-four hours, and entire yards returned to full functionality within two weeks. In fact, it was not until early in 1945 that the Fifteenth Air Force was able to launch large enough raids against Austria to guarantee marshalling yards being out of service for a week or more.[63] Bombing of railways had to be of tactical use and significance. As such, a raid on Auschwitz was only likely to be sanctioned if it was militarily necessary to assist the Red Army.[64]

The Allies had reconnaissance photographs of Auschwitz – particularly the industrial area around Monowitz – but the extermination part of the camp complex had not been the subject of the reconnaissance missions.[65] Auschwitz had been on the MAAF target list since December 1943 as part of plans to attack German chemical and oil facilities.[66] The Americans did attack Monowitz and the vast I. G. Farben complex in a series of air raids on 20 August, 11 September and on 18 and 26 December 1944. These raids caused extensive damage; production of methanol at the facility was reduced to 12 per cent.[67] It showed that bombing of Auschwitz was possible.

An area of concern with bombing the complex at Auschwitz I and the main killing facility at Auschwitz II (Birkenau) is to do with accuracy. Speaking in 1962 from a British perspective Noble Frankland observed that in 1941 Bomber Command found that only 20 per cent of its aircraft were dropping bombs within five miles of the target, and in attacks on more industrial areas only 7 per cent were landing bombs within five miles of the target.[68] For the American air crews, they found that even with Norden bombsights they still struggled to hit the target if it were hindered by cloud cover.[69] Late in 1943, the Americans tried to improve accuracy by using radar, but even then, the results were not always successful. Analysis by the Eighth Air Force showed that from twenty-seven radar bombing missions between September 1943 and January 1944 only 5 per cent of the bombs landed within one mile of the target.[70] The risks of causing significant harm to innocent civilians at Auschwitz are clear based on such inaccurate bombing capabilities. As Frankland elaborated further when discussing the accuracy of the Allied bombing campaign:

> This meant that the policy of precise attack upon oil plants, aircraft factories, particular industrial targets, and railway marshalling yards was largely futile. It meant that if the offensive was to be continued at all, it could only be directed against very large targets indeed and that meant, in effect, whole German cities. Thus, the policy of area bombing, whether strategically desirable or not, was made operationally inevitable.[71]

Criticism of the United States for not attacking Auschwitz appears to be largely unjustified. Although the Allies had been made aware of the mass-murder facilities at the camp, it is likely that MAAF leaders did not have that knowledge which would undoubtedly have influenced decision-making.[72] The bombing policy was to attack strategically and operationally significant targets. Bombing capabilities were erratic in their accuracy. Although the camp at Auschwitz-Birkenau covered a large geographical area, specific targets within the camp were small. The complex was attacked with raids against the I. G. Farben industrial plant at Monowitz, but those raids were militarily justified. Any broader attack against Auschwitz would only have occurred if it had been requested by the advancing Soviet forces to assist their advance across Poland.

As one of the victorious Allied powers, it fell largely to the United States (in conjunction with Britain, France and the Soviet Union) to lead the hunt and prosecution of Nazi war criminals. Most notably, prosecutions took place at the various Nuremberg trials. In the years since then, the U.S. response to Nazi war criminals has been inconsistent even though there is a legal obligation to prosecute any suspected war criminals.[73] Up until 1979, the deportation or prosecution of suspected Nazi war criminals living in the United States was done through the Immigration and Naturalization Service (INS), and was grossly unsuccessful. In fact, between 1945 and 1979 only two Nazi criminals were deported from the U.S.[74] Although the U.S. has statutory jurisdiction to prosecute war criminals, the legislative acts do not allow for prosecution prior to their enactment. Furthermore, the 1988 genocide statute does not apply to non-U.S. citizens unless the alleged crimes were actually against U.S. citizens.[75] It is also claimed by some sources that the INS may even have assisted former Nazis in their efforts to enter the U.S.

The Allied powers of the United States, Soviet Union, France and Britain made up the Allied Control Council for Germany (ACC), and on 10 September 1945, in Berlin, the ACC passed a resolution that ordered all Germans now living in countries that had been neutral during the war, and who had been involved as officials or intelligence agents of the Nazi regime, to return to Germany. Additionally, governments of countries where those Germans now lived were requested to deport them to the ACC area of control.[76] The ACC's Director of Prisoners of War and Displaced Persons was authorized to implement the resolution and created the Combined Repatriation Executive which was empowered to act through the embassies of the formerly neutral countries and territories of Afghanistan, Ireland, Portugal, Spain, Sweden and Switzerland, as well as the city of Tangiers and Vatican City.[77] The wanted people were defined as 'obnoxious Germans' – former members of the Schutzstaffel (SS), party officials and intelligence agents who, if they were still in

Germany, would be subject to arrest, interrogation, denazification and trials.[78] In Spain alone the British and U.S. Office of Strategic Services (OSS) were tasked to prepare lists of Germans of interest, which identified over 1,600 people to be repatriated.[79]

In just the U.S. zone of occupied German approximately two million people received some form of punishment and 400,000 were interned in civilian camps for varied periods.[80] A good definition of denazification refers to 'the full range of Allied/Soviet reform and punishment measures in occupied Germany' and often it describes 'the specific liquidation of the National Socialist Party (NSDAP) and the elimination of its influence'.[81] It is apparent that many Nazis were not arrested and punished, or that the processes of dealing with them were not always robust. Historians have debated the reasons for this. It has been argued that pragmatism on the part of the U.S. recognized that the numbers were too great and the focus was on rebuilding; others suggest that concerns about communism and the upheaval in Germany meant it was more practical to use the skills of former Nazis; others suggest that rehabilitation was faster once denazification was in the hands of Germans; and yet others suggest that U.S. ambitions changed when faced with the practicalities of post-war Germany. There appears to be consensus that the denazification policy did not live up to its aims.[82] The Moscow Declaration of October 1943 – issued by the U.S, Britain and the Soviet Union – included the need to conduct international trials of Nazi war criminals when their crimes crossed national borders.[83]

In Paris, in January 1945, the Central Registry of War Criminals and Security Suspects (CROWCASS) was created. It was intended to maintain three lists: one for people detained for war crimes, one for people wanted, and one of people who had been members of Nazi organizations.[84] Very quickly the list reached 80,000 people, not all of whom fitted the definition of war criminals. But some of that number continued to present a danger to Allied forces in Germany. It has been asserted that CROWCASS became overwhelmed and never fully managed to investigate all of the suspects on the list.[85]

More damning for the United States was the assistance offered to former Nazis. The geopolitical climate changed dramatically after the war, with growing distrust between the West and the Soviet Union. In this new world, it was apparent that some former Nazi personnel could be of use to the U.S. One of the most notorious examples is that of Klaus Barbie. He had served as an SS officer and was head of the Gestapo in Lyon from 1942 until late 1944. He was known to the French as 'The Butcher of Lyon'.[86] The French claimed that whilst in Lyon, Barbie had been responsible for the deportation and murder of thousands of Jewish and non-Jewish people (including orphaned children), the torture and murder of French Resistance members, and the assassination of Jean Moulin. In May 1947 and in November 1954, the French sentenced Barbie in absentia to death after finding him guilty of war crimes.[87] The French did not know the whereabouts of Barbie at that time. Barbie had been cited as a war criminal as early as 1944. In 1945, he was mentioned in the Central Registry of War Criminals and Security Suspects which stated that he was being 'sought by France for the murder of civilians and the torture of military personnel'. The French issued a warrant for him to be arrested for war crimes.[88]

As will be shown, the reason Barbie could not be located was that, after leaving France he returned to Germany, where, from 1947 to 1951, he was employed by the U.S. Army Counter Intelligence Corps (CIC), before being assisted to flee to Bolivia.[89] In March 1951, the CIC facilitated Barbie's journey to Bolivia, and also gave him a new identity, supporting documents and a passport. In Bolivia he lived freely for over thirty years under the new name of Altmann. He did not deny that he had been a Nazi and actually proclaimed his former Nazi affiliation. However, he did not reveal his real name or his links to the Gestapo.[90]

Barbie's freedom would not last. In January 1972, the Nazi hunter Beate Klarsfeld revealed Barbie's true identity when she gave a press conference in Bolivia. She told the assembled reporters that he was wanted in France as a war criminal. The French government requested his extradition but the Bolivian government – with which Barbie had a close relationship – would not cooperate. In 1983, a change of Bolivian government led to Barbie being handed over to France.[91] Barbie would eventually die in a French prison on 25 September 1991.[92]

In light of the U.S. involvement with Barbie, Attorney General William French Smith directed Allan A. Ryan Jr. to investigate the role that the U.S. had played. *The Ryan Report* was submitted to the attorney general in August 1983. Its key findings are summarized below by Mr Justice Goldberg:

(1) The CIC employed Barbie as a paid informant from 1947 until his flight to Bolivia on March 23, 1951.

(2) CIC officers, including the general in charge of CIC operations, concealed Barbie's continuous employment from both the American Military High Command and the High Commissioner for Germany.

(3) The CIC continued to employ Barbie despite a directive from the American Military High Command in 1949 that Gestapo personnel were not to be employed other than as short-term casual contacts.

(4) CIC officers and the general in charge of the CIC lied to the High Command and the High Commissioner when asked whether Barbie continued as a paid CIC informant after the 1949 directive.

(5) The CIC lied to French authorities who were seeking Barbie's extradition, and to the High Command and the High Commissioner, by stating that Barbie's whereabouts were unknown even though Barbie was lodged in a CIC safe house at the time.

(6) The CIC concealed its actions from French authorities, the High Command and the High Commissioner. The CIC illegally arranged Barbie's flight to Bolivia, providing Barbie with funds, a false passport and identity, and documents to facilitate his escape. The CIC utilized a so-called 'rat line' which enabled wanted Nazis to flee from Europe. It was operated, for substantial fees, by a fascist Croatian priest.[93]

Once the report was received, the U.S. officially apologized to France. It is apparent from the words of Allan A. Ryan Jr. that the CIC work with Barbie was covert and not known to either the American high command or U.S. high commissioner for Germany:

While I was serving in the Justice Department as Director of the Office of SpecialInvestigations, Criminal Division, the Attorney General appointed me to investigate allegations, levelled shortly after Barbie's expulsion, that Barbie had been employed by American intelligence after the war. I concluded that the Counter

Intelligence Corps (CIC) of the United States Army had indeed hired Barbie to spy on Soviet and German Communist activities between 1947 and 1951. The CIC concealed Barbie's employment from both the American Military High Command and the U.S. High Commissioner for Germany (HICOG).[94]

Ryan elaborates further to explain that the continued employment of Barbie by the CIC was counter to a 1949 directive from the American military high command:

> They continued to employ Barbie despite a 1949 directive from the American Military High Command stating that former Gestapo personnel were to be employed only as short-term contacts. Finally, the CIC spirited Barbie out of Europe to South America in 1951, providing Barbie with funds, a false passport and identity, and documents to facilitate his escape. I concluded that CIC officials were guilty of an obstruction of justice under 18 U.S.C. § 1505. I also concluded that prosecution of CIC officials was barred by the general five-year statute of limitations of 18 U.S.C. § 3282.[95]

A weak argument could be that in 1947 the U.S. was not at war with Germany and that, in fact, Germany was then a zone of military occupation rather than a sovereign nation. However, Barbie was a known war criminal and was on the list of those wanted for arrest. It matters not how useful he may have been to the CIC; he should have been arrested to stand trial. The tale becomes even more sordid when it is known that the CIC actively facilitated and assisted his escape to Bolivia. Barbie was not an isolated case. Goldberg mentioned the 'rat line' used to assist known Nazis to flee Europe. In April 1945, as Germany and Europe were being divided into zones of responsibility and control by the victorious Allies, the U.S. forces came across a tunnel complex at Mittelbau-Dora, in which forced and slave labourers had worked. The tunnels contained missile technology, which the Americans hastily acquired. They also detained scientists and engineers who had been involved in the design and manufacture of V2 rockets and other hitherto secret weapons. Many of the rocket engineers were moved to the U.S. and became part of the Apollo space mission project. Clearly their role in slave labour and suffering was conveniently ignored as they were deemed to be strategically useful.[96]

A number of U.S. firms – including General Motors, Chase Manhattan and Ford – worked with the Nazis. A November 1999 NBC News report showed that during the occupation, the French branch of Chase Manhattan froze Jewish accounts at the request of the German authorities. The Paris branch manager, Carlos Neidermann, liaised closely with the Germans and authorized loans to finance German war production. Contemporary companies that employed slave and forced labour during the war, including Bayer, BMW, Volkswagen and Daimler-Chrysler reached agreement in 1999 with the German government to establish a fund of $5.1 billion to pay victims. Opel, the German subsidiary of General Motors, agreed to contribute to the fund. Ford refused to take part in any settlement talks, claiming that the company did not do business with Germany during the war, and that its Cologne plant was confiscated by the Nazis.[97] General Motors was cited in a 1941 FBI report which quoted the company's director of overseas operations as saying he would refuse to do anything that might make Hitler mad.[98]

Henry Ford was leader of the America First Committee and actively sought to keep the U.S. out of the war.[99] Hitler and the Nazi regime admired Ford. He was avowedly antisemitic and first became known to Hitler through the publication of his pamphlet *The International Jew: The World's Foremost Problem*.[100] In 1923, Ford ran for the presidency. Hitler said in an interview with the *Chicago Tribune*: 'I wish that I could send some of my shock troops to Chicago and other big American cities to help.'[101] In *Mein Kampf* Hitler wrote: 'It is Jews who govern the stock exchange forces of the American Union ... Every year makes them more and more the controlling masters of the producers in a nation of one hundred and twenty millions; only a single great man, Ford, to their fury, still maintains full independence.'[102] In 1938, Ford was awarded the highest Nazi honour for foreigners, the Grand Cross of the German Eagle. By that time the brutality of the Nazi regime was well known.[103]

Records from the U.S. National Archives show that prior to the attack on Pearl Harbor, the Ford centre at Dearborn profited greatly from producing war matériel for the German regime, and the man who ran the German subsidiary was an enthusiastic supporter of Hitler. It is also suggested that Ford in Germany served as an 'arsenal of Nazism' according to a 1945 U.S. Army report.[104] In March 1998, a suit was filed in Newark, New Jersey on behalf of Jewish and non-Jewish victims against the Ford Motor Company and its German subsidiary Ford Werke in response to their use of forced and slave labour in the manufacture of trucks for the German military. Approximately forty slave labour cases were filed across the U.S.[105] On 1 February 1999, the then German chancellor, Gerhard Schröder, and the executives of 12 German corporations issued a joint statement that acknowledged responsibility to Holocaust survivors and making amends for the suffering caused in the past.[106]

The Washington law firm of Cohen, Milstein, Hausfeld & Toll sought damages from Ford on behalf of a Russian woman who had endured slave labour at the company's German plant. The judge threw the case out because the statute of limitations had expired. The company was not exonerated but the judge accepted the Ford rationale that 'redressing the tragedies of that period has been – and should continue to be – a nation-to-nation, government-to-government concern'.[107] A spokeswoman for Ford claimed that the Nazis confiscated the company's German plant and that, in reality, Ford had played a pivotal role in the war effort of the United States.[108] However, there is evidence that Ford continued to cooperate with the Nazi regime in Vichy France until at least August 1942 – eight months after the U.S. and Germany went to war. Furthermore, a report prepared during the war by the U.S. Treasury Department drew the conclusion that members of the Ford family encouraged executives of Ford in France to work with German officials. The report noted: 'There would seem to be at least a tacit acceptance by Mr Edsel Ford [Henry Ford's son] of the reliance ... on the known neutrality of the Ford family as a basis for receipt of favours from the German Reich.'[109]

The Ford Company claims that its French affiliate, Ford Société Anonyme Française (Ford SAF), deliberately slowed down production during the years of German occupation between 1940 and 1944.[110]

The director of Ford SAF, Maurice Dollfus, and the director of the French automobile industry under the Vichy regime, Francois Lehideux, appear to have struggled to defend the independence of Ford SAF from multiple influences which ranged from the company headquarters in Dearborn, the Vichy government, overseas affiliates in England, plus Ford Werke in Germany and the German authorities.[111] Dolfuss and Lehideux were arrested after the liberation and charged with collaboration. The charges were later dropped. They claimed to have been part of the resistance by deliberately slowing down production at Ford SAF. It has been argued however, that if production did slow down, it was not due to resistance, but was based on lack of materials, a shortage of workers and the Allied blockade. Additionally, the resistance assertion is brought into question when it is noted that Ford SAF was willing to work for the Germans during the period of occupation.[112] Keith Mann observes that any underproduction was not based on political or ideological resistance, but was based in Ford SAF interests. The company had been handsomely rewarded through German contracts and anticipated profiting from the new Europe that Germany would establish. It has also been pointed out that Ford was willing to accept German funds, even when the brutality of the regime was known and when Germany and the U.S. were officially at war. Ford SAF became a less enthusiastic partner after 1942 when it started to become apparent that Germany would lose the war.[113]

The United States is rightly seen as the country of liberators. Its political will and military might were essential factors in the Allied victory, and the eventual peace that followed. It was not occupied by German forces and as a nation it cannot be accused of colluding or collaborating with the Nazi regime in the way that some European governments and citizens did. But the U.S. is not above criticism. There was clear reluctance from many quarters – particularly the America First Committee – to the U.S. getting involved in the European war. There was resistance too from some in government, and elsewhere in American society, to the idea of helping Jewish refugees. It is probable that isolationism, nativism and some antisemitism influenced the hostility to those who were fleeing the horrors of the Nazi regime in Europe. That became most apparent in the concerted campaign to block the Wagner-Rogers proposal, and may have had a bearing on the plight of the Jewish refugees who sailed on the *St. Louis*. In the immediate post-war years there was selectiveness in how the United States dealt with former Nazis who may have been deemed useful due to their various areas of knowledge, skills and expertise.

History requires an honest assessment of the past. The land of the liberators was not without fault, prior to, during and after the war. This needs to be acknowledged if history is to teach us the relevance of the past to the problems and international crises of today.

Chapter 4

Great Britain

Great Britain differs from the United States in that part of its dependent territory was occupied by the Germans, it suffered sustained attacks against targets on the mainland, and it faced the very real threat of invasion. This chapter will mainly look at four key areas: appeasement, collaboration, the selectiveness of the *Kindertransport* and support for the Nazis.

The common assumption about the appeasement policies of the 1930s is that it demonstrated weakness and that Britain and France sought to secure peace with Germany by granting concessions.[1] Traditionally historians, and some politicians, have condemned the policies of appeasement as being politically naïve, and based on the false assumption that Hitler's ambitions and grievances were limited, which could be managed by concessions aimed at reducing the risk of another war in Europe. It has usually been asserted that the concessions over German rearmament, the Rhineland, Austria and the Sudeten region of Czechoslovakia actually worked to encourage Hitler rather than placating him.[2] It is further alleged that the appeasement policies diminished the credibility of Britain and France, particularly with regards to Poland.[3]

The critical view of British appeasement in the 1930s is largely due to the war memoires of Winston Churchill, which included the 'guilty men' thesis in which Churchill cited fifteen key policymakers as being responsible for appeasement at that time.[4] Opinions about appeasement have changed since then, but mainly in academic circles. It has also been observed that those who were alive and involved at the time did not recall believing that Neville Chamberlain had been wrong.[5] The long-accepted narrative about the appeasement policy in the 1930s was reinforced by the Soviet Union which regularly raised the subject of the Munich Agreement as proof that the Western diplomacy was deceitful.[6]

Critical historians suggest that a more confrontational approach may actually have helped to prevent the war, as Hitler would have been deterred, or that his recklessness would have been exposed in such a manner that he could have been overthrown by more level-headed politicians and the military in Germany.[7] Some suggest that a more aggressive approach by Britain and France could have led to the war starting earlier, at a time when it would have been more favourable to them.[8]

Most political decisions of the 1930s were considered in the light of the international order that had been established in 1919. France wanted security and to be treated as an equal partner. The French had formed an allegiance with the Soviet Union which impacted upon Britain's sense of security.[9] Appeasement was once viewed as an honourable part of the diplomat's toolkit of trying to avoid war by settling grievances through unilateral concessions. After the Munich Conference of 1938, appeasement came to be associated with cowardice, naiveté and the failure of diplomacy.[10] Winston Churchill famously described appeasement as being similar to someone feeding a crocodile in the hope that it will eat him last.[11] It must be acknowledged that Churchill, Eden and others had axes to grind and wished to be judged positively by history.[12]

British policy had been to aim for disarmament and arms control since the end of the First World War, but when Hitler came to power in 1933 it soon became clear that the Geneva Disarmament Conference, which began in 1932, was starting to falter.[13] Sir Orme Sargent was head of the Central Department of the Foreign Office from 1926 until 1933, and then assistant undersecretary to that department from 1933 until 1939. He was one of the key figures in formulating British foreign policy. The Central Department dealt with France and Germany.[14] Sargent and Sir Robert Vansittart were part of a group in the Foreign Office that opposed appeasement.[15] By January 1934 Sargent suggested that the former allies from the First World War had been trying to bluff Germany about disarmament since the Treaty of Versailles, but as Hitler showed that his intention was to rearm Germany, he had effectively called their bluff. Sargent was unsure whether the British and French had the courage to reciprocate, but he felt it was essential they did so before Hitler gained new allies.[16]

There were potential domestic obstacles faced by the British in confronting Hitler. The public may have believed that Germany had changed since the First World War and that it was no longer an imperialistic and militaristic threat. Or the public may have believed that

Germany should be allowed to focus its aggression and territorial aims on Eastern and Central Europe, which would reduce the risks that it posed to Britain.[17] Sargent did not believe that Germany had changed, but felt that the public would only realize this if there was a 'premature act of defiance' by Hitler. He was non-committal about the idea of Germany expanding its interests to the east.[18] Sargent believed that the British needed to stand up to German rearmament which was not only a breach of the Treaty of Versailles, but also encroached on British rights and interests.[19]

British documents from the 1930s were declassified in the late 1960s. This helped historians to realize that appeasement had not been a policy born out of idealism, but as a consequence of Britain's military weakness, poor intelligence, numerous threats and a fear of causing problems for the British economy.[20] The policies of appeasement also need to be considered in the context of the decline in British naval, commercial and financial power. It has been observed that in the 1930s 'the fighting strength of the British Empire was weaker in relation to its potential enemies than at any time since 1779'.[21] At the same time Germany was rising as a power. The British understood the threat from Nazi Germany but recognized that her limited military capacity and a poor economy prevented any action being taken until the situation had improved.[22] Ramsey MacDonald, Stanley Baldwin and Chamberlain all recognized that Britain was unprepared for war and that offering concessions to Germany would allow time for the British to rearm.[23] The government was equally aware that Germany would rapidly rearm and present a threat to the security of France. This view was reinforced by Germany's actions at the Geneva Disarmament Conference, but an awareness was maintained that even if Hitler appeared to respond to warnings from Britain and France, there was still the possibility of war.[24] When Germany withdrew from the disarmament conference and the League of Nations in October 1933, the British began to pursue a policy of rearmament in the full expectation that Hitler was preparing Germany for war at any time in the next three to five years.[25]

British concerns were well founded. By late 1934 Germany was covertly violating the Treaty of Versailles by building an air force approaching the strength of the RAF, and training an army of 300,000 men rather than the 100,000 permitted by the Treaty. The British focused on appeasement as a means of controlling German rearmament by legalizing it in order to slow it down. It was hoped that by accepting open rearmament they could persuade Germany to return to the League of Nations and conform to the Washington rules on arms control and disarmament.[26] By 1936 Germany remilitarized the Rhineland in violation of Versailles. Britain's response demonstrates that appeasement was by then part of a policy of buying time.[27] Following the Anschluss in March 1938, Chamberlain accepted that rapid rearmament was a priority over economic stability, but time was still needed before Britain would be ready for war. The surrender of the Sudetenland by Britain and France was also based on an awareness of military capacity rather than a misguided belief that war could be avoided.[28]

The 'buying time' argument as an explanation for appeasement is supported by the figures for British defence expenditure from 1930–9 (in £ million):

Year	Navy	Army	RAF	Total Expenditure	Defence Spending as a % of GDP
1930	52.3	40.2	17.6	110.1	13%
1931	51.0	38.6	17.9	107.5	13%
1932	50.2	36.1	17.0	103.4	12%
1933	53.4	37.5	16.7	107.7	14%
1934	56.6	39.7	17.6	113.9	14%
1935	64.9	44.7	27.5	137.0	15%
1936	81.0	55.0	50.0	186.0	21%
1937	101.9	72.7	81.8	256.4	26%
1938	132.4	121.5	143.5	397.5	38%
1939	181.8	242.4	294.8	719.0	48%.[29]

The clear reality of appeasement is that Britain was not in a position of strength militarily or economically when Hitler came to power in 1933. As Germany began rearming, the British sought to use the tried and tested diplomatic tools of appeasement as a means of trying to get Hitler to engage with international bodies and treaty agreements. British diplomats and politicians knew that Germany posed a danger, and that there was a risk of another European war. However, Britain was not in a position to fight a war at that time. Britain had to use diplomatic options to reduce the risks, even if that meant granting concessions to Hitler. The expenditure on rearmament increased significantly from 1933 to

1939 which suggests that Britain recognized that even as diplomacy was being tried, the likelihood of war was more realistic. Appeasement would therefore appear to have been a policy based on the optimism of traditional diplomatic methods, and the necessity of a nation that was ill-prepared for the conflict it knew was likely to come.

Britain experienced significant bombing during the war, aimed mainly at large urban centres, ports, airfields and industrial areas. However, the mainland was not invaded. The Channel Islands were occupied and the citizens there experienced first-hand the harsh reality of Nazi rule. The options for resistance and sabotage were limited due to the geographical isolation of island life. There was a necessary pragmatism required to survive and minimize harm. The resistance included hiding Jews and helping some of the foreign forced and slave labourers involved in German building projects through the Todt Organization.[30] It has been suggested that the 'resistance myth' developed in the post-war years as a means of apportioning all blame on the Germans in order to prove the innocence of everyone else. Guilt would involve collaboration, but innocence would imply resistance.[31]

But, as will be shown, there was also collusion and collaboration with the Nazis, including identifying, denouncing and handing over Jews. It has been argued that the islanders did not so much collaborate, but rather, they submitted to superior force and 'tactically' cooperated with the occupiers. Some islanders however, believed that their civic leaders overstepped the mark in their cooperation with the Germans.[32] It has been suggested that the islanders were selective with which individuals or groups they would protect and support. This was demonstrated in the help offered to British military personnel, Freemasons or Jews who were established islanders, whilst protection was less readily offered – and sometimes denied – to foreign Jews or offenders against the occupation laws.[33] Clifford Orange had previously worked with foreign immigrants on the islands. During the occupation he was employed as the Jersey Aliens Officer and his tasks included the registration of the Jewish population. It is known that he applied criteria that was overly inclusive which led to him registering people as Jews when they should not have been registered as such. It has been further suggested that his efficiency may have been the result of his pre-war role.[34] Orange interviewed residents of Jersey to ascertain if they were Jewish according to race rules laid down by the Nazis. Twelve people were registered as Jewish by him.[35] The youngest of these, a 21-year-old Romanian named Hedwig Bercu, then disappeared in November 1943 and was sought by the German authorities. Her photograph was printed in the *Jersey Evening Post*.[36] It is not known what happened to most of the twelve people identified as being Jewish, but some islanders believe that Bercu was captured and sent to a concentration camp.[37] The collaboration of islanders did not reach the levels it did in occupied continental Europe but it was there nonetheless. It must also be observed that the island authorities successfully managed to ensure food supplies and public health were maintained.[38]

The newspapers of Jersey and Guernsey during the first year of occupation became the mouthpieces of the German authorities. It was through the press that the rules of obedience were spelled out and the consequences of resistance were made clear. Reports were published of rudeness to the occupiers and petty acts of sabotage, which were denounced in the pages as 'stupid' and 'dangerous'. Warnings of punishment by military tribunal for sabotage received broad press coverage.[39]

The main victims of the Nazi occupation were Jews and the foreign labourers brought there to build the Atlantic Wall. Additionally, islanders were deported to German civilian internment camps, and some political prisoners (resistance offenders) were imprisoned on the islands and on the continent, with some being sent into the concentration camp system never to return home.[40] The building of the Atlantic Wall began in the summer of 1941, and over the next two years the islands became the most fortified section of Hitler's Atlantic Wall. The regime became stricter, with food shortages, security alerts and restrictions on movements. The largest deportation took place in September 1942 when 2,300 civilians were deported in retaliation for German civilians being interned by the British in Persia.[41] There was an increase in defiance by the islanders which resulted in arrests, imprisonment and deportation to concentration camps.[42] The Channel Islands were liberated on 5 May 1945.

After the liberation, Alexander Coutanche, the Bailiff of Jersey, sent a private memo to the Home Office in which he defended the Royal Court's registration of anti-Jewish orders by claiming that they had no option. Prominent islander Lord Justice du Parcq wrote a memo listing areas of concern, including the fact that the island government had assisted the Germans in deporting 2,200 islanders to German internment camps.[43] Furthermore du Parcq observed that Victor Carey, the Bailiff of Guernsey, had published an order in the local press which referred to Allied soldiers as the enemy.[44] The islanders were willing to denounce their own people on occasion. Frederick Page was reported to the Germans by the Jersey authorities for a 'wireless offence'. He stood trial and was deported to Germany where he died in 1945. The case originated in May 1943 when Jersey police were advised that a man named James Davey had wireless sets in his home. On searching the property, they found the wireless sets, two of which belonged to Frederick Page. The wireless ban had been introduced by the Germans and was punishable by imprisonment. The police could submit a report against a fellow islander, or risk being denounced to the Germans. The officer in charge spoke to Attorney-General Charles Duret Aubin, who advised the officer to decide where his conscience lay, but if a report was submitted it would have to be forwarded to the Germans. The report was received by Duret Aubin on 2 June 1943 and was indeed forwarded to the Germans.[45]

After the war it was reported that one of the most uncomfortable memories for islanders was knowing that many of their neighbours had been informers. It went against the accepted rules of neighbourliness associated with the islands. Islanders found that trust had been lost and care had to be taken about whom they spoke to and what they said.[46]

When planning for the liberation the British worried that they would see the sort of 'instant justice' that had been meted out to collaborators on the continent. It was therefore planned to administer swift justice to black marketeers and collaborators.[47] It is apparent that there may not have been a great deal of enthusiasm to raise the spectre of collaboration. In a report to the Home Office in the summer of 1945, C. W. Blackmore, financial advisor to Brigadier Alfred Snow, wrote:

> If at the outset we give any indication of our readiness to lend countenance to accusations of collaboration we shall be undermining the influence of the very instruments upon which we must rely to set the islands on their feet again, for it is only too clear from the information which is coming through to us that there is an element among the population dissatisfied with the conduct of the administrators who stood between them and their oppressors.[48]

Following the liberation, the British conducted investigations to consider evidence of cruelty against slave labourers, the behaviour of the island governments during the occupation, collaboration of a serious enough nature to be prosecuted and war crimes by the Germans. Uniquely among territories which had been occupied, no cases went to trial and no significant criticisms were offered against the islanders or the island governments.[49]

The *Kindertransport* is viewed as a noble endeavour that undoubtedly saved the lives of thousands of Jewish children by bringing them to the UK. The events of *Kristallnacht* on 9/10 November 1938 were the final straw for many Jewish families and brought into sharp focus the dangers they faced if they remained in Germany. It also stirred a response from the British government. Independent MP Eleanor Rathbone set up a Parliamentary Committee on Refugees, and on 14 November 1938 the home secretary, Sir Samuel Hoare, observed that emotions were raised not just in government but across the country.[50] Prime Minister Chamberlain also received a deputation from the Council for German Jewry. It was accepted that unlimited immigration was not an option, but the request was for Britain to provide temporary refuge to Jewish children.[51]

Some hesitance in helping Jewish refugees reflected concerns about antisemitism and hostility to foreigners. Indeed, the home secretary told the House of Commons during a debate on the refugee situation that there was an 'underlying current of suspicion and anxiety rightly or wrongly, about alien immigration on any big scale. It is a fact that below the surface there is the making of a definite anti-Jewish movement'.[52] As with the response to the Wagner-Rogers proposal in the U.S. there is a startling contemporary similarity to the hostility shown to refugees whose plight was known. On 21 November, Hoare advised the House of Commons that Britain would accept refugees who were trying to get to other countries. Britain eased its rules on immigration. As a result, whilst up until March 1938 only 11,000 Jews from Germany arrived, during the ensuing nineteen months approximately 50,000 Jews from Germany, Austria and Czechoslovakia were accepted into Britain. Included within that number were approximately 9,000 children under the age of 17 who came on the trains known as the *Kindertransport*[53] that transported the children from Berlin, Prague and Vienna to the Netherlands, after which ferries brought them to the UK.[54] In an ironic twist, the large numbers being admitted to Britain were partly the result of a British policy to prevent immigration of Jews to Palestine.[55]

The excellent study by Angel and Evans gives unique insights into the experiences and perspectives of survivors from that time. The journey of unaccompanied minors to a foreign land in which they understood neither the language nor the culture was undoubtedly traumatic. A survivor who was aged 7 at the time stated:

> My father would go every day early in the morning and get in line to different embassies to try and get visas for the whole family, but was unable to get even into the premises. So, in desperation they didn't know what to do, and after a lot of heart-searching, as you can imagine, they agreed for my sister and myself to come to England on this transport, which became known as *Kindertransport*.[56]

The emotional trauma was undoubtedly exacerbated by the British stipulation that the *Kinderstransport* children must be unaccompanied.[57] That insistence almost certainly condemned many thousands of adults to death during the later horrors of the Holocaust. About three-quarters of the *Kindertransport* survivors interviewed for the Angel and Evans study never saw their parents.[58] Most of those interviewed by Angel and Evans spoke of gratitude for the *Kindertransport* and the parallel Czech *Kindertransports* organized by Nicholas Winton. The interviewees also had mixed feelings about having to leave their parents behind. Many were critical that the number of children actually saved was small when compared to the number that could have been saved. As one interviewee said:

> I would say that to rescue 10,000 children when there were a million and a half that needed rescuing is pitiful. A million and a half children are not with us. That's a crime. One of the biggest crimes the world has ever seen. It doesn't matter whether I am alive or not. Those children deserved to live just as much as me. The children that were left behind in my class in Berlin. And relating that to the fact that a million people have become refugees over this last year or so. I think about that and I talk about it to the people here and I don't know what is going to happen to them.[59]

The harsh reality of the *Kindertransport*, and the willingness of the British government to accept Jewish refugees is not just the lives saved, it is the innocent lives lost because people were left behind to place their fate in the hands of a Nazi regime that was openly hostile and violent towards Jews. Hindsight would suggest that although the rescues were commendable, more could and should have been done.

Britain had its own lesser issues with fascism. Most notably this is associated with Sir Oswald Mosley who founded the British Union of Fascists (BUF) in October 1932.[60] Mosley had moved around the political spectrum. He was first elected to the House of Commons in 1918 as the Conservative MP for Harrow. In 1920 he crossed the floor and sat as an Independent MP. In 1924 he joined the Labour Party and in 1926 he was elected as Labour MP for Smethwick. By February 1931 he had left the Labour Party, and in March 1931 he founded the New Party which lasted for a year and a half.[61] British fascism differed from continental fascism in some ways but it was financially aided by Benito Mussolini and was intellectually influenced by both Mussolini and Hitler. It shared a clear similarity to the continental fascists in that Mosley allowed antisemitism as part of the BUF platform, and it relied on street-level support. The BUF was not electorally successful.[62] It also differed from its continental equivalents in that it was stopped before it caused millions to die; continental fascism was stopped only after the slaughter had occurred.[63] The potential success of fascism in Britain was effectively curtailed at the beginning of the Second World War when Mosley, his wife Diana, and over 700 of his supporters were incarcerated in May 1940.[64]

Mosley's route into fascism began in earnest following a New Party rally in Glasgow on 20 September 1931. Local communists attended and the event was disrupted by serious violence. The police had to intervene and Mosley and his contingent were forced to make a hasty escape. The following day he and his colleagues reflected on the previous day's events and Mosley is reported to have said, 'This forces us to be fascist and ... we need no longer hesitate to create our trained and disciplined force.'[65]

Most New Party rallies were marred by fights and violent confrontations with communists and other opponents. After the infamous 'Battle of Cable Street' in the East End of London in 1936, Parliament passed the Public Order Act which limited the ability of the BUF to organize street protests.[66] They also displayed a military style which was alien to

British politics at the time.[67] The militarism, ultra-nationalism and sense of service and discipline of fascism appealed to Mosley.[68] He saw fascism as 'a new creed for the twentieth century'.[69] Racism and xenophobia were a feature of Mosley's politics, and, in a similarity to Hitler's Nazis, he also had an interest in eugenics.[70] The BUF was primarily a street movement based on protests. Its membership was paltry and when it was shut down in 1940 it only numbered 9,000. It did have support from one element of the press, most notably on 8 January 1934 when Lord Rothermere wrote an article in the *Daily Mail* entitled 'Hurrah for the Blackshirts'.[71]

How much of a danger Mosley and the BUF posed is debatable. His ambitions were to limit the power of Parliament, create a one-party state and reduce the power of world Jewry.[72] Mosley opposed the war but tried to remain within the law in his advice to the BUF membership. He encouraged BUF members to join civilian defence units rather than the armed forces. In the military, orders are expected to be obeyed, whereas in units such as the Special Constabulary, Air Raid Precautions and the Nursing Reserve there was no obligation to obey instructions. Members of the BUF were further encouraged to join these civilian defence units so that they could spread propaganda.[73] Mosley's message which promoted an alternative version of the causes of the war, suggested that there should be a refusal to fight in a conflict that had been created by Jewish financiers. He suggested that the BUF would only fight if Britain was actually invaded.[74] Neil Francis Hawkins, the director-general of the BUF sent a letter to all BUF branches:

Young men likely soon to be called up have addressed many questions to Headquarters upon their position. The position of the movement is as follows: We have always been willing to fight for our country if Britain or her Empire is threatened. In fact, many of our members entered the Forces of the Crown before the War in case that ever happened. Members who are in any of the Forces of the Crown have been advised to obey orders. All members have been asked to do nothing to injure the country and to obey the Law. Those of us who are now free under the Law to decide the matter for ourselves are not offering our services to fight in this War BECAUSE WE DO NOT CONSIDER THAT BRITAIN OR HER EMPIRE IS THREATENED. It is a matter for the individual conscience of young men who are now to be called up whether or not they exercise the right which the Law gives them of appearing before the Tribunal.[75]

Special Branch observed that this letter was 'so couched as to leave no doubt in the reader's mind that the leaders desire those of their followers who are of conscription age to refuse to serve'.[76] MI5 observed :

The outbreak of war brought about no change in the policy or outlook of British Union ... For reasons which are obvious, Sir Oswald Mosley did not call upon his followers to perform illegal acts. He did not call upon members of the Armed Forces to refuse to obey orders. But, short of committing illegal acts, everything was done to ensure that 'financial democracy dictated by Jewish interests' was not victorious and that world Fascism remained undefeated.[77]

There seems to be little doubt that Mosley had sympathies and ambitions that were potentially harmful to Great Britain and the Allies. He endeavoured to profit from the social unrest and societal difficulties consequent to the First Word War and the Great Depression. He was a gifted orator, and prior to forming the New Party and then the BUF, he had successfully sat as an elected politician for the Conservatives, as an Independent and for the Labour Party. He was a rabble-rouser and garnered some mass appeal. Incarcerated for the duration of the war, his influence was therefore negligible, but his politics, and the existence of the BUF served as a warning during the war, and would spawn other far-right groups in the years and decades after the war. Politically, the BUF never won a seat. It was a small party but had the potential to be a malign influence on British life. Its successors have continued to promote toxic racism and ultra-nationalism

This chapter has not addressed the knowledge that the British government had of the mass murder of Jews, and was aware of long before public statements were made by Churchill and others. Those issues are addressed elsewhere in this book.

Britain was not above reproach prior to and during the war. It could certainly have done more to help save Jewish victims of Nazi terror. It had information about the genocide long before it became known to the wider public. Citizens of the Channel Islands showed also how – for multiple reasons – it was possible for those in occupied territories to cooperate and collaborate with the occupiers. This was more of an issue in the countries of continental Europe, which faced the full-force of Nazi brutality, and will be the focus of the following chapters.

Chapter 5

France

France in the 1930s had a reputation for offering asylum to those fleeing the oppressive regime of Nazi Germany. Indeed, no European country during the interwar years took in more refugees.[1] However, as the decade progressed, and economic conditions worsened, hostility to new arrivals grew. Laws were created that made it difficult for immigrants to enter oversubscribed job sectors such as medicine and the legal profession. Even in the film industry there were complaints about a Semitic invasion that was stealing jobs from native-born French workers. The film director Marcel L'Herbier cited the 1936 accession to power of Leon Blum as the point when 'Jewish immigrants' took over the film industry and began 'remaking it in their own image which is assuredly not our own'.[2] It is apparent that in some social, employment and political quarters there was established hostility towards Jews that predated the war and the invasion of France by German forces in 1940.

French collaboration with the Nazis and the murder of Jews will be addressed in due course. It is a country with a history of Holocaust denial and negationism. The earliest high-profile post-war negationist was probably Paul Rassinier, who has already been mentioned in the chapter on Holocaust denial. Rassinier had been beaten by fellow prisoners at Buchenwald after failing to pay his respects to the leader of the German Communists. As a result, he feared fellow inmates more than the SS. He was given a job in the infirmary at camp 'Dora' in the Harz Mountains where it appears he was relatively well treated by the senior SS officer. This seems to have prejudiced him in favour of the Nazis, about whom he wrote in defence of the criticism they faced. He denied that atrocities had occurred in the camps, disputed the existence of gas chambers, and claimed that the Jews had started the war.[3]

More influential, as an inspiration and supporter of negationists such as David Irving, Fred Leuchter and Ernst Zündel was another Frenchman, Robert Faurisson. He was particularly active in the 1980s and 1990s. He argued that claims of genocide, massacres and gas chambers were all part of a Zionist lie and a political and financial swindle designed to benefit Israel. His main focus was in trying to prove that the gas chambers at Auschwitz and other camps never existed.[4] He was eventually prosecuted by the French for crimes of inciting racial hatred, slander, and wilfully distorting history.[5]

France took a long time to confront the record of the nation and its people during the period of the Nazi occupation. The Second World War was not taught as part of the school curriculum until 1962, and the Holocaust was rarely mentioned in textbooks. Furthermore, no French leader until Jacques Chirac acknowledged the state's role and complicity in deporting Jews to Nazi concentration and death camps.[6] Years later, President Nicolas Sarkozy attended a commemoration event at the Paris Shoah memorial to remember the anniversary of the Vel d'Hiv round-up of Jews. He declined to add to the comments of former President Chirac.[7]

In February 2002 the minister of national education, Jack Lang, created a commission tasked with investigating extreme far-right activities at the University of Lyon III. The investigation was conducted by the noted historian Henry Rousso.[8] Rousso's report was made public in October 2004. It examined Lyon III and other French universities since 1968. It also looked at analysing the political and cultural roots of French negationism.[9] It noted an almost uniquely French phenomenon of persistent negationism in universities often among right-wing intellectuals with academic reputations. Of course, negationism was found among neo-fascists and the extreme right, but also – again, almost uniquely French – in groups of the anti-Stalinist extreme left.[10] In more recent times, Holocaust denial and negationism have been found in some Islamic groups on the fringes of French Muslim society.[11] As Rousso observed, the denial of the Holocaust by the far-right of post-war France is long established, and is almost a precondition of the rise of the extreme right after the failure of the Vichy government and 1940s collaboration with the Nazis. Negationism within the ranks of the extreme left has generally been confined to a few isolated militants. Negationism within some Muslim communities is part of a worldwide phenomenon and has links to Arab/Muslim antisemitism.[12]

One of the individuals cited within the Rousso report about Lyon III was Bruno Gollnisch, a deputy leader of the far-right, at the time a prospective candidate to replace Jean-Marie Le Pen as head of the Front National, and a professor of Japanese at the university. At a news conference he stated (after not even reading the report):

> I contest the legitimacy of this mission to police our thinking. Henry Rousso is a politically biased historian, a Jew, a respected figure, but his neutrality cannot be vouched for ... there is no serious historian who still agrees with the conclusions of the Nuremberg Trials ... I'm not denying the existence of concentration camps but, as to the number of dead, historians can certainly differ ... As for the existence of gas chambers, it is up to historians to make up their minds ... It is in the interest of many to deny this debate in Israel in its endless discussions over reparations.[13]

Gollnisch contended that his words were misreported as no journalist at the news conference had repeated the entirety of his statement which he claimed should have read:

> It is not unreasonable to fear that a Commission such as this might not respect the adage '*nemo judex in causa sua propria,*' 'no one should judge his own cause'. M. Rousso, a formidable historian of Jewish origin, Director of the Institute of Contemporary History (CNRS), a declared enemy of 'revisionists' who has wrongly declared Lyon III to be riddled with them, should have been considered a historian already against what he was asked to study. However, it seems that his report, if it is not the mountain that gives birth to a mouse, is at least a dash of cold water in the face of the persecutors of freedom of thought.[14]

These two statements highlight firstly, typical negationist language about the Holocaust, and secondly, a strange attempt to dismiss the credibility of Rousso's investigation and report on the basis that he is Jewish. Rousso identified the issues with negationism and antisemitism at Lyon III. His report was submitted to assist the government in addressing these problems. Gollnisch's response was to dismiss the validity of the report due to the faith and heritage of the author, and to resort to standard negationist arguments as a form of counterattack. The negationists describe themselves as revisionists – in France and elsewhere – but, it has been argued that whilst it must be possible to remember and represent some elements of the past differently, there are parts of the past that are absolute and cannot be reimagined.[15]

France has a history of Holocaust denial going back to the end of the Second World War. It also had, and still has, problems with antisemitism in some sectors of society. The hostility of some French people towards Jewish fellow citizens during the war manifested in collusion, collaboration and participation in the Nazi crimes of the Holocaust.

German forces invaded France on 10 May 1940.[16] On 22 June 1940, only six weeks after the Battle of France had commenced, the Armistice was signed.[17] The speed and success of the German victory astonished not just the French, but also allies of France who had believed in French military might and the capabilities of its defences. Half of France was occupied by German forces. In the unoccupied zones an authoritarian regime was set up, with its capital in the town of Vichy. The leader of the Vichy regime was former First World War hero, Marshal Philippe Pétain.[18] The Vichy regime enjoyed some popular support initially in 1940, but public opinion turned against it as the war and the occupation progressed.

Pétain and Vichy ministers all seemed to concur that there was a problem with Jews in France which needed to be resolved. They felt that Jews had some form of evil influence on French society and therefore had to be removed from the economy and from positions from which they could influence public opinion.[19]

As will be addressed later, there was little in the way of public outrage or protest when the regime enacted antisemitic laws in the summer and autumn of 1940, but there was reaction from citizens and some of the Catholic clergy when, in July 1942, the Vichy regime responded to German pressure and rounded up 12,000 Parisian Jews. They were held at the Vélodrome d'Hiver (commonly known as Vel' d'Hiv) before being deported to German-occupied territory in the east.[20]

Jews in France were divided roughly equally between the occupied and Vichy zones. There were approximately 150,000 Jews in Paris, of whom 60,000 were not born in France.[21] The Vichy government rapidly enforced anti-Jewish rules. As early as 13 July 1940, it was decreed that only men with French parentage were allowed to work in government. A matter of days later the right to practise medicine or hold positions in the civil service were similarly restricted. By 22 July 1940, those foreigners who had been naturalized since 1927 had their French nationality taken away. That legislation particularly impacted upon approximately 6,000 Jews, and was mainly felt by those refugees from Germany, and from Central and Eastern Europe.[22]

On 23 July 1940, citizenship was removed from anyone who was foreign born and had fled from France, and their property was seized. In August the Marchendeau Law was revoked. This law had been enacted in 1881 and protected religious and racial minorities from abuse in the press. It was an important law that defined the Third Republic and its liberal ideals.[23] Minorities were now open to any level of attack and abuse in the press with no legal protections available to them. On 3 October 1940, the Vichy government revealed a charter known as the Statut des Juifs, which defined Jewishness more strictly than Nazi Germany's Nuremberg Race Laws. It also prevented Jews from holding a range of professional, cultural and public positions. It allowed Jews to serve in the armed forces but they were not permitted to obtain commissions. Then, on 7 October 1940, Pétain's Vichy government repealed the Crémieux Decree, which, since October 1870, had granted the Jews of Algeria full French citizenship. In an instant, 170,000 Jews lost their civil rights.[24] In the four years of Vichy's existence approximately 400 laws, decrees, police measures and amendments to laws were introduced. They progressed from defining Jews, to counting Jews, dispossessing Jews, the issuing of ration books, the issuing of identity papers upon which the word 'Juif' was stamped, isolation from the majority population, being forced to wear a distinctive sign in the occupied zone, and ultimately, being transferred to camps for deportation.[25]

Evidence of hostility towards Jews, particularly foreign-born Jews, was found with the redevelopment of slum areas in Paris, known as *îlots insalubres* (literally insalubrious islets). As early as 1921, a memo from the Seine prefecture to the city council had identified these areas as being unsanitary with high mortality rates due to tuberculosis. One of the slums (*îlots*) was *îlot* 16, and of the seventeen identified in the memo, it was destined for special attention. It was known as an area where the majority of the residents were foreign Jews. In the 1940s, Guy Périer de Féral, the secretary-general of the Seine prefecture, described *îlot* 16 as 'sordid, inhabited by very poor people, the majority of whom are Jewish emigrants from Eastern Europe'.[26] Although the 1921 memo had identified seventeen *ilots* as being in need of eviction and redevelopment, it was not until October 1941, in the midst of war and occupation, that *ilot* 16, the only one known to house a majority foreign Jewish population was targeted for *actual* redevelopment.[27] It is questionable why this decision was made at that time. It has been observed that local urban redevelopment policies seemed to interact neatly with government policies of racial persecution against Jews. It has also been questioned whether the apparently urgent need to complete the redevelopment – at a time when France had other priorities – was part of a desire by the prefecture and city authorities to comply with national antisemitic policies.[28] The French law of 22 July 1941 determined the Aryanization of all government departments. Apart from that which was privately owned, all Jewish homes were to be seized. The law also demanded that the racial status of all people should be known.[29] Parisian housing organization archives for September 1942 have shown that the problems being faced by persecuted Jewish tenants of *ilot* 16 was an incentive to continue with the redevelopment. Furthermore, because some of the 639 Jewish families living there had actually left the area of their own volition, there was no need to rehouse them.[30] Backouche and Gensberger suggest that although the eviction and redevelopment projects were not inspired by state antisemitism, the actions helped normalize and trivialize it. In a positive twist, it transpires that 57 per cent of the 415 Jewish families that were evicted actually escaped deportation.[31]

France has had to come to terms with the fact some of Vichy's anti-Jewish and immigration policies were a continuum from the pre-war years. The French middle and professional classes had previously wanted governments of the Third Republic to introduce restrictive measures aimed particularly at foreign Jews. They found that Vichy not only agreed with their demands, but was also willing to carry them out. Pre-war, these policies were both economic and antisemitic. With the Vichy government the economic issue was resolved as Jewish businesses were dispossessed by state-appointed administrators.[32] It was not just the professional and middle classes that offered support for the Vichy government. There is evidence that the higher clergy of the Catholic Church also welcomed the new state as it was believed it promised to re-Christianize France.[33]

Furthermore, as the historian Max Hastings observes, the support for the Vichy government was widespread in the early years of the occupation, and thus there was also collaboration with the Germans.[34]

The most notorious act of French involvement in the crimes of the Holocaust was the round-up of Jews in Paris, their detention at Vel' d'Hiv, transportation to French sites of containment, and eventual deportation to Auschwitz and other Nazi camps. In May 1940, as German forces moved west, there was an influx of refugees into France. They included 8,000 Germans, of whom 5,000 were Jewish, and 10,000 people from the Netherlands and Belgium. These refugees were rounded up by the Parisian police and held in the Vel' d'Hiv and the Buffalo Stadium.[35] Worse was to come. The French Jewish diarist Hélène Berr noted on 15 July 1942: 'Something is brewing, something that will be a tragedy, maybe *the* tragedy.' Berr was warned that the Germans were planning a round-up of approximately 20,000 Jews. She added: 'A wave of terror has been gripping everybody else as well these past few days. It appears that the SS have taken command in France and terror must follow.'[36] The warnings were indeed true. The SS had planned the details of the first significant action in France following a visit by Adolf Eichmann. René Bousquet, head of the French police, informed his lieutenants that most of the operation would be manned and run by French police and other personnel. It was planned that they would detain 28,000 non-French Jews who had all been named on lists provided by the Jewish section of the Parisian police.[37]

The events of 16 July 1942 were summarized in a publication circulated a few months later by the Resistance:

> They took away women and children over the age of two, women in the seventh and eighth, and even the ninth month of pregnancy, sick people who were pulled out of their beds and carried on chairs or stretchers … it was especially the round-up of the children that must be emphasized. From the age of two they were considered candidates for the concentration camps! In a number of cases mothers were forcibly torn away from their little ones. Screaming and weeping filled the streets.[38]

The police and paramilitary operation led to the capture of 11,363 people, which was nowhere near the intended amount. More raids took place on 17 July, which increased the total to 12,884, of whom 3,031 were men, 5,802 were women, and at least 4,051 were children.[39] The numbers could have been much greater. The rumours of impending raids had been heeded. Many men ensured that they were not at home at the time. Foreign Jews, who were used to police raids, had prepared hiding places. Many police officers had leaked information to people they knew. Some police were less than thorough in knocking on doors and waiting for an answer. Some ignored Jews they saw sneaking away. The communist underground also released warnings in Yiddish.[40]

Despite the reduced numbers of captives, the raids had been carried out as planned. At 0400 hours on 16 July 1942, approximately 9,000 uniformed police officers and 400 members of a right-wing paramilitary organization, began the operation in six arrondissements. The captured Jews were to be placed in fifty buses, which had blackened windows, and then transported to appointed centres for sorting and deportation. The orders were intended to ensure that certain criteria were adhered to and that some excluded groups were not deported. The excluded groups were pregnant women, women with children under the age of 2, wives of prisoners of war, war widows, those married to exempted persons and registered employees of the Union Générale des Israélites de France (UGIF).[41]

Of the captives, nearly 5,000 were sent to Drancy. In excess of 8,000 Jews were sent to the Vel' d'Hiv in the 15th arrondissement, where they were held for over five days. The conditions there were terrible with no water supply, few toilets and a lack of food. Many of the Jews were distressed and in poor health. Dehydration was a problem. There were only about a dozen doctors and nurses available to try to deliver care.[42] It is worth noting that the camp at Drancy was guarded by French police officers until the summer of 1943 when the SS took over responsibility.[43]

From 19 to 22 July the Jews in the Vel' d'Hiv were walked in batches to the Gare d'Austerlitz, from where they travelled by train to the transit camps at Beaune-la-Rolande and Pithiviers. Between 31 July and 7 August four trains took adults and older children east to Auschwitz. David Cesarani notes that the passengers on the first transport were registered at the camp. Subsequent transports were subject to selections on arrival (i.e. selected as forced labour or to be killed). The majority of those on the transport of 5 August were sent to the gas chambers.[44]

The fate of most of these people was either immediate death in the gas chambers (if they survived the journey) or the slower death associated with starvation, disease, slave and forced labour, Nazi brutality and the general deprivations of camp existence. The *Auschwitz Chronicle* details information gathered from the archives of the Auschwitz Memorial and from German Federal Archives. The *Auschwitz Chronicle* confirms for 31 July 1942:

> 1,001 Jews arrive from the twelfth RSHA [Reich Main Security Office] transport from Drancy. There are 270 men and 730 women on the transport. After the selection, all the men and 514 women are admitted to the camp as prisoners ... the other 216 women are killed.[45]

It is unlikely that these were part of transport from France on 31 July. For 2 August 1942, the record states: 'The thirteenth RSHA transport from Pithiviers arrives. 693 Jewish men receive Nos. 55083–55775; 359 Jewish women receive Nos. 14156–14514.' It is presumed that this is the first transport of 31 July to which Cesarani refers.[46]

For 5 August 1942 the record states:

> 52 Jewish men and 982 Jewish women arrive with the fourteenth RSHA transport from Pithiviers. After selection, 22 men, who receive Nos. 56411–56432, and 542 women, who are numbered after the registration of the deported Belgian Jewish women, are admitted to the camp. The other 470 people are killed in the gas chambers ... 542 women sent from Pithiviers Camp in France with the fourteenth RSHA transport and classified as able-bodied receive Nos. 15102–15267 and 15269–15644.[47]

For 7 August 1942, the record advises that:

> The fifteenth RSHA transport arrives from Beaune-la-Rolande in France with 1,014 Jews. There are 588 men and boys and 426 women and girls in the transport. After the selection, 214 men who receive Nos. 57103–57316, and 96 women are admitted to the camp. The rest of the deportees (704) are killed in the gas chambers.[48]

For 12 August 1942, the record states:

> For 12 August 1942: 1,006 Jews arrive in a RSHA transport from Drancy. There are 525 women and 475 men in the transport, including 400 old people. Almost all of them were born in Germany. After the selection, 140 men and 100 women are admitted to the camp and receive Nos. 58086–58225 and 16337–16736. The other 766 deportees are killed in the gas chambers.[49]

Finally, the record for 13 August 1942 states:

> For 13 August 1942: 1,007 Jews from France, predominantly old people, arrive with the eighteenth RSHA transport from Drancy. After the selection, 233 men and 62 women are admitted to the camp as inmates and receive Nos. 58785–59017 and 17069–17130. The other 712 deportees are killed in the gas chambers.[50]

The scale of loss is alarming. These few transports brought 6,291 people to Auschwitz. A few days and weeks earlier they had been healthy. They had committed no crime, and were not deserving of any punishment. Of the 6,297 cited, 2,868 would be sent straight to the gas chambers. Their suffering and deaths were brought about through a combination of many factors including French antisemitism, German plans to destroy European Jewry, French collaboration, the actions of French police and paramilitaries, and, despite some leaking of information to warn of the round-ups, the apparent willingness, indifference or apathy of French citizens and officialdom to allow the deportations to occur.

The actions of the French militias were known to be extreme. Dr Charles Kaufmann was arrested by the SS in 1944, for helping members of the French Resistance. He was denounced by five members of the Milice, a militia formed by the Vichy regime in 1943 in collaboration with German forces. The Milice were reputed to be more brutal than the Gestapo, with a willingness to use torture and assassination against fellow French citizens.[51] Freda Wineman, born in Metz, Lorraine in 1923, is a Jewish survivor of the Holocaust. She describes how

In May 1944, my mother found a convent willing to give us shelter, but before we could go there, we were arrested. It happened on 17 May 1944. By chance the Milice (Vichy police) stopped my mother and found she was carrying our ration books, which identified us as Jews and told the Gestapo that there were six of us the family. My mother was arrested immediately.[52]

Freda and two of her brothers were arrested and interrogated by the Gestapo. A few days later Freda and the rest of the family were rounded up and arrested, before being put on a train to Drancy. Within a few more days the family were put onto a lorry and taken to Drancy station, where they were placed in a cattle truck to be transported to Auschwitz. Her mother, father and one of her brothers were murdered in Auschwitz.[53]

In recent years press reports in France have alleged that the *gendarmerie nationale* made use of wartime Jewish card indexes to organize round-ups. Such actions facilitated the oppression, deportation and ultimately the murder of Jews. A parliamentary commission of inquiry was convened but dismissed the case. However, it highlighted continuing political sensitivity to allegations of French complicity and participation in Nazi policies of Jewish persecution.[54] In the 1980s allegations against collaborators − including resistance fighters − were made public. Nazi hunter Serge Klarsfeld campaigned for a retrial of René Bousquet, the former head of the French national police, and Jean Laguay, who was Bousquet's representative in occupied France, for their role in the deportation of Jews. As has already been observed, Bousquet led the July 1942 Vel' d'Hiv detentions and deportations.[55] In June 1993, Bousquet was murdered in his apartment as he awaited trial. In 1994, Paul Touvier, a former member of the Milice in Lyon was found guilty of crimes against humanity. In 1998, Maurice Papon, was also found guilty of crimes against humanity, for his role in the deportation of 1,600 Jews from Bordeaux.[56]

In 1997, the French Catholic Church publicly asked to be forgiven for its failure to help Jews during the Holocaust.[57] The ceremony was aimed to coincide with the pope's visit to Paris from 21 to 24 August. The pope was going to admit to centuries of Christian intolerance. In 1994, the pope called on all Catholics to acknowledge the evils of antisemitism.[58] On 30 September 1997, at Drancy, from where the deportation of 67,000

French Jews had occurred, the bishop of Saint Denis, Olivier de Berranger, asked for the indifference and silence of the Catholic Church during the Holocaust to be forgiven. An acknowledgement that the bishop's words had been heard was made by Henri Hajdenberg, president of the Conseil Représentatif des Institutions Juives de France.[59] The apology needs to be considered in the context of longstanding antisemitism within the Catholic Church and among its members, and of centuries of targeting Jews as scapegoats. The apology seemed somewhat belated as it occurred long after contrition had been offered by the Church hierarchy in Germany, Hungary, Poland and even the United States.[60]

The apology ignited considerable debate. Until 1983 textbooks in France had maintained that the deportations of Jews were solely due to the actions of the Germans. It was not until 1995, shortly after being inaugurated, that President Jacques Chirac acknowledged the complicity of the State and the Catholic Church by admitting that France bore responsibility for the deportation to death camps of 25 per cent of the country's Jews.[61] When the apology and request for forgiveness was made, it was not universally welcomed. The then leader of the far-right Front National, Jean-Marie Le Pen, described it as absolutely scandalous.[62] Some would suggest that in reality, it was a necessary apology that came too late, and that the hierarchy of the French Catholic Church under the Vichy regime never offered any form of apology.[63]

There has been reluctance in France to accept the level of support the Catholic Church gave to the Vichy regime. When laws were imposed against Jews, no Catholic leader publicly protested against them.[64] Of course they did not publicly welcome the anti-Jewish measures of the Vichy regime either. It was not until 23 August 1942 that Jules Saliège, the archbishop of Toulouse issued a powerful declaration denouncing the round-ups that had taken place that summer.[65]

It has been argued that the 'politics of memory' affected the delay in an apology from the Catholic Church for the silence and inaction of French bishops during the Holocaust. Prior to the commencement of deportations not a single public objection was raised by the hierarchy of the Church about the treatment being meted out against Jews.[66] And of the seventy-six bishops in France, only six raised any objections once the deportations started. The objections soon quietened down as, in all probability, the Church saw benefits in silence and apparent loyalty to Pétain and the

Vichy regime which had brought religion back into education, provided funds for private Catholic schools, supported the idea of family values – however they could be defined – and was openly hostile to communism and the Freemasons.[67] The Vichy regime sought to appeal to Catholics and Protestants. It claimed to seek a return to some form of Christian order.[68] It is worth observing that such ideals are proposed by modern contemporary populist nationalist politicians. Michael Sutton suggests that behind the antisemitism and indifference of public opinion there was also centuries-old ingrained thinking. Additionally, for the formulators of opinion and the elites of France, there were modern variants of antisemitism during the years of occupation, and the appeal of 'Nazi-like' doctrines of a racist nature espoused by some of the collaborators based in Paris.[69]

Pétain actually sought out the Vatican's opinion on the anti-Jewish laws the Vichy regime had imposed. Vatican Ambassador Léon Bérard, in a letter dated 21 September 1941, provided assurance that 'an authorized person at the Vatican had said that the church would not start any quarrel over restricting certain citizens' access to jobs or over limiting Jews actions in society'. To cast doubt about any later ambiguities from the Catholic Church after the deportations commenced, a further letter from Bérard on 18 January 1943 advised that Pope Pius XII 'very warmly praised the work of the Marshal and took a keen interest in government actions that are a sign of the fortunate renewal of religious life in France'.[70]

Of course, many Catholics helped and undoubtedly saved Jews at great personal risk. Over 4,000 French citizens have been recognized as Righteous Among Nations.[71] Many members of the lower clergy opposed deportations, and eighty-five ecclesiastics have been acknowledged as rescuers by Yad Vashem.[72] But, the Catholic Church in France was very closely bound to the Vichy regime, and became so discredited that when General Charles de Gaulle was invited to attend an event at Notre Dame in thanksgiving for the liberation of France, he refused to allow Cardinal Suhard, the Cardinal of Paris, to be there.[73]

The Vichy government created anti-Jewish legislation that went further than the laws of the Nazis, and its legal system cooperated more than any other occupied nation. Jews were deported and also, 3,000 died in French-run internment camps.[74] Such was the enthusiasm of the Vichy regime that when the Nazis required the deportation of Jewish males aged 16–60, and Jewish females aged 16–55, Pétain's second-in-command Pierre Laval requested that children also be deported.[75] There was cooperation from the French police with the deportations of Jews from the summer of 1942, and round-ups occurred in the occupied and the unoccupied zones. Twenty-five per cent of the Jewish population of France – 76,000 – including 10,000 children were handed over to the Nazis and deported to be exterminated.[76]

It is of course well known that after liberation there were violent recriminations against Nazi sympathizers and collaborators. Several thousand people would die in what was to become known as *l'épuration* – the purification – which may have helped to expunge some sense of national guilt and shame. Following a post-liberation visit to Paris, the U.S. Army historian Forrest Pogue wrote: 'I soon found that the old bitterness against Jews and labor remained.'[77] The implication is that animosity towards Jews existed prior to, during and following the occupation. It was as much a French phenomenon as it was a German Nazi phenomenon. Max Hastings wrote:

To this day, France has not produced an official history of its war experience, and probably never will do so, because consensual support for any version of events would be unattainable. It is striking that the most persuasive modern studies of the French wartime era have been written by American and British authors: relatively few indigenous scholars wish to address it.[78]

In France, like many countries in Europe, the history of antisemitism predated the German invasion. Although France had accepted more refugees from Nazi Germany than any other country in Europe, it is apparent that multiple factors – economic, social, political and religious – contributed to an increase in hostility and intolerance towards foreign-born Jews, and also to French-born Jews. The Vichy regime cooperated and collaborated with the Nazis. The French police were actively involved in round-ups of Jews and detentions in internment camps. Three thousand Jews died in French internment camps and 76,000 Jews were deported to Nazi extermination and concentration camps. But there are still high-profile voices on the far-right of French politics that continue to deny the Holocaust and condemn any expressions of contrition, guilt, sorrow or remorse.

France and the French people suffered during the occupation and under the regime of Vichy. But there was collaboration, collusion and active participation in the crimes of the Holocaust. Of course, commendably, over 4,000 French citizens are recognized as Righteous Among Nations, and eighty-five ecclesiastics have been cited as rescuers by Yad Vashem. The Second World War history of France requires honesty and the acceptance of wrongdoing by citizens, police, the military, the Catholic Church, politicians, communities and wider society.

France is not alone among the formerly occupied nations for wrongs committed against Jews or that allowed the scourge of Nazism to take its toll on human life and cause untold misery. This will be explored further in the following chapters.

Chapter 6

The Netherlands

The people of the Netherlands are surely permitted to be proud that their country is second only to Poland with the number of its citizens – 5,778 – identified as being Righteous Among Nations.[1] But, of course, the Jewish population of Poland was much larger, and Poland was the primary territorial site chosen by the Nazis for the crimes of the Holocaust. As has been shown, and will be demonstrated elsewhere, the citizens of many occupied territories were also responsible for harming and murdering Jews, and the Netherlands is no exception.

When the war commenced in September 1939 with the invasion of Poland, both Belgium and the Netherlands remained neutral. They would, however, forfeit their neutrality should Germany invade France through their territories, as had previously happened in 1914.[2] Predictably, on 10 May 1940, German forces poured into Belgium, the Netherlands and France. Victory was rapid and all three countries were defeated within a few weeks, and, due to heavy bombing raids (particularly on Rotterdam), the Dutch capitulated only five days later. Those three countries would become occupied territories in which a strong German military presence would be maintained.[3]

The modern narrative and perception of the Netherlands during the occupation is of country that valiantly attempted to save and assist its Jewish population. And this narrative, is, of course, justified. The population of the Netherlands held a general strike in February 1941 as a demonstration of solidarity with the country's Jews. It was the only occupied nation where such an act occurred. It is estimated that between 3,000 and 4,000 Jewish children were saved by being placed with foster families by the student resistance movement. It is also estimated that out of a population of 8.8 million people, approximately 100,000 Dutch citizens offered some form of help to Jews during the occupation.[4] However, it has also been observed that in reality, relatively few citizens of the Netherlands offered up their homes as shelter for Jews. The pre-war Jewish population of the Netherlands was 140,000, of which over 100,000 would be murdered, the highest number in occupied Western European countries.[5] The Anne Frank House Museum suggests that the figures are 107,000 Jews deported and 102,000 murdered, which are similarly grotesque figures.[6]

Coming to terms with wrongs of the past is difficult for any nation, particularly those that fell under Nazi control, whose citizens suffered oppression and whose Jewish compatriots were destined to face the horrors of the Holocaust. In 2005 Roger van Boxtel, the chief executive of Nederlandse Spoorwegen (NS), the Dutch state railway, apologized for its role in the transportation of Jews to Westerbork Camp, from where most were then transferred to Nazi death camps in Poland.[7] Five years earlier, in January 2000, Prime Minister Kok offered official apologies for the treatment received by Jewish survivors of the camps when they returned to the Netherlands after the war.[8]

In a more specific gesture of contrition van Boxtel and NS agreed in June 2019 to pay compensation of €50m (£45m) to relatives of the thousands of people it was responsible for transporting. It is anticipated that compensation will be paid to approximately 500 survivors of the camps and 5,500 to next of kin.[9] The apparent nobility of this decision had been a long time coming. Despite the apology fourteen years earlier, NS had resisted the idea of paying compensation. It took a threat of legal action from a survivor; Salo Muller, a former physiotherapist at Ajax football club, lost both his parents who were transported from Westerbork and killed at Auschwitz. Muller, assisted by the Dutch human rights lawyer Liesbeth Zegveld, had threatened to take legal action which seems to have influenced the about-face by NS. Muller himself survived the Holocaust after being placed on a *Kindertransport*.[10]

NS profited from its role in assisting with the transport of Jews to Westerbork and the camps in the East, with payments from the Nazis equivalent to £2.2 million in today's money.[11] Other estimates suggest the payments received from the Nazis were nearer to £2.5 million.[12] The last NS train from Westerbork left on 13 September 1944, prior to many NS employees going on strike in an effort to end the German occupation.[13] In November 2018 NS acknowledged that it operated the trains for transportation on behalf of the German occupiers and also that it had done much more than that. As Dirk Mulder of the National Westerbork

Memorial stated on Dutch television in 2018: 'The NS complied with the German order to make trains available. The Germans paid for it and said the NS had to come up with a timetable. And the company went and did it without a word of objection.' As a result of the agreed compensation each survivor will receive €15,000, and widowed spouses of victims and children will receive €5,000–€7,000.[14]

Historians – and indeed the Dutch themselves – have long pondered why it was that so many Jews in the Netherlands died in the Holocaust: 75 per cent compared to 25 per cent of French Jews and 40 per cent of Belgian Jews.[15] There was a lack of unity among those with power and influence in the Netherlands following the German occupation. Queen Wilhelmina was opposed to any collaboration with the Germans. However, Prime Minister Dirk Jan de Geer, initially from his base with the Dutch government in exile in London, believed that the people of the Netherlands needed to cooperate with the Germans in a similar way to the French Vichy regime. After de Geer returned to the Netherlands in September 1940, he published a pamphlet advocating collaboration.[16]

As will be discussed further, a major contributory factor in the difficulties faced and experienced by Jews in the Netherlands was the role of the Dutch civil service, with most opting to assist the Germans as professionally as they could. It is noteworthy that in 1943, the Dutch government in exile stated:

> They [the civil servants] had spent their whole lives accustomed to obey, they were always – and rightly – so proud of the impeccable execution of their tasks and conscientious fulfilment of their duties, that they brought the same conscientiousness and same fulfilment of duty to the scrupulous organization of the plunder of our country, to the advantage of the enemy.[17]

Furthermore, civil servants signed forms confirming their Aryan heritage, and from November 1940 they complied with German requirements that all Jews be removed from public service. Additionally, when, in January 1941, the Germans demanded that every Jew should be registered, it was the Dutch civil service that complied with shocking efficiency. The registration lists would greatly facilitate the deportation of Jews to Nazi death camps.[18] In parallel to the early oppressive laws in Germany, and to regulations imposed on other occupied lands, by June 1940 a vast array of antisemitic laws and regulations were enforced which banned Jews from visiting public swimming pools, parks and cinemas; they were banned from attending non-Jewish schools, or to own radios, or to work in medicine and the law with non-Jewish clients.[19] When the Germans occupied France, Belgium and the Netherlands, they opted not to impose the oppressive style of regime that had proven to be so effective in Poland. In anticipation of working with the indigenous populations, the Germans left most of the bureaucracy to local authorities. Although the Germans encountered more Jews in these countries, they endeavoured not to alienate local populations with the terror and use of ghettos that had been employed in Poland.[20] They were, however, willing to employ some of the discriminatory and oppressive rules previously mentioned.

These oppressive measures were imposed at the insistence of Arthur Seyss-Inquart, the *Reichkommissar* for the Netherlands. Seyss-Inquart, an Austrian, had contributed to the downfall of Austria's Chancellor Schuschnigg in 1938. He had served as a deputy to Hans Frank in Poland and assisted in the subjugation of the Poles.[21] The Netherlands and Norway differed from France in that they were seen as Germanic nations. Thus, the Wehrmacht was not as necessary or influential in the Netherlands where, instead, an SS and Nazi Party civilian occupation was forced upon the country.[22]

Furthermore, the Germans were assisted by the Jewish Council, which cooperated in the deportation process, whilst protecting family members through the use of exemption certificates which were issued by the Germans in 1942.[23] All of these issues will be discussed in more detail.

The success of the Nazi regime – assisted by Dutch citizens, civil servants and the Jewish Council – produced the highest death rate of Jews in Western Europe. Over a two-year period, from 14 July 1942 until 3 September 1944, it is estimated that 107,000 Jews were transported to Nazi concentration and extermination camps in Poland. The final transport to leave the Netherlands on 13 September 1944 went to Bergen-Belsen in Germany.[24]

At the start of the occupation in 1940, there were 140,000 Jews in the Netherlands, of whom 22,000 were not citizens of the country. Of that number, approximately 75 per cent, or 16,500, were German Jews who had fled to the Netherlands before the German occupation. It has long been assumed that these foreign-born Jews, armed with knowledge of what to expect from the Nazis, elected to hide more often than their Dutch counterparts, resulting in greater chances of survival. However, research shows that German Jews did not have a higher survival rate than Dutch Jews.[25] It is true that foreign-born survivors have spoken of knowing what was to be expected from the Germans. Eva Schloss, whose family arrived in the Netherlands after fleeing Austria, observed:

> Our worse fears had come to pass. As of 15 May 1940, we were living under Nazi occupation, and we had nowhere else to go … After our experiences in Vienna and the reports we'd heard from the rest of Europe, we knew what was coming. The head of the new Nazi-appointed regime was Arthur Seyss-Inquart, the former Austrian Chancellor who'd been responsible for allowing the Anschluss with Germany in 1938. But the Nazis proceeded cautiously at first, not wanting to alienate the majority of the Dutch population, and so we waited in our apartment in Merwedeplein, keeping each other cheerful but deeply afraid of the future.[26]

Returning to the key theme of this book and this chapter – collaboration and collusion – Dutch historian Frank Bovenkerk suggests that 'the efficiency of the German murder machine would have been impossible without large-scale assistance from Dutch institutions, officials, and the public at large … the Nazis were able to reach their goals with minimal effort in the part of their own personnel. Throughout the Netherlands, for example, no more than 444 German police officers were needed; they were assigned to combatting the resistance'.[27] In his 1968 work, *Ashes in the Wind: The Destruction of Dutch Jewry*, Jacques Presser wrote:

> Did not the officials of Dutch municipalities collaborate in the registration of Jews and in placing the letter 'J' on Jewish identity cards? Did not virtually all government employees sign the declaration of Aryan descent? Did not the Dutch authorities collaborate in dismissing Jewish civil servants? The judiciary in dispensing German Justice? The Department of Social Affairs, the municipalities and the District Labour Office in allowing themselves to be used to deport Jews to the work camps? The municipal authorities in

Amsterdam in allowing all Jews to be concentrated in their city? The streetcars, the railways and the police, in helping during the deportations, and the gendarmerie in guarding Westerbork Camp? Did the Dutch authorities refuse assistance in confiscating Jewish radios and bicycles, in depriving Jews of telephones? Did banks and clearing-houses sabotage the transfer of Jewish effects to Lippmann, Rosenthal & Company, or the Stock Exchange the transfer of Jewish shares? Was not the government diamond agency involved in setting up a diamond industry at Vught? Did the Government Textile Bureau refuse to cancel the permits of Jewish textile merchants? Was not the Nederlandse Unie, the organization of hundreds of thousands of loyal Dutchmen, prepared to work loyally with the occupying forces although their rules and regulations were obviously antisemitic? What non-Jew had a clear conscience? And what Jew, for that matter? Did not the signatures of the two secretaries general, proud of their anti-German attitude during the war, appear under a proclamation to the Dutch people, describing resistance fighters, scores of whom were facing the death sentence in 1941, as 'reckless and criminal elements' – and this at a time when Dutch Jews were already being exterminated as vermin in Mauthausen?[28]

These words are a damning indictment of some of the Dutch wartime population and their role in the almost total destruction of Dutch Jewry.

The chronology and trajectory of harm against the Jews of the Netherlands followed the pattern of other German-occupied territories. They were discriminated against and segregated socially and economically. They were forced out of previously secure professional roles. Their freedom of movement was restricted. They succumbed to registration and being forced to wear yellow stars and having a 'J' in their passports. Finally, via the transit camps at Westerbork and Vught, they were transported eastward to Nazi concentration and extermination camps.[29]

Within a few months of the invasion, in September 1940, there was an increase in violence against Jews by the Weerafdeling (WA), a militant branch of the Dutch National Socialist Party (NSB).[30] By early February 1941, particularly in the sector of Amsterdam where most Jews resided, there was an escalation in violence between younger Jews and members of the WA. In response, Johann-Heinrich Böhmcker, who was Seyss-

Inquart's representative in Amsterdam, issued an order on 12 February 1941 for the municipal police to erect an enclosure of the Jewish Quarter, effectively the establishment of a ghetto, with a Jewish Council, similar to those of the Polish ghettos. The ghetto was in existence only temporarily, but the Jewish Council remained.[31]

Following enclosure of the Jewish Quarter, violence in that area of the city settled down, but it continued in other parts of the city. Discussions took place between Heinrich Himmler, *Reichkommissar* Seyss-Inquart and another Austrian, Hans Albin Rauter, the *Generalkommissar für das Sicherheitswesen* (General Commissioner for Security) and *Höherer SS-und Polizeiführer* (Higher SS and Police leader). A decision was made to arrest 427 young Jewish men and keep them as hostages. On 22 and 23 February 1941, the Ordnungspolizei (German Order Police) and others carried out round-ups.[32] There had clearly been anti-Jewish violence by Dutch citizens prior to this point. In complete contrast there was a major Dutch response in reaction to the arrests. The Communist Party organized a general strike in Amsterdam and Zaandam. On day two of the strike, which had spread to other parts of the Netherlands, there was brutal intervention by German police and the Waffen-SS. Several organizers of the strike were executed, many arrests were made, the burgomaster of Amsterdam and the chief of police were replaced by individuals who were pro-German, many workers were dismissed from their jobs, and the city was fined 15 million guilders.[33] The original hostages were sent to Mauthausen and Buchenwald where they all died. The Nazis ensured that their fate was known, so that fear of Mauthausen would act as a deterrent.[34]

The Germans issued orders in January 1941 that all Jews had to be registered. Questionnaires had to be completed with twenty items listed, including nation of origin. The questionnaires were distributed and checked by the burgomasters and the lists of names were sent to Jacob Lentz, director of the State Inspection of the Registry. All 497 Dutch municipalities complied.[35] Of Jews in the Netherlands, 57 per cent lived in Amsterdam. Of that number only 25.9 per cent survived the Holocaust.[36]

The nationality of origin of Jews in the Netherlands has already been referred to, particularly whether prior experience of the Nazis persuaded some to hide and therefore survive. From April 1933 until April 1938 a total of 12,910 newly arrived refugees were registered by the Dutch Jewish

Refugee Committee; however, government estimates were of 25,000 Jewish immigrants, of which 5,789 emigrated from the Netherlands. After April 1938, the totals for Jewish immigration and emigration are unknown. However, in 1941 the State Inspection of the Registry estimated a total of 140,001 Jews of which 22,821 were immigrants.[37] Research comparing numbers of betrayed Dutch and non-Dutch Jews from the second half of 1942 and the first half of 1943 concluded the chances of survival were not significantly impacted by nationality.[38] It has, however, been noted that Jewish refugees in the city of Groningen were more aware of the dangers the Germans posed than Dutch Jews. Furthermore, for Jews to find hiding places and avoid harm they would need the help of non-Jews. Newer arrivals – the refugees – would not have established the necessary social contacts and relationships to facilitate such support.[39]

Debate has also revolved around whether the social status of Jews in the Netherlands had a bearing on survival opportunities. This also encompasses the nationality of Jews. Prior to the Nazi occupation there had been an influx of Jews from Germany during the 1930s. These Jewish refugees had experienced first-hand the harmful legislation and attitudes that prevailed under Nazi rule. Many of the German Jews worked on the Dutch Committee for Jewish Refugees. In 1941, the committee became the Jewish Council. The Jewish Council was empowered to temporarily exempt Jews from being deported to Nazi camps. Most of these exemptions were given to German Jews and their relatives.[40] However, an administrative decree in 1940 forced German Jewish refugees, if registered as illegal, into what was then a refugee camp at Westerbork.

The Jewish Council was able to provide a variety of exemptions. Jews working in businesses or industries that supported the German war effort would be issued with passes such as the *Rüstungssperre* by the Germans, whilst the Jewish Council issued exemptions to those who they deemed to be useful to the Council or to the Jewish community. By giving the Jewish Council the facility to provide exemptions, the Germans hoped to gain cooperation in the deportation of Jews from the Netherlands. It has been suggested that Jews from higher or wealthier social classes had more success in obtaining exemptions.[41] The exemptions were only ever temporary, and ultimately even the members of the Jewish Council would become targets for deportation. Certainly, being in possession of an

Memorial statue of Polish courier and resistance fighter Jan Karski in Warsaw.

The MS *St. Louis* docked in Hamburg.

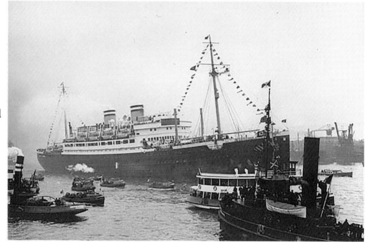

President Federico Brú of Cuba.

Klaus Barbie, the Butcher of Lyon.

British Prime Minister Neville Chamberlain.

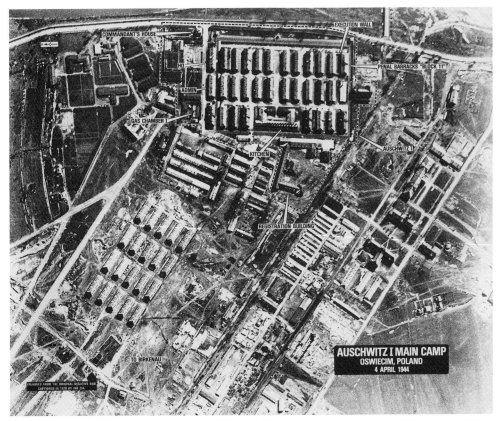

Aerial photograph of Auschwitz I taken by Fifteenth U.S. Air Force bombers on 13 September 1944.

German fortifications on the island of Jersey.

Eleanor Rathbone MP led the process that resulted in refugee support and the *Kindertransport*.

Oswald Mosley, leader of the British Union of Fascists.

Marshal Philippe Pétain, leader of the Vichy government.

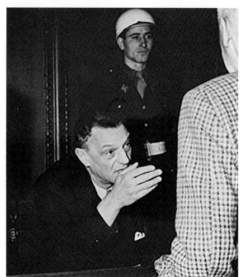

Arthur Seyss-Inquart at the Nuremberg Trials.

Westerbork inmates on the Appelplatz.

Kurt Schlesinger requested Jewish inmate control of Westerbork. He was an integral administrator at the camp.

Herbert Backe. mastermind behind the 'Hunger Plan'.

Brygidki prison in Lviv.

1943 Luftwaffe photograph of Babi Yar.

Paul Blobel, one of the organizers of the Babi Yar massacres.

Admiral Miklós Horthy.

Adolf Eichmann.

Raoul Wallenberg, Swedish diplomat and humanitarian.

Ferenc Szálasi, leader of the Arrow
Cross Party in Hungary.

Jedwabne Synagogue

Warsaw Ghetto uprising.
Jews being removed from a
bunker.

A German officer
supervising the movement
of workers during the
Warsaw Ghetto uprising.

The aftermath of the liquidation of the Warsaw Ghetto.

SS guards supervise a column of Jews during the liquidation of the Kraków Ghetto.

Scenes after the liquidation of the Kraków Ghetto.

exemption enabled Jews to seek safety and hiding, but after April 1943 no Jews were allowed to reside anywhere outside of Amsterdam, Westerbork or Vught.[42] An exemption that delayed transfer to Westerbork increased the possibility of not being deported to Auschwitz or Sobibor, but to a camp with a higher survival rate. It is known that 34,313 Jews from the Netherlands were killed soon after arrival at Sobibor, whereas it is probable that those who obtained delayed transfer to Westerbork are likely to have been among the 5,200 survivors of the camps that returned to the Netherlands after the war.[43]

The camp at Westerbork was not originally German, but Dutch. In February 1939 the government of the Netherlands built Westerbork to accommodate German refugees. The first German Jewish refugees arrived at the camp in October 1939.[44] Even after the German occupation of the camp, it remained under control of the Dutch authorities, albeit with a change of administration. In a further twist, Kurt Schlesinger, a German Jewish refugee who had arrived at Westerbork in February 1940, was able to convince the Dutch camp commander, Jacques Schol, to allow the Jewish inmates to run the camp. As such, the officials of the camp's administration were Jewish refugees, with Schlesinger in charge.[45]

As German was the main language spoken at Westerbork, the German Jews were able to take on administrative roles, which in turn potentially favoured those who shared their national heritage.[46] In July 1942 Westerbork became a transit camp whence Jews were transported to concentration and extermination camps beyond the borders of the Netherlands. It has been observed that German Jews at Westerbork, particularly those who held positions of influence, sought to keep other Germans from being deported.[47] It was known by the majority of Jews in the Netherlands that transfer to Westerbork, particularly once it became a transit camp, was usually followed by deportation to Nazi death camps in Poland. The thorough research of Marnix Croes asserts that Jews from the wealthier classes may have been more likely to survive. They could finance escape to neutral countries or secure a place to hide; they may have had better connections with non-Jews that could be useful to gain protection when in hiding; they could exert influence on the Jewish Council which could delay transfer to Westerbork and provide more time to hide or leave the country.[48] Of course, ultimately, even the wealthy or the members of the Jewish Council were often only delaying the inevitable.

The German Sichereitspolizei (the SiPo or Security Police) took over the command of Westerbork in July 1942 to prepare for the deportations that would begin two weeks later. The Jewish inmates, led by Schlesinger, maintained control of the registration of Jews in the camp through a department known as the *Registratur*. In total ninety-three trains left Westerbork between July 1942 and September 1944. All the Jews on those deportation transports were placed in that position by being on a list provided by the *Registratur*; the Germans merely requested numbers to fulfil a stipulated quota, so Schlesinger and his team decided who would make up those numbers.[49] In October 1942, SS-Obersturmführer Albert Konrad Gemmeker became commandant at Westerbork. One of his earlier tasks was to promote 2,000 German Jews to the status of *alte kamp-insassen* (literally 'old camp inmates'), thereby exempting them from deportation.[50]

It is of note that of the transit camps in the Netherlands only one, Herzogenbusch (also known as Vught from the nearby town), was managed by the SS-Wirtschaftsverwaltungshaupamt (WVHA, or SS Main Economic and Administrative Office). In the summer of 1942 Rauter created this larger camp for Jews prior to their deportation to the east. By December 1942, Vught had been placed under WVHA control as a concentration camp. It was patrolled by the Ordnungsdienst (Jewish camp police).[51] In the summer of 1943 more than 10,000 inmates of Vught were sent to their deaths at Sobibor.[52]

Returning to the earlier theme of whether social status or nationality of Jews in the Netherlands impacted upon survival chances, it is fair to observe that German Jews in Westerbork, through being helped by the *alte kamp-insassen*, stood a greater chance of delayed deportation and therefore survival.[53] The Dutch Red Cross or Nederlandsche Roode Kruis (NRK) attempted in 1947 to highlight differences in survival rates of Jews who had resided in the Netherlands during the Second World War. Using deportation lists, registered deaths and lists of survivors, the NRK estimated that 16,000 survivors were never deported due either to exemptions or having been in hiding. Approximately 5,500 deported Jews returned to the Netherlands, of which relatively more were women. It was also noted that nearly all Jews below the age of 16 and over the age of 50 died.[54] More contemporaneous research looking primarily at Amsterdam Jews has been undertaken by Peter Tammes. He notes:

While male Jews had a reduced risk of death, in the end their survival chances hardly differed from females. Though Jews aged 6–14 and 31–50 initially had a lower risk of death, in the end compared with Jews aged 15–30 they had lower survival chances, just as Jews aged 50+. For Jews aged 0–5, it was the other way around. Immigrants showed better survival chances than native Jews. German Jews showed better survival chances than Dutch Jews, but Polish and other Jewish nationals showed highest survival chances. Jews who had abandoned Judaism had better survival chances than Jews belonging to an Israelite congregation. Divorced, widowed and unmarried adult Jews had better survival chances than married Jews and their children; Jews married to non-Jews, however, had one of the highest survival chances. Jews in the two highest social classes had better survival chances than jobless Jews.[55]

Tammes suggests that survival chances were not random but were greatly influenced by socio-demographic factors.[56] Earlier research of the Yearbooks of the Netherlands State Institute for War Documentation has suggested that survival rates that were based on wealth which could be used to exert influence over the Jewish Council do not seem to be supported statistically. Undoubtedly, further debate will continue.[57]

So far, this chapter has looked at the process by which Jews in the Netherlands were isolated and marginalized, how they suffered loss of rights and the indignities of registration, how they were confined to Amsterdam and the transit camps at Westerbork and Vught, and how from there, they were deported eastward, mainly to the extermination camp at Sobibor and to the concentration and extermination camp at Auschwitz-Birkenau. As in all occupied lands the main guilt rests with the Germans, but the Netherlands – because it was perceived as being Germanic – was not subject to brutal military occupation as experienced in Poland, and 'enjoyed' the civilian administration of Seyss-Inquart. It has been noted that some Dutch citizens demonstrated their objections with a general strike in 1941, and, of course, many Jewish children were safely moved to foster placements by the student resistance movement. The role of the Jewish Council in the selective manner exemptions were issued and its involvement in compiling lists of people to be deported has been discussed. However, in a book about collaboration, collusion and guilt, what about the non-Jewish citizens of the Netherlands? The Dutch National Socialist Party (NSB) and its more militant branch, the WA, were actively involved in violence against the Jews of Amsterdam. But concerns reach beyond the NSB and WA.

It has been observed by some historians that the Netherlands did not have a strong antisemitic tradition such as was found in other European countries. Compared to the majority population, the Jewish community was small, and also generally secular and assimilated. As such, the Jewish population were somewhat invisible as they did not have a strongly identified presence away from the immediacy of their own community. Furthermore, although there was not a strong tradition of antisemitism in the Netherland, it does not automatically mean it was not present.[58] Scholars more often accept that there was antisemitism and anti-Jewish attitudes in the Netherlands before, during and after the war. Jews were seen as strangers within the wider society from a social rather than a racial perspective, and were unable to access roles or participation in areas such as student societies or the diplomatic services.[59]

It has been suggested that equality was something that the Dutch authorities sought to achieve before the war. Furthermore, there was not a great deal of enthusiasm for National Socialism and its policies.[60] However, after the rise of the Nazis in Germany many Jews were refused entry to the Netherlands, and after the war returning survivors of the Holocaust encountered a lack of empathy.[61] It is often a source of bemusement to historians that the Jewish population of a modern, democratic society could be almost entirely wiped out.[62] During the occupation there was extensive cooperation from elements of the Dutch civil service and the police. On 21 April 1941, Sybren Tulp was appointed as head of the Amsterdam police force. He was a former officer in the Royal Dutch East Indian Army and was an avowed and enthusiastic Nazi, which, it has been observed, was atypical, as most collaborators in the Netherlands were not Nazis.[63] Increasingly, research has studied official organizations, trade and industry, and professional bodies and shows that complicity and crimes against humanity during the Nazi occupation did occur.[64] However, it has been observed that many Dutch citizens who were involved in crimes against Jews, or events that led to mass murder, were not personally hostile towards Jews and neither were they sympathetic towards those who were persecuting them. It has even been suggested that cooperating with the deportation of Jews was contrary to the very principles such individuals would claim to hold.[65]

The Dutch historian Coen Hilbrink wrote about the conduct of train conductors (of relevance given the recent apology by NS) and other employees of the government during the occupation. He posed the question: 'How is possible that the Nazis managed to get the Dutch to cooperate on such a staggering scale in their efforts to achieve totally such criminal aims as the social isolation and the deportation of the Jews?'[66] Collaboration with the enemy had been a punishable crime for several decades before the war under the Dutch Criminal Code of 1886. However, in 1937, public servants and government employees were given *Aanwijzingen,* or instructions, in the event of any future hostile occupation of the Netherlands. It was advised that in the interests of the Dutch people, civil servants were to stay at their posts and continue their work to the best of their abilities. Perhaps some civil servants took this advice too literally.[67]

The people of the Netherlands, as is the case for those of other occupied territories, have had to debate the reality of memory. This requires honest analysis and acceptance, not just of past resistance and heroism, but also of wrongdoing, collaboration and crimes. It has been observed that it was not just those non-Jews in positions of authority, but also ordinary men and women, who, by action or inaction, bear responsibility for the deportation and death of so many of the nation's Jewish population.[68]

Critiquing the work of Dutch historian Bart van der Boom, fellow historians Evelien Gans and Remco Ensel suggest that van der Boom follows a trend of Netherland's historiography that seeks to minimize 'differences in position, feelings and motives' by levelling or equalling the role of victims, bystanders and perpetrators. Additionally, they argue that van der Bloom feeds into a narrative that seeks not to blame 'ordinary Dutchmen' for not giving enough help to their Jewish fellow citizens because they did not know what fate awaited them.[69] In fact, van der Boom is not so ambiguous. He suggests that in the Netherlands people knew about the round-ups sending people to Westerbork, that trains were taking Jews to Poland, and they knew about Allied warnings and German boasts of extermination and destruction. He opines that some elements were not known with any certainty but were assumed, such as forced labour and families being separated, but people may not have known the details of camps where many would die. He also asserts that part of the reality was neither known nor was it assumed: that three out of every four deportees would be killed on arrival at Sobibor and Auschwitz-Birkenau.[70]

It is known that Dutch police officers controlled the clearances of Jewish homes, and that they guarded the deportation transports.[71] In May 1942, a force of 2,000 volunteer Dutch policemen was formed to assist the Germans during raids on Jews. It has been claimed that the helpfulness of the Dutch police 'surpassed German expectations'.[72]

It is also known that some Dutch citizens denounced Jews for money, as occurred in other occupied countries. As survivor Eva Schloss observed following German losses in Russia and Africa: 'Rewards were offered for betraying Jews to the Gestapo.' This made the situation in hiding for her family more dangerous.[73]

In 1943, more than fifty Dutch police officers, members of the Colonne Henneicke (Henneicke Column), a group of Dutch Nazi collaborators, searched the country looking for Jews who had gone into hiding. When Jews were found, they were often robbed, extorted, abused and even sexually assaulted before being handed over to the Germans. One estimate is that approximately 8,500 Jews were victims of this group.[74] Previously, in September 1942, the municipal police in Amsterdam had been instructed to arrest Jews, but the officers became increasingly reluctant, so from October 1942 the Amsterdam police were used less often to assist with round-ups. From that time, they were carried out by special detachments directly supervised by the German SiPo and Ordnungspolizei. The Dutch units were the pro-Nazi Bataljon Amsterdam, the Voluntary Auxiliary Police and the aforementioned Colonne Henneicke, the latter paid by the German police. It is known that all of these groups were pro-German and consisted mainly of SS members and Dutch National Socialists.[75]

Of the 25,000 Jews who went into hiding in the Netherlands, one third were apprehended.[76] It is noteworthy that hundreds of Jewish children were saved by being placed with foster families; however, adults struggled to find a safe haven and many Dutch people were reluctant to provide lodgings to Jews.[77] Anne Frank is the most well-known victim of the Holocaust to have emerged from the Netherlands. Her family fled to the Netherlands from Germany soon after the Nazis came to power. Reflecting on reports of antisemitism in the Netherlands and rumours that German Jews would not be welcomed back to Holland after the war, on 22 May 1942, Anne Frank wrote:

> To our great sorrow and dismay, we've heard that many people have changed their attitude towards us Jews. We've been told that anti-Semitism has cropped up in circles where once it would have been unthinkable. This fact has affected us very deeply. ... I have only one hope: that this anti-Semitism is a passing thing, that the Dutch will show their true colours, that they'll never waver from what they know in their hearts to be just, for this is unjust![78]

Some historians ponder whether there was a Dutch inclination towards obedience and duty that was a contributory factor in the compliance of public officials and civil servants, and even the willingness of Dutch Jews to complete questionnaires and reside where ordered to. Historians also consider whether ignorance of the actual fate of the Jews when deported explains the obedience of the victims, and their reluctance to hide or flee. It is also questioned whether that same ignorance explains the lack of resistance and the cooperation of bystanders.[79] It was opined by the Israeli-French historian Saul Friedländer that whilst by late 1942 and early 1943 it was known in Germany and Eastern Europe that there were plans to exterminate the Jews, it is possible that only a minority of Jews knew with any certainty what their fate would be. He also asserted that for bystanders in Western and Southern Europe clear knowledge of the Holocaust may not have been common until late 1943 or even early 1944.[80]

On 3 May 1962, Loe de Jong, historian and director of the Dutch State Institute for War Documentation, addressed a lecture on television. He asserted that during the Holocaust in the Netherlands 'the large majority of people – Jews and gentiles – could not bring themselves to realize in time that, when the National Socialists spoke of the destruction of Jewry, they meant destruction in its most concrete form'.[81] De Jong still held that opinion in 1988 when he wrote:

> The reactions of Dutch Jews and gentiles are completely incomprehensible if one does not take into account the fact that virtually none of them realized in the years 1940–1945 what awaited

the deported – misery, yes, but extermination, mass murder in gas chambers? No, that was inconceivable. During the Occupation, Auschwitz or Sobibor was not a reality that was reckoned with – it only became so after the war. Then one knew what was not known during the Occupation and thus could not [have determined] people's behaviour.[82]

It is questionable whether such ignorance was widespread in government circles. On 9 July 1942 the Polish government in exile held a press conference in London which was attended by the British minister of information and by journalists. The attendees were made aware that the Germans were trying to exterminate the Jews of Poland, but it was not clear what the German intentions were towards other Jews in Europe.[83] On 29 July 1942, in a broadcast from London, Radio Orange spoke about Polish Jews being sent to gas chambers and mentioned Dutch Jews being dragged out of the country. This shows that there *was* an awareness of the gas chambers and therefore the fate of the Jews that went beyond closed government or military circles.[84] On 3 August 1942, the underground newspaper *De Waarheid* published an article with a direct plea to Dutch police officers: 'Think of your human and professional duty – arrest no Jews and only make a show of carrying out orders directed against them. Let them escape and go into hiding. Remember that every man, every woman and every child you arrest will be killed and that you are their murderer.'[85] De Jong's assertion that the dangers Jews were facing was a secret or not widely known is belied somewhat by his own experiences. He fled to London in 1940 and became a newsreader at Radio Orange. It was de Jong who read out the Allied declaration of 17 December 1942 which observed that the Germans were carrying out Hitler's plan to exterminate the Jews of Europe. Additionally, de Jong's own research showed that in the Netherlands during the war there were witnesses to the horrors of mass shootings and the extermination process at Auschwitz-Birkenau. Many of these stories were being reported in the underground press.[86]

National memory is in part dictated by the education system and by politicians. Authoritarian states, or those that have suffered under authoritarian regimes, have understandable but often misguided ideas on the narrative of history. Democratic nations can be equally selective. Former European imperial powers view their days of empire as being glorious times that were fruitful and beneficial for all, rather than times when subjugated populations suffered in order to provide territory and resources to their oppressors. The current prime minister of the Netherlands, Mark Rutte, is a historian and former state secretary for education, culture and science. He has continued to teach history of a regular basis. Yet, in April 2012, he was asked by a Jewish journalist whether he knew the Hollandsche Schouwburg, a former Amsterdam theatre which was used by the Nazis as an assembly point for Dutch Jews, prior to dispatch to Westerbork and deportation to Auschwitz and Sobibor. Hollandsche Schouwburg has been a war memorial since 1958, and was the subject of a Dutch feature film which was released in 2011. Mr Rutte claimed not to know what Hollandsche Schouwburg stood for, even though it is as significant to the Holocaust history of the Netherlands as Westerbork and the Anne Frank House.[87]

Marc L. F. van Berkel undertook to review Holocaust education in the Netherlands. In the process he analysed nineteen Holocaust-related textbooks that have been used in the education of 15- to 18-year-olds from 1960 until 2010.[88] His research found that school history focused on maritime history, the Dutch East Indies and the Second World War; and up until the 1960s there was a national narrative of the 'resistance myth' – the stoic bravery of a nation under siege.[89] Within this national narrative the Holocaust did not feature significantly. The Second World War was taught as a struggle of freedom and democracy, with the racism of the Nazi occupation not being a key subject. For many years neither the former resistance movements nor a series of governments recognized the significance of Jews as victims. This changed somewhat after the broadcast of the NBC television series *Holocaust* in 1979. Indeed, the selectiveness of memory was such that until the early 1970s there were only two monuments dedicated to Dutch Jews, and one of those was a gift to the people of Amsterdam from the Jewish community.[90]

The historiographical narrative in the Netherlands changed after the trial of Adolf Eichmann in 1961, following which a number of historical studies were published. The image of the Dutch people during the war is now that of casual bystanders, with some citizens being actively involved in Jewish persecution. It has been accepted that antisemitism existed in the Netherlands before, during and after the war, with marked indifference to the fate of the Jews, and that the Dutch were 'the best student in the Germanic class'. It is accepted that there is a need to accept national failures when there is evidence that they occurred.[91] Holocaust history as taught in schools, and as depicted in textbooks, has improved, but van Berkel's research suggests that there is still a tendency to portray the Holocaust as a purely German event, with the Dutch displayed as heroic resisters or innocent bystanders. The focus still tends to be on the heroism of the general strike of February 1941 and the story of Anne Frank. The participation of Dutch officials in the registration and deportation of Jews is still neglected.[92]

Why the people of the Netherlands cooperated so efficiently with the Nazis continues to puzzle historians. But the reality is that many did, with fatal consequences for approximately 102,000 of their fellow citizens. Recent apologies and offers of compensation signify progress. The nature of Holocaust education is also progressing from the traditional narrative of heroic resistance, to one that also encompasses national guilt. The Netherlands stands out as an example of a peaceful, cultured and educated democracy that, given the right circumstances, could fall under the spell of a brutal and destructive regime. It is a lesson that modern societies should heed.

Chapter 7

Ukraine

In the territory of what is now modern Ukraine many brutal acts of harm against Jews occurred. These were, as elsewhere, primarily perpetrated by German forces, but, as has been shown in previous chapters, and as will be shown in subsequent chapters, there was also local participation. Some of this participation was at the behest of the German occupiers, but some was enthusiastically and willingly led by Ukrainians.

It is generally accepted that Ukraine is where the Holocaust truly began, months before the extermination camps with their gas chambers were established. Most Ukrainian Jews were rounded up by *Einsatzgruppen* (mobile killing units) before being shot and buried in mass graves. This was done in public and witnessed by the villagers, townspeople and citizens of Ukraine, some of whom were compelled to participate or were actively involved. The Holocaust in Ukraine remained hidden to the outside world for many years after the war due to the secrecy and antisemitism of the Soviet state.[1] There are some 2,000 mass graves of Jewish victims in Ukraine. Increasingly, Ukrainians are marking these sites as memorials and are actively promoting Holocaust education. There are also plans for Ukraine to join the International Holocaust Remembrance Alliance.[2]

Following the invasion and occupation of Ukrainian territory, the Germans were able to take advantage of local hostility towards Jews by feeding established social, cultural, political and religious prejudices. They also inflamed hatred by introducing new elements including associating Jews with the dangers of Soviet Bolshevism. In Ukraine, this would find a receptive audience as it was a nation that had first-hand experience of life, suffering and death under Soviet influence and control. It is often asserted that in Eastern Poland and Western Ukraine the violence of local populations towards Jews was due to a widely held belief that Jews had collaborated and worked with the Soviet authorities.[3] Most notably, as will be discussed, many in Ukraine – particularly rural peasant farmers

– suffered greatly during the *Holodomor* or terror famine of 1932/3, in which millions starved to death as a result of Soviet policies.

The discussion also needs to consider the fact that Jews (who mainly lived in urban centres and as such suffered less during the famine) were demonized because of they survived the famine better than Polish or Ukrainian urban dwellers. The Nazi invaders understood the nature of Ukrainian national memory and the hostility of some towards the Stalinist Soviet Union. By the power of propaganda, they were able to utilize this hostility and associate Jews with Bolshevism – and therefore Ukrainian suffering. It is also worth noting that relations between Jews and Ukrainians before the war were not particularly hostile in western Volhynia, eastern Galicia and central Ukraine, although there was some mistrust between communities.[4]

Modern Ukraine occupies territory that was both Polish and Ukrainian at the time of Operation Barbarossa, the German invasion of June 1941. For the purposes of this chapter Ukraine will be referred to in its current geographical context, but where possible, focus will be on what was Soviet Ukraine.

As alluded to already, the invading German forces were adept at suggesting that Jews and Soviet Bolshevism were somehow intrinsically linked. However, hostility towards Jews predated the *Holodomor* and can be traced back to the end of the nineteenth century. Polish and Ukrainian populations of the territory associated Jews with being involved in free professions which prevented middle-class Ukrainians and Poles from achieving their potential, and also hindered the modernization of Ukrainian society.[5] Added to this, was the oppressive nature of the Soviet regime, which, by the time of Operation Barbarossa and the subsequent German occupation, was fuel for the hatred of Jews – who were perceived to have profited from Soviet rule – to be linked with equal hatred of the Soviets themselves. Jews and Soviets were seen as one and the same.[6] By making a propaganda connection between Jews and Stalin's Soviet Union, the Germans were able to portray the invasion of Ukraine as a liberation of an oppressed population from the rule of Jewish Bolshevism.[7]

Operation Barbarossa commenced on 22 June 1941. German forces moved east across territories previously occupied by the Soviets since the invasion of Poland in 1939, and farther afield. In Ukraine, people – including some Jews – at first welcomed the Germans as liberators.[8]

In large areas of the Ukraine farmers saw the opportunity to fight back against Soviet-imposed collectivization and modernization. They took back their farms and destroyed the modern machinery that they had been forced to use.[9]

The *Holodomor* may be a major factor in the success of such propaganda in igniting Ukrainian hostility towards Jews based on the suffering of rural communities. However, unlike Poland where documents are available to study the persecution of Jews, in Ukraine a lot of such information is still classified.[10] During the *Holodomor*, Stalin's Soviet Union forced farmers into collectivization, forced modernization on their farming methods, and imposed quotas on grain and other produce in order to feed the military and industrial workers of the wider Soviet territories. The borders were sealed and the resulting famine caused the suffering and death of millions, particularly in rural communities. Some argue that the *Holodomor* was a deliberate act of genocide; that although the harvests of 1932/3 were poor, they were also adequate. However, unrealistic grain requisitions made it inevitable that people would starve and die.[11] It has also been argued that the Soviet policies of grain procurement, collectivization and enforced modernization were aimed at destroying Ukrainian nationalism which had increased during the preceding decade. Furthermore, the Soviet regime was aware of the crisis, yet it chose not to offer assistance and even declined international aid.[12]

For a long time estimates of the numbers who died varied from the tens of thousands up to 10 million. Demographers in Ukraine have more recently looked at numbers tabulated at district and provincial levels during that period. It has been accepted that the causes of death on certificates may have been falsified in some instances but that the numbers have not been changed. Demographers looked at those deaths that were excessive to the norms of the time and also included lost births compared to the usual rate. Based on that information it is estimated that there were 3.9 million excess deaths and 0.6 million lost births, giving a total of 4.5 million deaths during the famine.[13]

The guilt of Stalin and the Soviet Union for the suffering in Ukraine has been debated by scholars and historians who question whether there was intent or deliberate unwillingness to help. Ukraine had been more rapidly collectivized than other regions. A directive by Stalin of 22 January 1933 closed the borders between Ukraine and the North Caucasus, preventing outward migration of those who were starving, in spite of the fact that Ukrainian officials had warned Moscow of the likelihood of famine as early as 1932.[14] Furthermore, in a letter of 11 August 1932 to Lazar Kaganovich, Stalin had outlined his suspicion of the Ukrainian peasants and fear of losing the territory. Additionally, Molotov led an Extraordinary Commission in Ukraine which decreed measures on 18 November 1932 that resulted not only the confiscation of grain, but also meat and vegetables. The resulting famine was ominously predictable.[15] In Ukraine and the North Caucasus extreme measures were taken against villages and collective farms for perceived failures in procurement; all foodstuffs were taken, there was a banning of food imports, and peasant farmers were deported.[16]

The famine of 1932/3 would still have been raw and fresh in Ukrainian memory at the time of the German invasion of June 1941. The Germans had been aware of the famine at the time it was happening as their diplomats described it in reports to Berlin. Additionally, Goebbels had referred to the famine and five million deaths in a speech to the Nazi Party Congress in 1935.[17] The Nazi occupiers of Ukraine were willing to use the famine in anti-Soviet propaganda. They needed to positively reach rural Ukrainians as their labours would provide food for the German military and the wider Reich. Propaganda posters depicted starving peasants with messages attributing their suffering to Stalin and the Bolsheviks.[18] In 1942/3, the tenth anniversary of the famine, newspapers increasingly tried to win over Ukrainian peasants. One article in July 1942, in the popular agricultural newspaper *Ukrainskiy Khliborob*, stated:

All peasants remember well the year of 1933 when hunger mowed people down like grass. In two decades, the Soviets turned the land of plenty into the land of hunger where millions perished. The German soldier halted the assault, the peasants greeted the German army with bread and salt, the army that fought for Ukrainians to work freely.[19]

The Nazi media also sought to conflate the famine, Soviet rule and the role of Jews. As elsewhere in Nazi-controlled territories Bolshevism was identified as being the creation of Jews. Efforts were also made to suggest that Jews had not only survived, but had remained comfortably wealthy. When an antisemitic film was shown about the famine in Kyiv, the consequence was the murder of a Jewish secret policeman.[20] It is known that some Jews did help their Ukrainian neighbours during the famine. Indeed, as most Jews were not farmers, they did not experience the hardship and losses due to Soviet requisitions.[21] This also meant that Jewish survival rates during the famine were higher, and thus easily exploited in subsequent propaganda campaigns as proof that they benefitted from allegiance to the Soviets, rather than the reality that they survived because they were not targeted for grain and other produce requisitions in the same manner as were farmers.[22]

Ukraine had one of Europe's largest Jewish populations when it was invaded in June 1941. Whilst exact figures are not known, it is estimated that at least one and a half million Jews were killed in Ukraine.[23] Most of the murders were committed by the Einsatzgruppen – special forces tasked with killing civilians, primarily Jews, deemed to be enemies of Germany. Most Ukrainian Jews were not deported to camps, but were shot in situ by German troops and local collaborators.[24] (Not all Ukrainians collaborated in the violence against Jews, and indeed, there are 2,634 Ukrainians who have been recognized by Yad Vashem as being Righteous Among Nations.[25]) However, early on during the occupation, the Germans established local Ukrainian administrative structures to assist with conveying the orders of the new regime and securing public order.[26] In the occupied areas of Ukraine that had either civilian or military administration, the Germans would only allow local participation at regional level, but mayors, village elders and district leaders had access to useful local manpower even if they were not permitted to form a Ukrainian collaborationist regime.[27]

In the earlier days of the invasion of Ukraine the Germans embarked on a concerted programme of anti-Jewish propaganda through posters and pamphlets, proclamations, radio broadcasts and via the Ukrainian print media.[28] At the time that German troops arrived at the outskirts of Lviv on 30 June 1941, there were some 150,000 Jews in the city. It is reported that the Jews remained frightened and hidden in their homes, whilst the majority of Ukrainians welcomed the Germans with great enthusiasm, perceived as they were as liberators.[29] There was also a perception that the Germans would improve standards of living, which was particularly well received in the rural farming communities.[30]

A key theme of this book is to explore beyond the crimes that were committed solely by the Nazi regime, and to examine where there is evidence of local participation, particularly in some of the occupied territories. Ukrainian historians of the Holocaust have, in recent years, looked at collaboration from Ukrainian citizens, government agencies and the auxiliary police.[31] As elsewhere, in considering the history of formerly occupied territories, historians have been assisted by the available survivor testimonies, most notably written documentation and, since the 1990s, audio and video interviews obtained by Yad Vashem and the Survivors of the Shoah Visual History Foundation.[32] In those territories that fell under the post-war Soviet sphere of influence it has been asserted that survivors either tried not to remember, or at least tried not to talk about the events that they witnessed and experienced. Furthermore, it is possible that post-war memories influenced wartime memories, and additionally, survivors struggled to identify individuals involved in criminality, and some had difficulty recalling details of dates and chronology.[33]

The testimonies of survivors and other witnesses are not the only sources of evidence. The historian Yuri Radchenko wrote about the Holocaust in Kharkiv. He accessed the State Archive of the Kharkiv Oblast, within which is held Kharkiv Municipal Council documentation from the occupation period, and decrees issued by various senior local officials. The archive also contains witness testimony obtained after Kharkiv was liberated in August 1943.[34] The archive of the Kharkiv Oblast Administration of the Ukrainian Security Service contains documentary evidence of those involved in the creation and guarding of ghettos, murder and the theft of Jewish property. This documentation is made up of witness and defendant testimony, the latter of which may have been obtained under duress. These testimonies were gathered during the final years of the war and the decade following. It has also been asserted that collaborators sought to conceal or deny their involvement in activities against Ukrainian Jews, and tried to claim that they had been forced into such activities by the Germans.[35] Nonetheless, there is a wide variety of primary and secondary source witness and defendant testimony, Ukrainian government documentation, and both contemporaneous and later accounts.

Hitler's motivation for the invasion of Soviet Ukraine was in part to avail Germany unfettered access to the vast, fertile agricultural land in the territory, and the abundance of other resources. Blockades during the First World War had led to mass hunger and starvation in Germany. Hitler saw the occupation of Ukraine as something that 'would liberate us from every economic worry'.[36] There were no concerns for the welfare of Ukrainians or other citizens of the Soviet territories. Indeed, there was a deliberate plan to starve them. The 'Hunger Plan' was conceived by Herbert Backe, the Nazi tasked to deal with food and agriculture. He believed that the war could be won if the Wehrmacht was fed from Russian (Soviet) lands, and that such supplies would also feed the population of Germany. However, this could only happen if the Soviet population was deprived of food. Backe's aim was that this famine could result in some 30 million Soviet deaths.[37] Backe issued economic policy guidelines in May 1941, and a memorandum to a thousand German officials in June. The policy guidelines are clear and unambiguous:

Many tens of millions of people in this territory will become superfluous and will have to die or migrate to Siberia. Attempts to rescue the population there from death through starvation by obtaining surpluses from the black earth zone can only be at the expense of supplying Europe. They prevent the possibility of Germany holding out in the war; they prevent Germany and Europe resisting the blockade. With regard to this, absolute clarity must reign.[38]

Additionally, Heinrich Himmler, who was in charge of *Generalplan Ost*, the Master Plan for the East, wanted to turn Ukraine into a German colony which was free of Jews and inhabited by the local German *Volksdeutsche*.[39]

It has been observed that in the Ukrainian and Polish memories and narratives of the German occupation they perceive themselves as being the primary victims. There is an understandable glorification of resistance fighters and national struggle, but this makes it difficult to confront and address any participation in, and collaboration with, the crimes of the Nazis.[40] There have been constructive efforts to address the past but how history is perceived depends on geographical factors. Since the collapse of the Soviet Union and Ukraine becoming truly independent and sovereign, governmental and parliamentary commissions have investigated the

Organization of Ukrainian Nationalists or Orhanizatsija Ukrains'kykh Natsionalistiv (OUN) and the Ukrainian Insurgent Army or Ukrains'ka Povstans'ka Armiia (UPA). In eastern Ukraine these organizations are seen as Nazi collaborators and war criminals, whilst in western Ukraine they are seen as heroes who fought against oppression.[41] Interestingly, international lawyer Philippe Sands visited the western Ukrainian city of Żółkiew (Zhovkva) in the summer of 2014 when making a documentary with Niklas Frank (son of Hans Frank) and Horst von Wachter, the son of Otto von Wachter who created the Waffen-SS Galicia Division in the spring of 1943. Sands, Frank and von Wachter were invited to a ceremony organized by a local nationalistic Ukrainian group which sought to remember and revere the fallen soldiers of this SS division.[42] This group may well not be representative of the majority of Ukrainians, but their actions appear to celebrate the Nazis and they are allowed to conduct remembrance services with impunity. The role of the OUN will be considered elsewhere.

National historical narrative can be influenced by many factors. Formerly occupied nations may need some form of redemption in how memories of that time are reflected upon. After the war Ukraine once again came under the Soviet Union's control. Trials were conducted by the Soviets of Ukrainians who had cooperated with the Nazis. Those trial files may be useful for historians to obtain biographical details, but trials conducted in the period 1943–5 and immediately after the war were prejudiced and could lead to entire communities being condemned as collaborators, resulting in mass arrests, deportations and sometimes death.[43] Later investigations in Ukraine and NKVD (security police) surveillance reports reveal more reliable information about those Ukrainian officials who were known or suspected to have cooperated and collaborated with the German occupiers.[44]

When Operation Barbarossa commenced in June 1941, the Germans were joined by two battalions raised by the OUN. They hoped to create an independent Ukraine, and had probably been deliberately misled by the Germans into believing this was an achievable ambition.[45] When members of the OUN declared independence in Lviv some days later, the German response was violent, and by December 1941 both arms of the OUN were declared illegal and their leaders sent to Sachsenhausen.[46] However, there is no subtlety to be seen in this statement from the

OUN in June 1941 in which an allegiance to the German invaders is clear:

The newly emerging Ukrainian State will cooperate fully with the Great Nazi German Reich, which under the guidance of its *Führer* Adolf Hitler is forming a new order in Europe and the world and which will help the Ukrainian Nation liberate itself from Muscovite oppression.[47]

When German forces entered Lviv on 30 June 1941, the leading military personnel were accompanied by two battalions of Ukrainian troops with codenames *Nachtigall* (Nightingale) and *Roland*. These were Ukrainian exiles who had been recruited from the ranks of the OUN that had been operating in independent Poland. After the Soviet annexation of the east of Poland, they had moved to Berlin where the Abwehr, German military intelligence, began working with them. The *Nachtigall* and *Roland* battalions were assisted by German officers.[48] The *Nachtigall* militias that marched into Lviv were organized by OUN-B. It has been asserted by Polish writer Jerzy Wegierski that they were involved in helping with the round-ups of Jews in Lviv and participation in the subsequent prison actions; however, the Polish historian Andrzej Zbikowski suggests that whilst the 600 members of *Nachtigall* who entered Lviv were involved in the pogrom and prison massacres, they were not the main perpetrators.[49] Conversely, the Ukrainian-Jewish historian Iakov Khonigsman has suggested that *Nachtigall* troops were involved in perpetrating atrocities against Jews immediately upon entering Lviv. He cites the testimony of Kazmira Poraj, a history teacher from Lviv:

The streets near the City Hall are covered with shattered glass. The Ukrainian-speaking soldiers wearing SS emblems humiliate and brutalize the Jews. They make them sweep the street with their own clothes – with blouses, dresses, and even hats. They made Jews pick up shattered glass with bare hands and carry it to the carts. From Galyts'ka street to Krakivs'ka street, the road is drenched with blood flowing from the people's hands.[50]

It is apparent that there is some disagreement between historians about the level and degree to which *Nachtigall* personnel were involved in anti-Jewish actions in Lviv, due to varying levels of corroboration.[51] In Volhynia, Jews faced dangers from the Polish Home Army, German forces, Soviet partisans and members of the OUN-UPA (Ukrainian Insurgent Army). Many Jews were in hiding, having fled from the ghettos, but members of the OUN-UPA frequently murdered Jewish individuals and groups that they met. However, the UPA would spare some Jews if they were deemed to be useful due to their professional background and skills.[52]

A key part of the Nazi plan following the commencement of Operation Barbarossa was the extermination of the Jews in the German-occupied territories. Administrative bodies were established to assist with this process, and the local non-Jewish populations were integral in filling these roles. An example of such a structure was the Kharkiv Municipal Government.[53] Furthermore, although OUN policies towards the Jews may have changed in the latter stages of the war, they certainly complied with German anti-Jewish measures following the initial stages of the invasion.[54] Ukrainian press reports accused Jews of denouncing Ukrainian resistance fighters during Soviet rule.[55] The resolution at the Second General Congress of OUN-B in April 1941 (two months before the German invasion) clearly demonstrates pre-existing hostility towards Jews that would be ripe for exploitation by the Germans. It stated:

> The Jews in the U.S.S.R. constitute the most faithful support of the ruling Bolshevik regime and the vanguard of Muscovite imperialism in the Ukraine. The Muscovite-Bolshevik government exploits the anti-Jewish sentiments of the Ukrainian masses to divert their attention from the true cause of their misfortune and to channel them in times of frustration into pogroms on the Jews. The OUN combats the Jews as the prop of the Muscovite-Bolshevik regime and simultaneously it renders them conscious of the fact that the principal foe is Moscow.[56]

On 17 July 1941, Hitler ordered the introduction of civil authorities in the newly occupied territories of the east. Accordingly, on 1 September 1941, the Reichskommissariat Ukraine (RKU) was established. By September 1942, the territory of the RKU had expanded to include the administrative units of Wolyn and Podill'ia, Zhytomyr, Kyiv, Dnipropetrovs'k, Mykolaïv and Tavriia.[57] The Germans had learned from experience – as demonstrated in the chapters on France and the Netherlands – that as an occupying power they needed to work with the local population. Some historians argue that this often required necessary cooperation from locals rather than collaboration.[58] However, as has been shown elsewhere, this almost inevitably resulted in harm and grave danger for the Jews in occupied territories. Undoubtedly, Ukraine and the other Soviet territories differed from those of Western Europe in that Nazi Germany had planned and accounted for tens of millions of deaths, whether they were Jews or not.

In those parts of the Ukraine with large populations of ethnic Germans, the *Volksdeutsche* were given leading positions in local administrations as they were considered to be both ethnically and politically reliable. However, they were soon found to be unprofessional and incompetent.[59] In primarily rural areas west of the Dnieper, both branches of the OUN (OUN-Bandera and OUN-Melnyk) had some success in inserting their chosen candidates into key positions in the local administration.[60] It is apparent that up until early autumn of 1941 the Germans were reasonably tolerant towards the OUN presence, but this changed. Wary of Ukrainian nationalists, between late autumn 1941 and early spring 1942, the Germans removed anyone suspected of having such links from having roles in the administration.[61] Some argue that the OUN did not seek influence in local administrations with a specific aim of helping to implement the mass murder of Jews, but, by joining a system that played a role in supporting those crimes, they certainly helped to facilitate the actions of the German occupiers.[62] There are examples that show OUN members demonstrating an antisemitic bias before the Germans arrived. In Litin, west of Vinnista in late July 1941, a local militia group ensured restrictions were placed on the free movement of Jews in that area.[63] It is likely that social status and material gain was part of the motivation of the Ukrainian auxiliary police for seeking work as local administrators.[64] It has also been argued that there was a desire to conform with the occupiers.[65]

In the first three days of July 1941, two pogroms took place almost concurrently, in Lviv and Boryslav. A major factor in these pogroms related to the activities of the Soviet NKVD as they fled from the advancing German forces. The speed of the German advance prevented the NKVD from evacuating inmates from local prisons. These inmates were mainly members of the OUN, plus political and public figures, as well as Poles, army and police personnel and members of the resistance. In the three main prisons of Lviv – Brygidki, Lackiego and Zamarstynów – the NKVD committed acts of mass murder. In Boryslav the prison was located in the courthouse that was also the NKVD headquarters. Here too the NKVD massacred the inmates.[66] News of the massacres soon became known, and despite the guilt of the NKVD, and initial blame being placed on the Communists, the locals soon apportioned blame on the Jews.[67] There has long been a debate among historians about the usefulness and validity of survivor and witness testimonies, with them often being dismissed as subjective, and therefore unreliable. However, whilst most historical research and documentation will show *what* happened, in so much as events, dates and places, it does not always address what was *felt* and *experienced* by those who survived war and genocide. This is where survivor testimonies become most useful.[68]

Historian Vladimir Melemad cites the accounts of some Jewish survivors as they describe the ensuing events. Leszek Allerhand described what happened on 2 July 1941:

On the third day of the German invasion, we were confronted by the Ukrainians on the street. The Ukrainians wore the blue-and-yellow armbands. It happened on Plac Kapitulny [Cathedral Square]. They put us down on the ground and started beat us. Then they forced us on our knees and made us move in the direction of the Brygidki prison. They kept hitting us and shoved us. On the way to Brygidki, they kicked me out; my mother managed to escape, but my father was taken to the prison. He returned home in the evening, terribly beaten.[69]

Kurt Lewin, 16 at the time and another witness, described the first day of the German invasion:

When the Germans arrived [30 June 1941], the city was decorated with blue-and-yellow flags, because the Ukrainians believed in German support for an independent Ukraine. The second day was also quiet and then the pogrom started. On the third day, my father, accompanied by two senior members of the community, went to Metropolitan Andrei Sheptytskyi. Rabbi Lewin was seeking Metropolitan's intervention to stop the violence in the streets, for it had become known that the Ukrainians were attacking Jews and there were instances of looting. I was waiting in the apartment for my father return. Suddenly, four or five Ukrainians came in. They took me out on the street, beat me, and dragged to the Brygidki prison. The Ukrainians did not touch my mother, they took only men. They made Jews walk in the middle of the street; Ukrainians and Poles were standing on the sidewalks clapping, enjoying the spectacle. At the Brygidki prison we had to dig out prisoners murdered by the NKVD before the Soviet retreat.[70]

The testimony of the Jewish survivor Daniel Hochman in Boryslav describes visceral scenes:

When the Germans arrived in the town, a few Ukrainian hooligans started to beat up Jews in the streets. Then hundreds of peasants from the mountains joined them. It was a pogrom, like in the Middle Ages. It lasted for three days, from July 1 to July 3. They attacked Jews with knives, axes, hammers, pitchforks, and stones. These people were like beasts. The Poles stayed away from that. The Germans kept observing without interfering for two days. On the third day, a German commander halted the riots. There were about 300 bodies on the streets. We were hiding in the house of my uncle, outside the town. My grandfather and grandmother were killed in the streets. It was my first direct experience with the Ukrainian atrocities.[71]

It is estimated that the NKVD murdered at least 3,000 prisoners before they retreated in front of the German advance. Many Ukrainians – and indeed many Poles – held a belief that the NKVD was dominated by Jews, so, rather than blaming those who were actually responsible for the murders – Soviet guards – they started blaming the Jews. Members of the OUN formed militias, which, along with Ukrainian civilians, captured Jews, took them to the prisons, and forced them to exhume the bodies.

Those Jews were violently mistreated and eventually killed.[72] On 1 July, law professor Maurycy Allerhand witnessed Ukrainians beating Jews with whips and sticks. Large crowds gathered outside the prisons and Jews were made to run the gauntlet through these mobs. Some Ukrainians captured Allerhand's son, Jonatan, and he was taken to the Brygidka prison where he was forced to exhume and clean corpses. Estimates of the number of Jews murdered during this pogrom are between 4,000 and 8,000.[73]

Other pogroms occurred. Over the period 25–28 July 1941, the Jews of Lviv suffered gravely at the hands of Ukrainians as they commemorated the assassination of the nationalist leader Simon Petlyura in 1926. He had been killed in Paris by a Jew. During the pogrom Jewish men and women were taken to a prison and subjected to terrible cruelties.[74] These 'Petlyura days' were permitted by the Germans. Ukrainian auxiliary policemen, peasants and individual Poles were able to rob, torture and kill Jews without fear of punishment. These actions were not spontaneous: the Jewish intelligentsia was deliberately targeted by the auxiliary police.[75]

It is apparent that the murder of prisoners by the NKVD was a factor that led to the pogroms, but pogroms also occurred in communities where there had not been prison murders. It has been observed that local populations were also incited by the Ukrainian nationalist task force known as *pokhidny hrupy*. It is not known whether they were acting on the orders of the Germans or had been instructed by the OUN.[76] As an indicator that greed was also a motivation, it is notable that as well as acts of violence against Jews, they were also robbed and blackmailed.[77]

The Ukrainian militia was dissolved by the Germans early on during the occupation and was replaced by the Ukrainian auxiliary police. This force was known to be involved in violent activities against Jews, including murder.[78] Actions against Jews – including murder – in rural and forested areas, were undertaken by Ukrainian partisans even after hundreds of thousands of Jews had already been killed. Antisemitism may have strongly influenced the partisans.[79] The Germans were indeed tolerant of Ukrainian violence against Jews: an order by SS Chief of Police Reinhard Heydrich recommended inciting such violence, but with the Lviv Pogrom, the violence and killing had started before the arrival of Sonderkommando 4b, and as such it is unlikely that the pogrom was influenced or encouraged by the Germans.[80] Certainly, later during the occupation, there is testimony that supports German and Ukrainian cooperation. Milka Levine described hiding with her family in 1942: 'We stayed under the floor for 15 days. From time to time, the SS, Gestapo and Ukrainians came back to the ghetto and were still looting, screaming and shooting.'[81] It is known that orders issued by local Ukrainian administrators demonstrate discrimination against Jews that preceded the German occupation, but the motivation for Ukrainians to work as administrators may have been the financial benefits of Jewish valuables and property.[82] It is estimated that approximately 4,000 Jews were murdered by Ukrainian mobs in Lviv.[83]

Between late July and mid-August 1941, Himmler met with leaders of the SS and Einsatzgruppen. He wanted the rate of executions increased, and to include those who were not obviously involved in anti-German or communist activity. The process of eradicating the Jews was to formally begin. A written order of 1 August was given to the SS Cavalry Brigade which instructed them to clear out partisans and resistance fighters in the Pripet Marshes, with the added proviso that 'All Jews must be shot. Jewish women to be herded into the marshes'. The rate of killing increased significantly, including the murder of Jewish women and children. Entire Jewish communities were annihilated.[84] In order to create ghettos and complete the process of murdering hundreds of thousands of Jews, Himmler required extra personnel. German units of SS and infantry were drafted in with 19,000 additional men employed in the killing process. Einstatzgruppen D also enlisted the help of Ukrainian auxiliary police units.[85]

The vast majority of the killing in Ukraine was perpetrated by Germans – most notably the Einsatzgruppen and Einsatzcommando which followed the Wehrmacht into the territory. The most infamous massacre occurred on 29/30 September at the ravine of Babi Yar on the outskirts of Kyiv. In total it is estimated that approximately 100,000 Jews and non-Jews were killed at Babi Yar over several months. The post-war narrative of history was somewhat dictated by the antisemitism of Stalin's Soviet regime. Stalin wanted to send Jews east after the war, and in official Soviet history Babi Yar did not even exist until it was acknowledged by the Khrushchev regime and a monument was erected to commemorate those who had died during the German occupation.[86]

Babi Yar was one of the most extreme consequences of the German plans for the invasion of the Soviet Union. German forces had been issued with guidelines including that they should take 'ruthless and energetic action against Bolshevik agitators, irregulars, saboteurs, Jews and total elimination of all active and passive resistance'.[87] Following the commencement of the invasion on 22 June 1941, SS and police units (including the Einsatzgruppen) followed the Wehrmacht into Soviet territories. On 2 July they were given specific orders to execute all Communist functionaries, people's commissars, 'Jews in party or state positions' and 'other radical elements'.[88] In August the Hungarians transported approximately 18,000 Jews and marched them into south-west Ukraine to Kamenets-Podolsk. SS Brigade Commander Freidrich Jeckeln added these new arrivals to the local Jewish population of approximately 8,000, and over a three-day period had 23,600 men, women and children shot.[89] The village of Belaya Tserkov, 70 kilometres from Kyiv, had an established Jewish community that had existed for over 300 years. Between 8 and 19 August, the Waffen-SS, assisted by Ukrainian militia, shot and killed several hundred Jewish men and women at a rifle range near the barracks.[90]

Prior to the German invasion some 160,000 Jews lived in Kyiv. Approximately 100,000 left the city ahead of the Germans who entered Kyiv on 19 September 1941.[91] Kyiv was incorporated into the RKU, which was headed by the Nazi district leader Erich Koch. Early in the occupation of the city there were two major explosions – probably set off by Soviet engineers – which destroyed part of the city centre and the German headquarters. These explosions were used as a reason to kill the remaining 60,000 Jews in Kyiv.[92] Following the arrival in the city of Einsatzcommando 4a, posters were placed around the city ordering Jews to assemble on 29 September near the Jewish cemetery or risk being killed. Thousands did as instructed and were directed towards Babi Yar. The Germans created an environment that gave the appearance of registering these Jews, but their documents were discarded. In groups of thirty or forty the Jews were forced to strip naked, rings were removed from fingers, and then they were pushed to the edge of the ravine where they were shot. Young children were thrown in alive.[93] Ukrainians joined Germans in guarding this process, which is of course relevant to the theme of this book. Over the two days of 29/30 September 33,771 Jews were murdered at Babi Yar.[94] It is estimated that in total over 100,000 people (including non-Jews) were killed at Babi Yar over the ensuing months, but the events of 29/30 September constitute one of the biggest single massacres of the war.[95] The main perpetrators were of course the Germans led by *Standartenführer* Paul Blobel.[96] However, it is known that Ukrainian police units assisted in the massacre.[97] Additionally, Ukrainian police units, the Germans of the SS and Einsatzgruppe C, under the jurisdiction of the army's XXIX Corps, were assisted by allied Hungarian soldiers.[98] Paul Blobel was ultimately indicted for the atrocities of Babi Yar, and executed after standing trial at Nuremberg.[99]

By mid-July 1941, Jews were forced to wear identifying armbands. Soon they were prevented from using public transport. Food and other goods were in short supply across Ukraine: Poles and Ukrainians bought food at low prices and sold it to Jews at much higher prices. Additionally, when Jews started being moved into ghettos, they would be beaten and robbed by Germans and locals, who would then help themselves to the contents of their homes. Survivors have stated that Jews in hiding were found by the Germans due to help from the local population.[100] Ukrainians were not averse to profiting from the suffering of their Jewish neighbours, and indeed, in Ostrog, for example, locals queued to purchase the possessions of those who had been murdered.[101]

From the end of October 1941, the Germans began establishing Jewish ghettos in various urban centres. This was done in conjunction with registering Jews for labour and the formation of Jewish councils.[102] During the first ten days of December 1941 the local government in Kharkiv was actively involved in the identification of Jews during the census. Jews were forcibly moved by Ukrainian building directors to the ghetto in the barrack accommodation of the Kharkiv Tractor Factory and the Machine-Tool Factory. Any Jews who escaped would be betrayed to the police, which often resulted in their death.[103] The local council worked in cooperation with German soldiers to prevent those who escaped from receiving assistance from non-Jews, and was actively involved in the murder of Jews in the ghetto and the looting of their property.[104] The commandant of the barracks at the Machine-Tool Factory, Mykola Kucherenko, was instrumental in the murder and persecution of Jews, and even encouraged local teenagers to assault Jews being taken to the ghetto.[105] He was also witnessed to personally murder Jews, including an incident in January 1942 when he and others shot and killed seven teenage Jewish boys and girls. His accomplices were Ukrainian security guards.[106]

At the start of December 1941, before being transferred to the concentration camp at Pechora, Jews in Shpikov had to hand over their valuables to an OUN-B member called Sokor, who was also head of the local administration. Furthermore, they were forbidden to use main roads and were ordered to wash themselves regularly as 'dirty Jews' would be shot.[107] It has been observed that only in exceptional circumstances were local administrators directly involved in the mass shooting of Jews, but that their knowledge and support were essential to the preparation and follow-up work of the Germans in the extermination process. Without local support the Germans lacked the necessary manpower to complete the procedures. Local auxiliary administrators were involved in identifying, registering and isolating Jews, and, after mass-murder events, they were able to acquire the property of the dead Jews which provided a personal income for mayors and local administrators.[108]

The Jewish quarter in Lviv was surrounded by German security police and Ukrainians on 12 November 1941 and the district effectively became a place of containment. Over several days approximately 10,000 Jews were removed from the area and killed by the Germans. Elsewhere checkpoints were set up to which young women were taken and made to remove their clothes before being robbed of belongings, beaten and sexually assaulted. Additionally, Germans and Ukrainian auxiliaries would frequently raid the homes of wealthy Jews.[109] The liquidation of the Kharkiv ghetto commenced on 27 December 1941, with several hundred Jews being taken from the ghetto to be shot at Drobitskyi Yar. Eventually the Nazis would murder 9,000 Jews there.[110] The local government was actively involved in the hunt for Jews who had survived the liquidation of the ghetto; indeed, on 23 January 1942, after the ghetto ceased to exist *Oberburgomeister* Kramarenko issued a decree stating that

until the last Jewish Communist and bandit-Bolshevik trash and all suspicious persons in general have been uncovered, and with the goal of protecting the values of our city, each district ... must organize a section composed of three groups to assist the authorities and the police.[111]

Prior to and following the murder of Jews, local administrators assigned to Ukrainian authorities in towns and villages the role of determining how much money the Jewish community had to transfer into the local budget. Additionally, after Jews had either been murdered or moved to ghettos, local administrators registered remaining property and transferred it to the Germans, or, in the case of Babi Yar, ensured it was distributed to the local Ukrainian population.[112]

Collaboration, as a concept, is complex, with multiple factors to consider. What may be seen as collaboration by some, may also have been necessary cooperation in circumstances that are difficult to comprehend today. Soon after the invasion and occupation by German forces in the summer of 1941, the collaborators were inspired by nationalistic propaganda and a desire for revenge which the Germans encouraged. This was the time of riots, looting and pogroms, which has been referred to 'a settling of pre-war scores'.[113] It is known that the rawness of the *Holodomor* was still fresh in the memory of Ukrainians, and that many saw Jews as being favoured by the Soviet regime, and even that they had prospered while others suffered and died. Anti-Soviet sentiments and hostility towards Jews became somewhat intertwined. Hatred of the Soviets and hatred of the Jews were conflated. Whilst the Final Solution was a German project, and German forces were responsible for the vast majority of murders and massacres, it is also known that Ukrainian administrators and auxiliary police forces played an essential and effective role in its implementation, particularly in small towns and villages.[114] A significant body of research into the cooperation of local Ukrainians with the Germans has looked at the various branches of the auxiliary police, and has been assisted by war crimes trials in Canada, the United States and elsewhere. Unfortunately, there has been too little research into local administrators during the occupation.[115]

As this chapter has shown, there was an enthusiastic welcome from many of the Ukrainians (including Jews) for the invading German forces in June 1941. They were perceived as liberators from the Soviet regime of Stalin. Some, such as the OUN, had already nailed their colours to the mast of the German regime and had been advocating support and antisemitic sentiments prior to the invasion. Indeed, part of the OUN, the *Nachtigall*, had been working with German military intelligence in Berlin. The OUN may have cooperated in anticipation of furthering their nationalistic ambitions, which were soon thwarted by the Germans, but the OUN and UPA, along with auxiliary police forces, local administrators and civic leaders actively engaged with the Germans in identifying, registering and isolating the Jewish population.

It has been suggested that the Holocaust truly began in Ukraine, but that it was mass murder by shooting rather than in concentration and extermination camps with gas chambers, slave labour and conditions that were insufficient to sustain life. Estimates are that 1.5 million Ukrainian Jews were killed in Ukraine. Their killers were primarily Germans but also included Ukrainians; the weaponry of murder was beating, and the use of whatever tools came to hand. The Ukrainian-led pogroms were brutal and bloody affairs.

Ukraine had suffered before the war due to the oppressive policies of the Soviet Union. It was then occupied by the 'liberators' of Nazi Germany who proved to be a destructive power, before being once again 'liberated' by the Soviet Union. The territory remained under Soviet control until gaining true sovereignty in 1990. The history of the Soviet–German–Soviet eras of Ukraine is a history of difficult times. The difficulties continue in 2021 with the ongoing territorial disputes and conflict with Russia. In Ukraine, as in Poland, there is much to remember about the past, but there is also much to forget. Some still glorify and revere the OUN, whilst others condemn the OUN as Nazi collaborators. There are reasons to be hopeful. Carl Gershman, former United States ambassador to the United Nations Human Rights Council, wrote a positive article in *The Washington Post* in May 2019, following the election and inauguration of Volodymyr Zelensky to the presidency of Ukraine. He suggested that the new president would help to consolidate the democracy that had been developing in Ukraine since 2014. Gershman also expressed positivity that Holocaust education and remembrance were likely to become the norm in Ukraine.[116]

The late 1980s and early 1990s saw Ukrainian politicians, historians, wider society and the diaspora acknowledging, researching, writing and speaking of the *Holodomor*, that terrible famine that took so many millions of lives. There commenced honest reflection on the Soviet era and how it impacted upon Ukraine. There is a need for that honest reflection to also include the period when Ukrainian territory was invaded and occupied by the forces of Nazi Germany. That occupation was the true start of the Holocaust and that is a reality of Ukrainian history which needs to be acknowledged, spoken about honestly and accepted as part of the past.

Chapter 8

Hungary

Hungary may well be known in the history of the Second World War as the final country of mass deportation. The Jews of Eastern Europe, particularly Poland and Ukraine, were murdered where they lived and called home. The majority of Jews in Hungary were transported en masse to Auschwitz-Birkenau and to almost certain death. The Jews of the Netherlands and France were deported in huge numbers, and many, too many, died in Eastern Europe, but their numbers pale when compared to those deported from Hungary.

Hungary was an ally of Germany. Its soldiers had fought alongside German forces during Operation Barbarossa and the invasion of Soviet Ukraine. Hungary had also been on the losing side in the First World War, and, like Germany, had suffered huge loss of territory and other punishments due to post-war treaty impositions. Similarly, Hungary's sense of identity and national pride became factors in the years leading up to the Second World War. Hungarian nationalism also manifested in racial and religious intolerance towards its minority communities. Indeed, the first anti-Jewish law in Europe of the twentieth century was enacted in Hungary, and would be followed by further legal edicts which negatively impacted upon its Jewish population. These laws were Hungarian laws and were not imposed by, or intended to mirror, the laws that were being enforced in Nazi Germany. Actions against Jews occurred long before Hungary was occupied by Germany on 19 March 1944. Prior to and following the occupation, Hungarian militias, police, government officials and citizens were actively involved in hostility against Jews. When Germany, despite the evidence of impending defeat, demanded the deportation of Hungary's Jews to Auschwitz-Birkenau, Hungarians willingly and enthusiastically assisted.

The memory of the Holocaust in territories that were occupied by Germany can vary, as has already been shown. National memory is further impacted by the influence of post-war Soviet occupation or authoritarian influence in the decades that followed. Hungary in 2021 has a nationalist government that demonstrates hostility towards minority communities – migrants and refugees – and has been influential in some of the antisemitism that is once again becoming noticeable in the circles of the far-right and far-left. Of course, Hungary had its examples of heroic acts to save and protect Jews. Citizens of Hungary have been acknowledged by Yad Vashem for that heroism. But, accepting guilt for aspects of the Holocaust has not always been apparent. In a book about collaboration and collusion, it is necessary to consider Hungary, a nation that, in the final months of the war, deported almost the entirety of its Jewish population to Auschwitz-Birkenau, where the majority died soon after arrival. Many others were deported to provide slave labour for the German military machine, and they too, would have experienced dreadful hardships, suffering and often death.

The dangerous antisemitism and ultra-nationalism of Hungary, which manifested after the First World War can be linked to defeat in that conflict. That defeat, alongside Germany and other allies, resulted in the Trianon Treaty, with huge loss of territories and population groups, that seriously damaged national pride. Hungary had other similarities to Germany after the First World War. It was a country of violent social and political upheaval. There was even a brief period when the country had a communist government led by Béla Kun, a man of Jewish origin.[1] This would prove to be a factor in subsequent Hungarian antisemitism and the linking of Jews with communism.

The communist takeover in 1919 resulted in the emergence of many anti-communist groups, often made up of former officers from the Austro-Hungarian army and ex-civil servants. These groups rallied at the south-eastern Hungarian town of Szeged to fight against the new dictatorship.[2] It was here that the first signs of Hungarian fascism began to appear among a group of 'professional' right-wing thinkers who preoccupied their time on such issues after the loss of their military role.[3] Elsewhere, in Vienna, conservative landowners gathered around Count István Bethlen. As time progressed there were some political chasms developing around the counter-revolutionaries – such as Gyula Gömbös and Béla Imredy, who were ideologically more inclined to fascism and wanted an alliance with Germany – and the anti-revolutionary thinkers such as Count Bethlen and Admiral Miklós Horthy. The group represented by Bethlen and Horthy were of a political type that was likely to serve fascism by default rather than by design, as they were generally ambivalent about national and foreign policy. They were admirers of the fascism promoted by Mussolini in Italy. Admiral Horthy was favoured by all the groups and thus became their leader.[4] The fight against the communists became known as the White Terror. It lacked clear ideological thinking on broader issues beyond combating communism, but the *Szegedi Gondolat* (the Szeged idea/philosophy) was marked by nationalism, chauvinism, anti-communism and antisemitism. The antisemitism was primarily nationalistic and economic in character but it developed into a more racial outlook.[5]

Admiral Horthy became regent of Hungary on 1 March 1920.[6] The country had suffered defeat in the First World War, the period of post-war dictatorship resulted in 587 people being killed in political clashes, while militants of the White Terror murdered between 5,000 and 6,000 people, including many Jews in pogroms. The definition of Hungarians as Magyars – combined with nationalism, provincialism and Christianity – unleashed aggressive, racist attitudes.[7] The instability was exacerbated in 1919 by Hungary losing its monarchy, becoming a republic, having a Socialist and then a Communist government, followed by the viciousness of the White Terror counter-revolution. Horthy, in taking on the title of regent from the absent monarchy, did not have the powers previously held by the Crown.[8]

In the post-war negotiations the initial Hungarian government under Károly Huszár had to deal with the Americans regarding a peace treaty. The relevant parties – including Count Albert Apponyi on behalf of the Hungarians – gathered at the Trianon Palace in Versailles.[9] The Hungarians brought maps and various experts, but they were isolated and forbidden even to have contact with an envoy in London (but secretly managed to). The Trianon Treaty was signed on 4 June 1920 and was devastating for Hungary, which came off worse than all of the defeated powers. The new states of Yugoslavia and Czechoslovakia took substantial chunks of Hungarian territory, while Romania took Transylvania and some territory that could properly be defined as Hungarian.[10] The population of Hungary was reduced from 20 million to 8 million, and the country lost two-thirds of its territory. Three million Hungarian speakers were now living in different states.[11] The three-fifths of the Hungarian population lost as a result of Trianon were mostly minority populations in the borderlands, which included the territory of Subcarpathian Rus.[12] One thing united Hungarians of the left and right during the years 1918 to 1920, and that was to preserve Hungarian territory that had existed prior to the First World War. The acceptance by Admiral Horthy of the Trianon Treaty compounded the sense of loss that all Hungarians felt.[13] Hungary also lost its only seaport, to Italy, and rights to self-determination were invoked in those territories for those who wished to sever ties with Hungary, but the same rights were denied if they were to favour Hungary. The country was also compelled to pay reparations. Trianon is still perceived by some Hungarians as the most traumatic event in the nation's history.[14] It damaged both national pride and the economy, with the need to revise the treaty becoming the most important issue in Hungarian politics.[15] Jews, who made up a mere 6 per cent of the population, and who regarded themselves as Magyars, were made the scapegoats for the consequences of Trianon.[16]

The Hungarian government was the first in Europe to pass anti-Jewish legislation, when it introduced the *numerus clausus* rule in 1920, which ensured that only 6 per cent of students in higher education could be Jewish.[17] Further anti-Jewish laws would be passed by the Hungarian government, often quite independently of German influence and control. Act 15 of 1938 stipulated that only 20 per cent of people employed in the free professions could be Jews. Act 4 of 1939 reduced the number of Jews allowed to work in the free professions to 6 per cent, and also sought to define Jewishness. Act 15 of 1941 broadened the definition of a Jew and brought it more into line with the definition in the Nuremberg Laws. Act 14 of 1942 allowed for Jewish men to be conscripted into labour battalions in the Hungarian army. Act 15 of 1942 permitted the confiscation of Jewish-owned land.[18] The labour battalions had existed since August 1940.[19] The turnaround in the legal protections previously afforded to Jews had been rapid. In 1895 – only twenty-five years before *numerus clausus*, Jews had been given freedom of religious practice and their religion was recognized by law. Yet, on 21 September 1920, the Hungarian parliament voted fifty-seven in favour and seven against to pass the *numerus clausus* legislation. Claims were made that rather than being antisemitic, it was a law passed to protect Christian interests.[20] István Haller, minister of education in 1920, entitled a chapter in his

1926 autobiography 'As long as there is a Trianon there will be a *Numerus Clausus*'. Some of Hungary's political elite wanted Jews to do more to help restore Hungary's pre-war borders and territories. In a speech to the Hungarian parliament, Count Kuno von Kleselsberg stated: 'Give us back the old Greater Hungary, then we will abrogate the *numerus clausus*.'[21]

German propaganda did influence the rise of Hungarian fascism. Its development was quite probably aided by Horthy's attempts to placate and pander to the various competing groups – those who had been involved in the White Terror, the Szeged men, the special squad officers, newly formed political parties and societies, and those who were part of the political elite.[22] As the Nazi Party was achieving increased popularity and political success in Germany, by coincidence, in 1932, Gyula Gömbös became prime minister of Hungary. He was an avowed admirer of Hitler, and, when Hitler became chancellor of Germany in 1933, he was the first head of state to visit him.[23] There were immediate mutual benefits as Germany and Hungary signed an economic agreement: Hungary would export agricultural produce to Germany, whilst importing materials for rearmament and modernization. These economic ties would continue to strengthen.[24] Germany assisted and supported Hungary with a major rearmament programme in the late 1930s. As well as allowing Nazi-sponsored organizations to work in Hungary, the country was also influenced by Nazi propaganda which was being disseminated to the German Swabian minority community. Hungary became susceptible to German '*volkish*' ideas. Furthermore, the army was becoming increasingly radicalized by right-wing influences.[25]

Hungary was an ally of Nazi Germany, but it would not be occupied by the Germans until 19 March 1944. The anti-Jewish legislation in Hungary until then was homegrown and fully independent of the Germans'. It was reflective of Hungarian attitudes towards Jews and other minorities, and also of the Hungarian sense of Magyarism and of victimhood after the First World War, Trianon and a need to reassert national identity and pride. Hungary was also the country with the last sizeable Jewish population by the time of the German occupation. In 1838, the Jewish population of Hungary was approximately 445,000. In November 1938 and in March 1939, Hungary was rewarded for its loyalty to Hitler and Germany with territory from Czechoslovakia. Further territory from Romania was granted in August 1940. These land acquisitions added approximately 320,000 people to the Jewish population of Hungary. Unfortunately, they were poorly integrated into the Hungarian Jewish population, and were often seen as foreigners – even to Hungary's Orthodox Jews.[26]

During the years between the wars the ruling classes became increasingly xenophobic and preoccupied with ethno-nationalism and the idea of the 'Magyarization' of the nation. This would exclude minority populations. Horthy was particularly concerned with the large German minority population, a concern for Hungarian nationalists since the mid-nineteenth century.[27] Some, such as Bálint Hóman, the minister of culture and education from 1932 to 1942, believed it was necessary to deport Romanians, Serbs and Carpatho-Ruthenians from Hungary. The opinion of Henrik Werth, head of the army's general staff in 1941, was more radical in his thinking. He wanted to expel Hungary's Jewish, Slav, Romanian and Roma populations. More widely within the nation the concept of 'Greater Hungary' helped to foment the potential for violence as an option.[28] There are reports of Hungarian soldiers committing 'small-scale' massacres against Carpatho-Ruthenians when they marched into the territory in March 1939. There was also targeted violence against Jews.[29]

The Hungarians had enjoyed a good relationship with Stalin's Soviet Union. During the period of the pact between Hitler and Stalin, the Soviets had returned Hungarian standards from the war of 1849, and in return the Hungarians released the Communist Mátyás Rákosi from prison. On 23 June 1941, the Soviets conceded to Hungary's territorial claims on Romania but Prime Minister László Bárdossy did not release the report. In what is believed to have been a joint German–Hungarian plot to seek an excuse to declare war on the Soviet Union, foreign aircraft dropped bombs on the town of Kassa. On 22 June 1941 the German invasion of the Soviet Union commenced, with 40,000 Hungarian troops participating in the invasion of Soviet Ukraine. The Hungarians also provided grain and bauxite to the Germans.[30] After initial successes, the Wehrmacht stalled at Moscow in December. The Hungarian general Ferenc Szombathelyi and István Horthy, elder son of Admiral Horthy, were aware that problems lay ahead. Matters were exacerbated following Japan's attack on Pearl Harbor on 7 December 1941 and the resultant entry of the United States into the war. For reasons best known to himself,

Bárdossy, following Hitler's lead, unilaterally declared war on the United States without consulting either the cabinet or Horthy.[31]

Hungarian troops were brutal during their occupation of Yugoslavia. One Hungarian unit massacred 700 Jews at Újvidék (now Novi Sad) in Serbia on 21–23 January 1942.[32] Earlier, in August 1941, Hungarian troops forced 18,000 Jews across the border into German-occupied Ukraine to Kamenets-Podolsk, where most would be massacred.[33] Whilst Hungarian troops may have offered some protection to the Jewish labour battalions which accompanied them into Soviet territory, this was no guarantee of safety. One Hungarian officer murdered all of his Jewish unit. It is estimated that 30,000 Jewish conscripts serving in the Hungarian labour battalions never returned from the Soviet campaign.[34] Jewish personnel may largely have been protected from the violence being directed at other (civilian) Jews, but they were cruelly treated, poorly fed and suffered great hardship, being forced to march long distances. Their tasks were arduous and often dangerous, such as mine-clearing.[35]

Whilst Jews across German-occupied Europe were in grave danger and ultimately murdered in their millions, the Jewish population in Hungary had largely, but not entirely, remained safe from the reaches of the Nazi regime. That does not, however, exonerate the Hungarians during this time. The Hungarians occupied the south-western region of Subcarpathian Rus in November 1938, and immediately began expelling Jews from the territory. In March 1939 the Hungarians took control of the whole area and began to broaden the expulsions. Initially Jews were deported to the no man's lands that fell between the Czech, Slovak and Hungarian territories, but were soon deported to occupied Poland. By the end of 1939, the Hungarians had deported several thousand Jews from Subcarpathian Rus.[36] In July 1942, when Hungarian forces briefly controlled East Galicia during Operation Barbarossa, it was used as an opportunity to violently transfer larger numbers of people from Subcarpathian Rus. On 10 July 1941, Miklós Kozma, commissioner for Subcarpathia, wrote to László Bárdossy, the prime minister: he proposed that starting the following week he would push across the border all non-Hungarian Galicians (meaning Jews), plus Ukrainian agitators and Gypsies (Roma).[37]

On 15 August 1941, Hungarian leaders actually halted mass deportations of Jews into German hands, primarily because German forces in East Galicia wanted the deportations to stop.[38] It is, however, known that at least 15,000–20,000 Jews had been deported from Subcarpatho-Ruthenia by that date, with many killed by Germans and local Ukrainians, including the massacre at Kamenets-Podolsk.[39]

It is estimated that in 1942 there were approximately 750,000 Jews in Hungarian and Hungarian-controlled territory.[40] The government was unwilling to deport all of the Jews from its areas of control: in part this was due to Admiral Horthy waiting to see which way the war was heading. There was also concern amongst many about the Kamenets-Podolsk incident in 1941. In March 1942 the pro-Nazi László Bárdossy was replaced as prime minister by Miklós Kállay, whom Horthy saw as being more pragmatic. In putting off further mass deportations of Jews, Horthy was already showing an awareness that it might not be in the interests of Hungary to actively cooperate with the Germans in the process. He realized that if the Allies were victorious such actions would result in consequences.[41] However this did not totally protect Hungary's Jews. In May 1942, a Hungarian infantry commander in Munkács used Jewish homes as a site for a 'partisan exercise' which rapidly turned to violence and looting as the Jews became real targets.[42]

The situation for Jews in Hungary became perilous from 19 March 1944 when the country was occupied by Germany. Horthy representatives had been testing the waters with the Allies to try to find a way of extracting Hungary from the war. Hungarian forces had suffered greatly fighting alongside German forces at Stalingrad, where the Hungarian Second Army was annihilated with half of the 200,000 troops killed and most of the rest wounded or captured. These losses were significant to Hungarian thinking.[43] There was also pressure on the Hungarian government due to some thirty-eight intelligence reports detailing exactly what was happening to the Jews at Auschwitz. The Polish government issued a press release on 21 March 1944 stating: 'It is not possible to estimate the exact figure of people put to death in gas chambers attached to crematoria but it certainly exceeds half a million, mostly Jews, both Polish and from other countries.' The Polish press release was published in several newspapers in the United States, and three days later President Roosevelt observed:

As a result of the events of the last few days hundreds of thousands of Jews, who while living under persecution have at least found a haven from death in Hungary and the Balkans, are now threatened with annihilation as Hitler's forces descend more heavily upon these lands.[44]

Clearly Roosevelt was suggesting that at the time Hungary was a place of safety for Jews. This would almost certainly have put added international pressure on Horthy.

Prime Minister Miklós Kállay requested that nine Hungarian divisions be withdrawn from the Eastern Front. In response, in early March, Hitler set in motion Operation Margarethe, the plans for the occupation of Hungary. Horthy was summoned to meet with Hitler at Scloss Klesshein near Salzburg on 18 March. Hitler demanded that Horthy sign consent to German forces occupying Hungary. He refused to do so.[45] Hitler compelled Horthy to dismiss Kállay and appoint the pro-German Döme Sztójay in his place, while Horthy conceded to Germany's demand that 100,000 Jews be sent to the Reich as forced labour.[46] Hungary was not just home to a large Jewish population, it also possessed raw materials, stocks of food and other supplies that the Germans would be able to avail themselves of once they took control of the country.[47] As Horthy headed home two Wehrmacht divisions entered Hungarian territory. Horthy was accompanied by Ernst Kaltenbrunner, the head of the RSHA, and Edmund Veesenmayer, who had been appointed the German plenipotentiary. Once in Budapest they selected a new government to serve under Prime Minister Sztójay. Horthy was permitted to maintain his own position, which gave tacit legitimacy to the new regime and the subsequent actions against the Jews.[48]

A report by Veesenmayer on 30 April 1944 offered the opinion that the Hungarians perceived the Jews as

a guarantee for the position of 'Hungarian interests', and they [Hungarians] believe that through the Jews they can provide proof that they waged this war alongside the Axis powers only out of necessity, but that in practice they have indirectly made a contribution to the enemies of the Axis powers through hidden sabotage [by not handing over the Jews].[49]

The impact on Hungary's Jews was immediately noticeable. Trude Levi, was a 19-year-old nursery school teacher living in Budapest at the time of the German occupation. She observed: 'It seemed that we had escaped the fate of all the Jews of Europe. It was obvious that Germany was losing the war and we hoped that soon it would all be over.' However, 'on 19 March 1944 we found German tanks, soldiers and machine guns lining the banks of the River Danube. When no one expected it any more, we were occupied'.[50] She describes how Jews were forced to buy yellow stars and wear them on their clothing. She also describes how 'Courageous Christian friends offered to hide me in Budapest'.[51] And it is worth noting that 867 Hungarian citizens have been recognized as Righteous Among Nations by Yad Vashem.[52] Ibi Ginsburg also survived the Holocaust in Hungary. Her testimony highlights that although the Jews of Hungary were aware of what was happening to Jews elsewhere in Europe, the impact of the invasion and being confined to a ghetto did not immediately lead to fear of being killed:

I was nineteen and a half years old when the events I am about to describe happened. I was the eldest of four girls in a family of practising orthodox Jews. Until the spring of 1944, I lived with my family in Tokai, a middle-sized town in the centre of the wine-growing region of Hungary. Life was relatively peaceful. Hungary was an ally of Germany, and until 1944 was allowed to run its own affairs. The news of the fate of the European Jews, which filtered through to us in Hungary, seemed unbelievable. So when Germany occupied Hungary on 14 March 1944 [sic] and we were locked into a ghetto near our town; our trauma was more connected with our loss of freedom, home and belongings than with fear for our lives.[53]

John Chillag was aged 17 when German forces invaded Hungary. He observed:

The fortunes of the war had changed on all fronts and preparations for the 'invasion' were progressing. No one in Hungary thought that the Germans would occupy Hungary at that stage. But on 19 March, 1944, they did.[54]

He recalled that within two weeks of the occupation, the Nuremberg Laws were enacted in Hungary, plus the indignities of having to wear the yellow star, having radios, bicycles and valuables confiscated, and telephones disconnected.[55] The SS began to convey a daily message that the Jews were going to be moved to somewhere in the east to work for a German victory. The Jews knew that the war was gradually coming to an end, and with many unaware of the details of the Final Solution, they moved to the ghettos anticipating a short period of discomfort.[56]

Eichmann wished to prevent Jewish resistance, to avoid the problems encountered in Warsaw. Two of his senior lieutenants, Hermann Krumey and Dieter Wisliceny, decreed that senior Jewish leaders were to meet them at the Hotel Majestic. The night before the meeting 200 Jews were detained at Kistarcsa internment camp, and over the next few days 2,000 more Jews would be detained there. The message from Krumey and Wisliceny was that SiPo, the security police, were now in control of Hungary's Jews. The Jews of Budapest were forbidden to have contact with Jews in the provinces, and were ordered to maintain calm or face severe consequences. They were assured that if they behaved well no harm would befall them. They were also ordered to form a Jewish Council which, under the leadership of the well-respected Samuel Stern, came into existence on 21 March.[57]

In early April Eichmann attended a conference chaired by László Baky and senior members of the Einsatzkommando. Also in attendance were László Endre and Colonel László Ferenczy, commander of the 20,000-strong Hungarian gendarmerie. They divided Hungary into six zones and planned how they would register and relocate all Jews from the rural areas and concentrate them in the urban centres. The Jews would be stripped of their wealth and assets. It was believed that by focusing on 'foreign' rural Jews that this would reassure the Jews in Budapest. The task of rounding up the Jews was entrusted to the chiefs of police and the gendarmerie with assistance being provided by civilian militias.[58]

The speed and success of the relocation of the provincial Jews, plus those from Transylvania and Subcarpathia, is testament to the role of the Hungarians. In mid-July Veesenmayer reported that 437,402 Jews had been escorted out of these areas by enthusiastic Hungarian gendarmes dutifully following their orders. The gendarmerie allegedly met little resistance.[59] The round-ups commenced on 16 April 1944. In just twelve days 194,000 Jews in Zone I – Carpatho-Ruthenia and north-eastern Hungary – were forced into newly built ghettos. Between 3 and 10 May, the 98,000 Jews of Zone II, which included northern Transylvania and Kolozvar/Cluj, were trasnferred to ghettos. Between 5 and 10 June, the 53,000 Jews of northern Hungary – Zone III – were moved. Between 16 and 26 June some 40,000 Jews in Zone IV – which included Debrecen and Szeged – were relocated. The 29,000 Jews of Zone V in south-western Hungary were forced into ghettos between 30 June and 3 July. Finally, approximately 24,000 Jews living in areas around Budapest were also relocated. The approximately 200,000 Jews living in Budapest were moved into 'yellow star' houses.[60]

In early May 1944 the SS began deporting Jews to Auschwitz-Birkenau. By the time the transportations ended on 9 July, the majority of the 437,000 Jews had been killed immediately after their arrival.[61] These deportations were primarily led by the Hungarian gendarmerie, under the guidance of the SS.[62] The murder rate was astonishing even by the standards of Auschwitz-Birkenau. The *Auschwitz Chronicle* notes that on 25 May 1944 the resistance movement in the camp was reporting that over 100,000 Hungarian Jews had already been killed. Those SS men directly involved in the killing process were having to work forty-eight-hour shifts followed by an eight-hour break.[63]

The transportations from Hungary to Auschwitz-Birkenau was ahead of schedule. Initially it was the Jews from Kistarcsa. Then, between 15 May and 7 June, ninety-two trains transported 289,000 Jews from Carpartho-Ruthenia and Transylvania (Zones I and II); twenty-three trains transported 59,000 Jews from Zone III between 11 and 16 June; fourteen trains transported 41,500 Jews from Zone IV began starting on 25 June; and eighteen transports took 55,000 Jews from Zone IV between 4 and 8 July.[64] In just eight weeks 437,403 Jews had been transported to Auschwitz-Birkenau, of whom 70–75 per cent were killed on arrival with the rest selected for labour.[65] It is estimated that only 25,000 of the Hungarian Jews sent to Auschwitz were registered and admitted to the camp (a factor that influences negationists when they question the totals of lives lost), and 80,000 were held in the camp for a few weeks until they were sent as forced labour to the Reich, required as essential labour because of the lack of surviving Jews in the camp system in Germany.[66]

Deporting the provincial Jews had been managed successfully without major incident. What to do with the Jews in Budapest was likely to be more complicated. The Budapest police were not seen as being trustworthy, so

Eichmann decided that two provincial gendarmerie divisions which had successfully distinguished themselves, should be brought in for the task.[67] The planning very much revolved around the use of Hungarians and ploys to make the containment and deportation of the Jews more manageable. The Germans would use right-wing Hungarian civil servants to round up the Jews. They also planned to use local tradesmen, and tram and bus drivers as guides for the provincial gendarmes operating in Budapest. Furthermore, a curfew would be imposed. Additionally, Veesenmayer planned that to prevent Jewish protests and resistance, he would ensure that Jewish 'plots' and 'attacks' on police would break out just before the deportations were due to start.[68] (Horthy had been under sustained international pressure to stop the deportations in July 1944, and it has been suggested that he could have stopped them as early as May. He was ultimately forced to resign on 15 October and the fascist Arrow Cross Party took power. The Arrow Cross continued the crimes against Jews with a vengeance, pursuing a campaign of murder.[69])

Some of the pressure on Horthy and the Hungarian government was quite inventive on the part of the Allies. The Americans launched an air raid on 2 July 1944 against Budapest and when the citizens emerged after four hours of bombing, they found that not only were large parts of the city ablaze, there had also been a major leaflet drop from the bombers. Such leaflets impacted upon a nation already at breaking point, and fully aware of the Soviets advancing from the east and the western Allies advancing through Italy and France.[70] Some of the leaflets fell into the hands of Jews who were accommodated in restricted housing. They were aware that their destiny was to be forced into cattle trucks by the gendarmerie and to be sent away, in all probability never to return. Any information that could offer a glimmer of hope was to be welcomed.[71] The leaflets gave news of developments in the war, and made clear that the treatment of the Jews was not going to go unpunished. It stated:

> The United States government demands of the relevant Hungarian authorities that they publish the procedure to be adopted with respect to the Jews under arrest in ghettoes or concentration camps. In particular the United States government demands that it be stated whether the Hungarian authorities intend to restrict food rations in a manner which is discriminatory; whether there is to be deportation

to Poland or to any other place and/or adoption of any measures which, in common with those noted above, are ... tantamount to mass execution. The United States government wishes to remind the authorities in Hungary that it is [closely] following the persecution of the Jews and other minorities [and views it] with extreme gravity. The United States government wishes to remind the Hungarian authorities of its decision that all those responsible for carrying out such orders [to persecute the Jews] will be dealt with in the manner stated by the President of the United States in his public warning on the 24th of March 1944.[72]

Hansi Brand and Rudolf Kasztner, a Hungarian Jew, negotiated with Eichmann in May and June 1944, to arrange to transport a train load of Jews to Switzerland as a gesture to placate the Allies. Eichmann was receptive to the idea as he knew it would show good faith on his part, and it was also a means of extorting money from the Jews who would travel.[73] Kasztner would later be assassinated in Israel after the war, in part because he had made sure that many of his own relatives and Jews from his hometown of Cluj were on the train. Indeed, 388 of the 1,684 passengers came from Cluj.[74] The Jews on the Kasztner train were not actually taken to Switzerland, but were transported to Bergen-Belsen, where part of the camp had been set aside for these 'exchange Jews' whom the Germans might use for ransom purposes.[75]

While Kasztner and Brand were negotiating with Eichmann and arranging the transport, they were well aware of what was happening to Jews in Auschwitz. In April 1944 two Slovakians – Rudolf Vrba and Alfred Wetzler – escaped from the camp and managed to return to their homeland. They detailed what they knew about the camp, and also information that they had been given by Filip Müller, one of the Sonderkommandos working at the gas chambers and crematoria. The Vrba–Wetzler report clearly described details of the extermination process. It began circulating in Budapest in May; by late June it had reached London, and by early July it had reached Washington.[76] Additionally, other sources of information were revealing what was happening in Auschwitz. The Archbishop of Canterbury received a cable from the World Council of Churches in Geneva on 24 June. He was informed that 12,000 Jews a day were being transported to Auschwitz, and that

400,000 had already been killed. The cable would have passed through censorship and its contents would therefore have been known to British intelligence services. On 27 June, the archbishop received a letter from Alexander Easterman, political secretary of the World Jewish Congress, which advised of reports coming from the Polish underground stating that 100,000 Hungarian Jews had been killed at Auschwitz. The discrepancy in the total deaths is irrelevant: the mass murder of Hungarian Jews is the key common detail.[77] The Vrba–Wetzler report was incendiary in its impact and resulted in Horthy being contacted by such diverse figures as Roosevelt, the king of Sweden and the pope. As Gennaro Verolini, a papal diplomat in Budapest, observed, there were concerns even before the Vrba–Wetzler report became known: 'Gradually we came to the conclusion that "compulsory work abroad" meant deportation. And deportation meant extermination, annihilation. We then protested very vigorously, at first to the nuncio himself, and then with other diplomats.' The papal nuncio for Hungary issued 15,000 letters guaranteeing safe conduct to some of the Jews of Budapest.[78]

Despite the pressure being put on Horthy, Eichmann began to consider the issue of the Jews in Budapest. Since May 1944, there had been 170,000 Jews living in 1,900 'yellow star' premises and another 120,000 Jews residing illegally in Christian properties. Eichmann planned to start the deportations on 6 July, but in the meantime, he imposed a curfew and forbade the Jews from receiving guests.[79]

Pressure on Horthy was not just from outside Hungary: even Count István Bethlen wrote to the admiral from his rural hiding place and said: 'all Christian Hungary will soon be irreversibly contaminated.' The churches in Hungary also began to privately denounce the deportations and threatened to do so publicly.[80] On 26 June, a meeting of the Crown Council agreed to stop the deportations. The main Hungarian organizers – Minister of the Interior Andor Jaross, and his secretaries of state Baky and Endre – were dismissed from their positions. Horthy moved loyal troops to Budapest to stop further deportations. The last transport from Hungary reached Auschwitz-Birkenau in mid-July.[81]

Unfortunately, this did not end the suffering of the Budapest Jews. The transports to Auschwitz might have stopped, but for the remaining Jews there was still danger. Many were helped by Raoul Wallenberg, the Swedish diplomat and humanitarian, who organized false identity papers and located safe places for them to hide.[82] After stopping the Auschwitz transports Horthy once again courted the Allies to make peace, and in early October a Hungarian delegation in Moscow actually signed a peace deal. The German response was swift and effective. On 15 October Otto Skorzeny, an SS officer, led a team that kidnapped Horthy's son Miklós in Budapest. He was rolled up in a carpet and taken to Mauthausen concentration camp in Austria. Horthy was blackmailed by the Germans and compelled to hand over power to Ferenc Szálasi, leader of the Arrow Cross Party. Horthy spent the remaining months of the war incarcerated by the Germans in a castle in Bavaria.[83]

On 8 November 1944 the Hungarians forced over 70,000 Jews into the Ujlaki brickyards in Obuda, before leading them on a forced march into Austria, where the survivors arrived in late December. During the march thousands were shot or starved to death.[84] Eichmann had made plans with Szálasi to deport the Jews to Reich territory where they would become forced labourers for the German war effort. They were forced to walk because of the lack of available transport. By the end of November more than 27,000 Jews were walking the 100-mile route to Austria, with plans for 40,000 more to follow.[85] In an apparently strange twist, a group of SS officers – including Rudolf Höss, former commandant of Auschwitz – complained to Otto Winkelmann, the Higher SS and Police Chief for Hungary. Höss had not suddenly developed compassion for those he had hitherto been involved in slaughtering, but he knew that the Jews would not be fit for work when they arrived in Reich territory.[86]

Himmler received a complaint about Eichmann's actions from Kurt Becher, an SS officer. Eichmann and Himmler met on board Himmler's private train in the Black Forest in November 1944. In a complete switch in what had been standard Nazi policy towards the Jews, Himmler ordered Eichmann to stop the deportation of Jews from Budapest. He stated that, 'If until now you have exterminated Jews, from now on, if I order you, you must be a fosterer of Jews'. As with Höss, this was not the sudden onset of compassion, but a pragmatic realization that the Jews could be useful in any future negotiations with the Allies. Himmler was also very aware that the Red Army was rapidly approaching Hungarian territory.[87]

The Jews of Budapest may have been granted a temporary reprieve from deportation by the Germans, but they were still in danger from the Hungarians. In November 1944, the Arrow Cross forced them into a ghetto. It is estimated that between December 1944 and the end of January 1945, the Arrow Cross murdered as many as 20,000 Jews on the banks of the Danube and dumped their bodies into the river.[88] On occasions Arrow Cross executioners would tie two people together so that one bullet would cause both to fall into the freezing waters of the Danube.[89] Agnes Grunwald-Spier writes that her mother had relatives and friends who were killed this way and that her mother said that 'the Blue Danube turned red'.[90] Anna Sondhelm, in her testimony to Agnes Grunwald-Spier, described an Arrow Cross raid on the parents' home of a friend of hers. The parents and grandmother of Anna's friend were taken to the Danube and shot. The friend considered herself to be 'lucky' because she was 'only raped' by the Arrow Cross men.[91]

In a final throw of the dice, aware of the Soviet advance, Eichmann planned, in January 1945, to kill the remaining 70,000 Jews in Budapest. The massacre was to be conducted by both the SS and the Arrow Cross. Raoul Wallenberg, the Swedish businessman, diplomat, and humanitarian, had been working closely with Pál Szalay, a senior policeman and one of the leaders of the Arrow Cross. On behalf of Wallenberg, Szalay spoke to German General August Schmidthuber and told him that if the ghetto massacre went ahead as planned, then after the war Wallenberg would ensure that Schmidthuber would be held responsible and hanged as a war criminal. The planned massacre was cancelled.[92]

Advancing Soviet forces had encircled Budapest by late December 1944. Hitler ordered the defenders of Budapest to fight to the death. During the battle some 40,000 civilians died. Budapest eventually fell to the Soviets on 13 February 1945,[93] German resistance ended on 11 February.[94] The siege of Budapest did not stop the persecution and murder of the city's Jews. On 24 December members of the Arrow Cross arrived at children's home in Munkácsy Mihály Street. The children and their carers were forced into the courtyard of the Radetsky barracks where they were made to stand in front of a machine gun. It was only the timely arrival of the Red Army that caused the would-be executioners to flee. Sadly, the parents of the children had already been killed.[95]

Estimates in 1946 suggest that 70,000 Jews survived in the Budapest ghetto. A further 25,000 survived in protected houses, 25,000 more survived by hiding and 11,000 survived during forced labour services.

Another 50,000 returned to the city from deportations. Approximately a third of the Jews of Budapest died or were killed, and half of the Jews in the post-Trianon territory.[96] A more specific estimate is that 105,453 Jews in Budapest died or disappeared from mid-October 1944, to the fall of the city on 13 February 1945.[97] Yad Vashem offers a total figure of 565,000 Hungarian Jews who perished during the Holocaust.[98]

As discussed in other chapters the Holocaust has a deep impact on the national memory of those nations that were occupied and experienced it first-hand. It also has an impact on nations with a large number of citizens with direct links to the horror of that time. Those nations that fell under the Soviet sphere of influence after the fall of Nazi Germany have a more complex national memory, with added scars attributable to the decades of communist totalitarianism. Hungary, of course, is one such nation. Hungary had not only been on the losing side in both world wars, but it also fell behind the iron curtain in the years after 1945. Other countries across Europe had been occupied by the Germans but for countries such as Hungary and Poland the possibility of coming to terms with – and commemorating – the past differed from the open western societies that emerged in the post-war years.[99] Those open societies included West Germany.

Hungary and Poland are also sensitive to any criticism of their citizens during the years of occupation; particularly when there is any suggestion of collaboration and collusion with the crimes of the Holocaust. In 2015, at the annual dinner of the United States Holocaust Museum, the then director of the FBI, James B. Comey, was critical of Hungary and Poland for the way they had complied with the genocidal policies of Nazi Germany. Both governments summoned the United States ambassadors, expressed anger, and denied any complicity in the Holocaust.[100] The sensitivities about the past – particularly in nations with perpetrator and victim histories – can clearly lead to an international crisis if not dealt with carefully.[101] Research by Hirschberger, Kende and Weinstein sought to address the role of historical memory within modern contemporary intergroup processes. In brief summary they found that:

> First, it shows that representations of history play an important role in the relationship between in-group identification and prejudice; Second, it shows that representations of history can be primed

and exert an effect above and beyond the influence of in-group identification; Third, it shows that the ghosts of history and the prejudice related to them influence contemporary international relations.[102]

Other research concurs that Hungarian memory and politics is characterized less by consensus and more by conflict, and that in Hungary the government was unable to establish a commonly agreed narrative of the past, even when, in 2014, it erected two memorials and introduced the Holocaust Memorial Year.[103] Hungary currently has one of the largest Jewish populations in Europe, the majority of whom live in Budapest, which also had a higher survival rate of Hungarian Jews during the war, compared with those who lived in rural Hungary. The *Zsidónegyed*, or Jewish Quarter, is one of the more popular tourist destinations. But Hungary has had its reputation tainted in recent years by reports of antisemitic incidents.[104] When the Hungarian government made 2014 Holocaust Memorial Year, it was in part an attempt to have the country viewed more favourably, but it has been suggested that the government did not succeed in its objective.[105]

Hirschberger et al refer to 'defensive representations of history' to describe how Hungarians perceive their group in the Second World War as either victims or resistance fighters of forced (as opposed to willing) collaborators. They also acknowledge that many Hungarians genuinely believe that one of these descriptions best represents the role of their group during the war, even if the evidence suggests otherwise.[106] The research showed that if a group is accused of causing harm, with evidence to prove that it did, the group will tend to adopt a victim status which protects their moral image.[107] This has been referred to as competitive victimhood represented by a defensive response to any threat to the moral image of the group. The research also found that there was a relationship between hatred of the victim group and defensive representations of the Holocaust.[108]

It is also acknowledged that whilst there was official and widespread collaboration by Hungarians with the Nazis, there was also resistance from the Magyar Front and members of the Hungarian Social Democrat Party.

Part of the problem with the Holocaust, as the most researched genocide in history, is that the rules of discussion are sometimes too narrow. It has been suggested that there is a need to deconstruct the concepts of the Holocaust and antisemitism in order to best investigate and understand the events of that time.[109] As mentioned in the chapter on Holocaust denial, there is a long-standing debate between scholars regarding the *intentionalist* or *functionalist* interpretations of the Holocaust. There are also debates about the Holocaust within the bigger picture of Nazi colonialism and mass violence that reach beyond any disagreements on a simple concept of antisemitism. Most discussions focus on the planned genocide in Polish and Soviet territories.[110] The Holocaust in Hungary has its own complexities. Of course, as has been shown, there was homegrown Hungarian antisemitism and violence against the Jews. Indeed, there was also homegrown fascism and anti-Jewish legislation that predated any allegiance with Hitler's Nazi Germany. The Hungarian Jews who were transported to Auschwitz-Birkenau were murdered by the Germans. But they were transported by Hungarians who handed them over in Kassa. The Hungarians 'ethnically cleansed' their territory of Jews, but, at Auschwitz-Birkenau, it was the Germans who killed them. These are two specific and separate acts of mass violence which achieved the same ultimate end.[111]

Returning to the work of Hirschberger et al, they found that Hungarian nationalism was associated with antisemitism, and that high nationalism was associated with higher endorsement of defensive representations of the Holocaust, which was also associated with more antisemitism. Low nationalism was associated with greater acknowledgement of in-group responsibility for past crimes and was also associated with less antisemitism. One of their other studies showed defensive representations of the Holocaust increased negative attitudes towards Israel, conspiratorial antisemitism and secondary antisemitism.[112] It would be expected that two groups which perceive themselves to have been victims of the same traumatic history would have a sense of affiliation and closeness. Yet, there is a competitive element to co-victimization which may have a bearing on what is seen in Hungary and other territories that were occupied by the Germans.[113] Of course, part of the motivation to distort collective memory may be a desire to exonerate a certain group from any responsibility for the crimes of the Holocaust. It allows the narrative to be changed so that in

Hungary, for instance, rather than acknowledging the well-documented crimes and collaboration of the Arrow Cross government, it is easier to claim that Hungarians were themselves victims of the Nazis and were forced to collaborate against their will.[114] As mentioned in the chapter on Holocaust denial, a common tactic among negationsists is to claim that those who fail to challenge the accepted history of the Holocaust do so in part because of pressure from Jews. This could fall under the concept of co-victimization, in that it exonerates the perpetrator group. Furthermore, defensive representations of history can be disproven by historical victim groups, which in turn leads to claims that the victim group is putting unfair pressure on the perpetrator group.[115]

George Soros is the founder of the Open Society Foundations. He was born in Hungary and lived through the Nazi occupation. In 1947 he moved to London where he studied philosophy with Karl Popper, author of *The Open Society and its Discontents*. After immigrating to the United States in 1956, Soros amassed a fortune through working in finance and investment. He used the money to fund philanthropic projects that best reflected Popper's philosophy that 'no ideology is the final arbiter of truth, and societies can only flourish when they allow for democratic governance, freedom of expression, and respect for individual rights'.[116] George Soros is also Jewish. Some of the attacks upon him resonate with many of the traditions of antisemitism. He and his Open Society Foundations are accused of subverting democracy by staging rigged elections, funding non-independent news media and being labelled as foreign agents or spies. Most of these accusations emanate from countries where right-wing populism has gained a hold and where the established norms and accepted human rights have been changed drastically. These activities have happened in varying levels in Poland, the Czech Republic, Turkey, Venezuela, Cambodia, the Philippines, Azerbaijan, China, Russia and Soros's former homeland of Hungary.[117] It is notable that in Europe Germany, France and the Netherlands each have right-wing and far-right populist nationalist political parties, but none has gained power, yet; but Hungary, along with Poland and the Czech Republic in 2020 is more obviously led by a far-right government.[118] This has raised concerns in many quarters.

Laurence Rees has written and narrated numerous television documentaries on the subject of Hitler, the Nazis and the Holocaust.

He has also written a number of carefully researched books on the same topic. In *The Holocaust: A New History*, published in 2017, Rees observes:

> The recent background to anti-Semitism in Hungary would have been familiar to Eichmann. Hungarian anti-Semites – like German and Austrian anti-Semites – had pointed to the influence that Jews were alleged to possess in the media and key professions, and also to the supposed links between Judaism and the hated creed of Communism.[119]

The United States Holocaust Memorial Museum observed that:

> Today Holocaust history in Hungary is under serious threat. The rise of antisemitism there in recent years has coincided with efforts to rehabilitate wartime political leaders and others who allied Hungary with Nazi Germany and collaborated in the murder of hundreds of thousands of Hungarian Jews during the Holocaust.[120]

Hungary has received criticism from other quarters, particularly regarding the politics of the government under the leadership of Viktor Orbán. Writing in *The Wall Street Journal* in December 2018, William A. Galson, former deputy assistant for domestic policy for President Bill Clinton observed that Hungary, with a population of 9.7 million people which makes up less than 2 per cent of the population of the European Union, is able to punch above its weight within the Union. As such when German Chancellor Angela Merkel wanted the EU to admit more than a million refugees and to share responsibility between member states, it was Orbán's opposition to such a policy that ultimately thwarted it and inspired other nations to follow suit.[121] It is not just on the international stage that Orbán's government has acted in ways that have attracted criticism. In 2018 more than 400 private news outlets were brought under the control of a holding company run by close allies of Prime Minister Orbán, which included his personal lawyer from within the Fidesz Party. It has been suggested that this is an attempt to return to a centralized state media similar to the communist era. The controlling company is protected from scrutiny following a decree issued by Orbán.[122] The government has also created a parallel court system with the selection and promotion of judges controlled by the justice minister. Furthermore, the government shut down the Budapest campus of the Central European University, which was founded by George Soros, in what many see as an attack on academic freedom and integrity.[123] During the 2018 election campaign there was a rise in antisemitic episodes in Hungary, and the use of antisemitic rhetoric by Orbán that has not been heard in mainstream European politics since the Second World War. A magazine closely linked to the Orbán government featured a cover picture of the head of the Federation of Jewish Communities with money emerging from his forehead. There were calls for this to be condemned but Orbán claimed that to do so would inhibit freedom of the press.[124] Controversially, Orbán also appointed Maria Schmidt as the head of a new Holocaust museum which intends to depict the role of Hungary and Hungarians more favourably than the existing museum, which acknowledges Hungarian collaboration in the deportation and murder of Jews. Maria Schmidt has been critical of the Nuremberg trials and has defended antisemitic figures. When she herself was criticized by some within the Hungarian Jewish community, she responded that 'some groups would like to consider their ancestors' tragic fate an inheritable and advantageous privilege', before adding that when they do so 'they exclude themselves from our national community'.[125] During a time when far-right populist nationalism is on the rise in Europe and elsewhere, it is necessary that liberal and democratic institutions and societies keep a close watch on Hungary.

It is not all negative though. In March 2015 Hungary assumed the chairmanship of the International Holocaust Remembrance Alliance (IHRA). During the Budapest plenary meetings in June 2015, Minister János Lázár spoke of Hungary's responsibility for the past and stated: 'The main focus of the Hungarian Chairmanship programme will be on tackling anti -Semitism, promoting Holocaust education, the issue of the Roma genocide and increasing visibility and importance of the IHRA.' This must give some hope to counterbalance the justifiable criticism of the current Hungarian government.

Hungary was politically, economically and militarily an ally of Nazi Germany for much of the Second World War. It is a nation with a history of homegrown antisemitism that included enacting the first anti-Jewish legislation in twentieth-century Europe. From the early days of the Horthy government Hungarian fascists were able to influence domestic policy. Hungary – as with Germany – was on the losing side in the First World War. The period after the war was one of political and social upheaval and included a brief communist dictatorship and the White Terror. Hungary was also treated severely with a post-war treaty (Trianon) which led to it losing most of its pre-war territory and population. With similarities to Germany, this led to blame being directed at the victorious First World War allies, the communists and, of course, the Jews.

Hungarian national memory of the Holocaust has been impacted by the post-war years under the influence of communism and the Soviet Union. Some Hungarians see themselves and their community as being the principal victims of the Germans, and will claim that collaboration, when it occurred, did so because people were forced to collaborate. The historical evidence suggests that collaboration was willingly entered into, and that many Hungarians were enthusiastic and independent participants in the crimes of the Holocaust. There is commendable acknowledgement of the Holocaust and Hungary's role in it. This was tacitly and openly spoken about when Hungary took the chairmanship of the International Holocaust Remembrance Alliance in 2015. There are also concerns about a rise in antisemitic incidents and rhetoric in recent years and the hostility of some within Hungarian politics and society to minority groups, migrants and refugees. Some have suggested that the political language voiced in Hungary today would be immediately familiar to the likes of Adolf Eichmann, which is not something Hungary should wear as a badge of honour.

Holocaust education is needed in all societies, but most importantly in the countries that suffered most or that were active participants in those crimes. This, it would seem, is something that Hungary needs to address if it is to come to terms with its past and learn from that period of history.

Chapter 9

Poland

It is clear that the Polish government and elements of Polish society are sensitive to any suggestion of Polish involvement in the crimes of the Holocaust and against the Jewish population of that country during the German occupation. As will be shown, there is abundant evidence of Polish antisemitism prior to, during, and following the period of occupation. Of course, antisemitism in and of itself, does not necessarily equate with the criminality of the Holocaust. In Poland, as elsewhere in Europe, antisemitism has existed as long as there had been a Jewish community. Mistrust and hostility between communities is a reflection of the tribalism of society that will manifest most obviously when there are discernible cultural, religious, linguistic and other differences. That tribalism alone does not explain the violent and often murderous hostility towards the Jews that some Poles demonstrated. This chapter will explore some of the evidence against elements of the Polish society during the years of German occupation. Some of the most notable research into this area has been undertaken by the historians Jan Grabowski and Jan T. Gross. There has been mixed response to their work, which has included outright condemnation and suggestions that they are in some way anti-Polish. In July 2016, the Polish minister of education, Anna Zalewska, was asked on national television about the perpetrators of the 1941 Jedwabne massacre and the Kielce pogrom of 1946. In reference to Jan Gross's book *Neighbours*, which explores the Jedwabne massacre, she stated: 'The facts need to be checked again; historians are not sure,' before elaborating that 'Gross writes lies, it's the anti-Semites who killed them'.[1] Grabowski expands on this theme by noting that Jaroslaw Szarek, director of the Polish Institute of National Remembrance (IPN), also attributed the killings at Jedwabne to the Germans, contradicting previous findings by the IPN that identified Poles as the perpetrators.[2]

These examples are identified by Grabowski as being indicative of a Polish history policy that is contrary to the evidence gathered over the previous twenty-five years.[3] Schlomo Netzer, writing about the Jewish historiography of the Holocaust in Poland noted: 'the rewriting of history, which is one of the outstanding characteristics of historiography, reflects the viewpoint of the contemporary generation as it looks to the past.'[4] He elaborated on this theme by observing that up-to-date perspectives and research add to what is known.[5] Reflecting on this, it has been suggested that Gross's book asked the question of Poles: 'Is it possible to be simultaneously a victim and a victimizer?'[6] Gross has caused Poles to rethink their traditional perceptions of history, particularly regarding the Holocaust.[7]

Scrutinizing the work of Grabowski and Gross, one can see that their methodology was thorough and appears to be balanced. They share similarities in their approaches to the evidence. Grabowski refers to his methodology as a 'triangulation of memory'.[8] By using three types of sources Grabowski endeavours to see the evidence of the wartime period from different perspectives. Firstly, he considers the testimonies of Jewish survivors which were obtained shortly after the war and filed with the Central Committee of Polish Jews (CKZP) before being transferred to the Jewish Historical Institute (ZIH) in Warsaw. Some 7,000 testimonies are held by the ZIH, and most were obtained between 1945 and 1948 which should add to their contemporaneous value.[9] Secondly, Grabowski compares the Jewish survivor testimonies with the records of Polish courts during the late 1940s. The court records particularly refer to those of the 'August Trials' which took place following a decree on 31 August 1944 regarding 'the punishment of Fascist-Nazi criminals, guilty of murders and mistreatment of civilians and prisoners of war and traitors of the Polish nation'.[10] Thirdly, Grabowski considers West German justice system sources from investigations conducted during the 1960s.[11]

The work of historians investigating the Holocaust and Polish involvement is greatly assisted by the variety of source material. It has been observed that the greater the number of sources that offer similar accounts – particularly witness testimony – the more reliable that information must be considered.[12] If there are multiple sources but some give similar accounts, it is reasonable to assume that, on balance, those accounts may be more reliable.[13] There is a risk with witness testimony that multiple individuals may be involved in obtaining the accounts and documenting them, which may impact upon the quality of recorded memories.[14] Similarly, the greater the time between the events recalled and the documenting of evidence, the more likely there is to be concern about the accuracy of recollected detail. As such, contemporary diaries or other records documented at the time are probably going to be seen as more reliable.[15] Furthermore, there is a risk of polyphony when other people put into writing that which is orally stated by a witness. A witness testimony that has not been authored first-hand may be subject to deliberate or unintentional changes that directly affect the initial context.[16] Similarly, whether self-penned or not, testimonies are subject to a number of influences and traditions that impact upon how an account is compiled or perceived – what Beate Müller describes as 'the discursive consequences of assuming and staging of the survivor's voice'.[17] However – and this is reflected in the work of historians such as Grabowski and Gross – there are basic methodologies that many disciplines share, and a desire to know if the information obtained is reliable and trustworthy.[18] Of course, one must also consider the motivation of witnesses when giving testimony. Grabowski observes that witnesses interviewed by the Central Committee of Polish Jews sought only to ensure the historical evidence of the Holocaust was preserved and did not appear to have any ulterior motive.[19] It is asserted herein that witness testimony should, on the whole, be accepted for its validity and veracity. All witnesses, whatever the trauma and whatever the time between the event and giving an account, will have difficulty recalling specific details, but the general observations of personal experiences become more acceptable when greater numbers are consistent in the evidence they provide.

The massacre at Jedwabne has been central to much of the debate on Polish criminality against the Jews during the German occupation. It is suggested that half of the population (gentiles) killed the other half (Jews) during one day of extreme violence on 10 July 1941. Estimates have been as high as 1,600 men, women and children murdered.[20]

As cited by Gross, a Jew from Radziłów, named as Menachem Finkelsztajn, reports a number of horrific events at this time. Finkelsztajn suggested that on 5 July 1941 some 1,200 Jews were killed in Wąsosz, on 7 July 1,500 Jews were killed in Radziłów, and that 3,000 were murdered in Jedwabne. In a later written testimony, he suggested that the number killed in Radziłów was actually 800, and overall Gross asserts that his estimations of the total number murdered at each place is double the actual number killed.[21] Finkelsztajn reported that the killers were 'local hooligans' acting with the consent of the Germans.[22]

Some events preceded and may have set the template for Jedwabne and other massacres of Jews. On 27 June 1941, soon after the Germans commenced Operation Barbarossa and deployed their forces to the east, Ordnungspolizei Battalion 329 entered Białystok to seek out Soviet forces. Jews were forced to clear the town of statues of Lenin and Stalin as Soviet music was played. Jewish men were seized, some were shot immediately and ten were killed inside a small synagogue.[23] The Germans detained women and children, and over 1,000 Jewish men. They were forced into a synagogue surrounded by machine guns. Gasoline was poured onto the building and set alight, killing all of those within.[24] Historian Timothy Snyder suggests that a certain logic applied to the German actions: the Jews were responsible for the Soviet occupation and in order for Poles to be liberated the Jews had to be killed. He opines that this logic was clear to the local population who had been led to believe in the 'Judeobolshevik myth' which had been promoted by the Polish right in the years since the First World War.[25]

The events in Jedwabne closely mirrored those in Białystok except that here, the Germans initiated what happened but the Poles perpetrated the massacre. Some activities, such as Jews being forced by Poles to carry Lenin's statue and a red banner, were acutely similar to Białystok two weeks previously. There was a clear implied link between Jews and the communism of the Soviet occupation.[26]

The hostility towards supposed Soviet collaborators manifested on 25 June 1941 when six alleged collaborators were tortured, beaten and lynched by local Poles in Jedwabne. The victims were three Jews and three Poles.[27] Over the following days and ultimately leading to the massacre at Jedwabne, there was increasing hostility and violence directed at Jews, which, it has been suggested, was tolerated by the Germans.[28]

Interestingly, communism had little support in the Jedwabne area, and although the anti-Soviet Polish underground movement had been betrayed during the Soviet occupation, it was not by a Jew, but by a Pole. The Germans provided the Poles with the opportunity to blame the Jews for the Soviet occupation, and to take retribution through elimination.[29]

Polish academic Krzysztof Persak examined court papers and witness testimonies associated with investigations into the Jedwabne massacre.

These revealed a consistency in how the events were described that concurs with findings from other historians. Persak's research also challenged some of the narratives that apportioned all or most of the blame onto Germans. His description of the events in Jedwabne concurs with other accounts. On 10 July 1941 the Jewish residents of the town were assembled in the market square, made to weed between the cobblestones, and forced to perform humiliating exercise routines. The younger male Jews were compelled to destroy a statue of Lenin and then the Jews were forced to conduct a funeral for Lenin, including carrying the remains of the statue around the market square whilst singing Russian communist songs. They then had to bury the statue in a grave before the Jewish group were murdered at that site.[30] This description is consistent with other accounts of that day. Later that evening the remaining Jews were forced into a barn which was set alight. They died in that building. Several hundred Jews were killed on that day.[31]

Responsibility for the massacre at Jedwabne is placed by witnesses on local Polish residents and some from nearby villages. They had varied roles, from assembling the Jews, to killing them individually, to driving them into the barn, to stealing from Jewish homes, or merely being part of a hostile mob.[32] Witnesses attribute organization of the massacre to the local municipal authorities led by the mayor, Marian Karolak.[33] As noted by Gross, Karolak is cited in almost all dispositions as being the coordinator of the Jedwabne massacre and being actively involved throughout the process.[34] Furthermore, the Polish population were cited as perpetrators.[35]

There was some official Polish acknowledgement of the massacre. One monument has an inscription stating – falsely – that 1,600 Jedwabne Jews were killed by the Nazis, whilst another, erected after 1989 states: 'To the memory of about 180 people including 2 priests who were murdered in the territory of Jedwabne district in the years 1939–1956 by the NKVD, the Nazis, and the secret police,' which somehow omits to mention the Jews killed or that there were 1,600 victims murdered by Polish neighbours.[36]

Polish historiography and the narrative associated with the crimes at Jedwabne and elsewhere must be influenced by post-war court proceedings. Some of the Jedwabne perpetrators stood trial in 1949 and 1953. It is apparent that the investigative process and the trials were ineffective.[37] It appears that local residents and the defendants were not wholly cooperative and may even have conspired to remain silent on key issues.[38] Persak's analysis of investigations into the Jedwabne case in the 1960s and 1970s suggests that efforts were made to blame the Germans and deny the involvement of Poles.[39] It is possible that investigators realized that the whole town of Jedwabne could have been implicated and therefore sought ways to minimize the scope of the prosecution cases.[40]

A factor in the trials of the Jedwabne defendants was certainly the 'August Decree' of 31 August 1944 regarding 'the punishment of Fascist-Hitlerite criminals guilty of murder and ill-treatment of the civilian population and of prisoners of war, and the punishment of traitors to the Polish Nation'. Of note, Article 1, Clause 1 of this decree says that those found guilty of collaboration with the Germans of the murder of civilian or military personnel would be sentenced to death.[41] Article 5 of the decree allowed for mitigation if a person acted under threats or command.[42] Interestingly, in the context of the Holocaust law, approximately 20,000 people were convicted and sentenced due to the August Decree. Most were sentenced by 1951, and the majority were almost certainly Polish.[43] This suggests that Polish courts – and the state – in the immediate post-war years, acknowledged that some citizens were involved in crimes associated with the Nazi occupation. The prosecutor in the Jedwabne case allowed for the charges to reflect that the defendants 'were involved in capturing twelve hundred persons of Jewish nationality, who, as a mass, were burned in a barn by the Germans'. In doing so, blame for the murders was placed on Germans not Poles. Of the twenty-two defendants who stood trial at Łomża District Court in May 1949, only one was sentenced to death; ten were acquitted.[44]

Jan T. Gross has been foremost in documenting the history of the Jedwabne massacre. When his book *Neighbours* was first released in Poland in 2000 it initiated a mixed response. Poland's Institute of National Memory (IPN) commissioned extensive research into the massacre.[45] The research was published in July 2002.[46] Most notably, the research found that the massacre was planned in advance by locals, with limited direct involvement from Germans.[47] It concurred with other research detailing the scenario of individual killings, the amassing of Jews in the market square, the burning of Jews in a barn, and the murder of most Jews in the town.[48] It acknowledged that Jewish property was plundered, and observed that 'executors of this crime, in the strict sense of the word, were

Polish inhabitants of Jedwabne and vicinity – at least 40 males', with it being difficult to explain the passivity of the rest of the population.[49] As Martin Winstone damningly observes about Jedwabne:

> Polish historians have produced an immense body of research in recent years which paints a compelling picture. Using previously ignored or inaccessible resources – including the accounts of survivors compiled immediately after or even during the war, German documents, post-war court proceedings and modern interviews with surviving eyewitnesses – it has been irrefutably demonstrated that a significant minority of people were more than mere bystanders.[50]

A similar pogrom occurred on 7 July 1941 eighteen kilometres away from Jedwabne in Radziłów. It is claimed that German military or police personnel arrived in the town and ordered the local Polish authorities to gather the Jewish population in the market square on the premise of weeding grass from the cobbles. The Germans are alleged to have suggested that the Poles should burn the Jews in a barn, which duly occurred before the local population plundered the homes of the Jews.[51]

Persak notes that the massacres at Jedwabne and Radziłów were among approximately thirty violent anti-Jewish incidents that occurred in an area that had been under Soviet occupation for nearly two years. The Germans were greeted as liberators and there was a strong sense that revenge should be taken on those who had collaborated with the Soviets – which, for the Poles, included all Jews.[52] The Germans had already associated Jews with Bolshevism – *Judeobolshevism* – and had promoted the idea that Jews and Soviets were inextricably linked. In those territories that Snyder refers to as being doubly occupied, the Germans reinforced the hostility towards Soviets as being legitimately directed against Jews.[53]

The concept of double occupation or 'double statelessness' has been written about at length by Timothy Snyder. In those areas where the Polish state had been destroyed either by the Germans, or the Soviets, or by both occupying forces, nearly all Jewish residents were murdered.[54] Snyder observes, with validity, that the Holocaust commenced in those areas where the state was rapidly destroyed twice – firstly by the Soviets, and then by the Germans.[55] In the double-occupied areas of eastern Poland the Germans recruited locals and killed by open-air mass shootings;

whereas in areas that had been under German control since 1939, the mass killings by gassing, deportations from ghettos and Jew hunts really commenced in 1941.[56] This leads to the next area of discussion.

Thus far some significant evidence has been cited, based on contemporaneous witness testimony, court records and academic research, which identifies Poles as being responsible for participation in the mass murder of Jewish neighbours. These murders happened in urban areas with established and sizeable Jewish populations that were easily identifiable to the German forces or known to their Polish neighbours. Away from the urban centres, in smaller villages and rural communities, another phenomenon developed – the *Judenjagd*, or Jew hunt. The targets here were Jews who had fled the urban ghettos, or who lived in smaller Jewish communities. The perpetrators were Polish neighbours, and the Polish 'blue police' (officially the Polish Police of the General Government, whose uniforms were blue).

David Cesarani, citing Jan Grabowski, notes his estimation that 250,000 Jews sought to avoid deportation by hiding in the Polish woodlands, of which only 50,000 survived the war.[57] Shmuel Spector estimated that by the time of the liberation, only 9 per cent of Jews who had hidden or taken flight were still alive.[58] Grabowski himself suggests that, of the 2.5 million surviving Polish Jews in the summer of 1942, the 200,000 potential victims of the *Judenjagd* never really stood a chance.[59] The Germans used a combination of incentives and fear to get Poles to help identify and locate Jews, and without the Polish familiarity with the environment and the people, the Germans would not have been as successful in finding them.[60] The Poles, often led by police officers or elders, would roam in organized groups seeking out Jews in hiding. Sometimes this was done to gain favours from the Germans, but often these hunts occurred independently of German influence.[61] Jews in hiding would sometimes need to enter urban areas, but ran the risk of their identification papers being checked by Polish police, who would rob them, hand them over to the Germans or kill them.[62] Jews living in ghettos needed on occasion to seek resources and barter and trade with the community outside of the ghetto. As survivor Kitty Hart-Moxon observed about the Lublin ghetto:

You paid dearly for every contribution from outside. Throughout history there has been a strong antisemitic feeling in Poland among certain elements, and now they not only allowed the Germans to do what they liked with Polish Jews, but actively collaborated with the invader. A few showed genuine compassion and courage, but others were only too glad to find Jews in hiding and hand them over to the Nazis.[63]

From late 1943, the Germans turned their focus to dealing with partisans, which gave the Polish police free rein to seek out Jews.[64] To add to the terror for Jews in hiding, the women were particularly vulnerable. Some women offered sex to pay for help, but would be sexually exploited anyway, and some Polish partisan groups actually sought out Jewish families in hiding specifically to find their women.[65] The historian Martin Winstone asserts that the numbers of gentiles participating in the process of murder were a minority, usually involved as part of the security services such as the Polish blue police. The blue police were used in ghetto clearances and in the *Judenjagd* in the more rural areas.[66] The subject of the police will be referred to later in more detail. Cesarani, citing Jan T. Gross, notes that murder, rape, torture and extortion of Jews by Poles were not crimes conducted by a few rogue elements on the fringes of society, but were considered acceptable social practice.[67] Furthermore, many, including supposedly upstanding citizens – mayors, police, elders and firemen – participated in order to profit from Jews.[68]

Studies of the *Judenjagd* in Dąbrowa Tarnowska found that of 239 documented murders, only seven are known to have involved the German police acting alone. In most of these cases Jews were killed either by peasants or Polish police officers, or were handed over to the Germans.[69] Of course, it is known that the Germans often kept meticulous records, but these do not provide verifiable information about those murders in which the Germans were not involved. It is asserted by Winstone (and others) that there were possibly thousands of murders of fugitive Jews – sometimes preceded by rape and torture – committed by Poles acting independently.[70] A cited diary entry from Symcha Hampel notes:

Poland is probably the only country in the world where practically the whole society betrayed and handed over to the Germans each hidden

Jew, their fellow citizen. I want to stress that thousands of Jewish children have been caught this way, handed over to the German murderers and sent on to the gas chambers. The Poles worked hard and well [to make it possible] … The entire Polish society is to be blamed, and the Polish clergy most of all. Only now, living among the Poles, can I see how deeply entrenched is antisemitism in Polish society … the priests often discussed the Jews in church and thanked God that these parasites were gone once and for all. They were grateful to Hitler for having done the dirty work [for them].[71]

Others disagree about the breadth of Polish society's involvement. Martin Winstone, for example, asserts that not only did a minority of Poles help Jews, but also that a minority were actively involved in persecuting them. However, in Poland as elsewhere in occupied Europe, the majority of the society was indifferent with mixed levels of sympathy or hostility towards Jews.[72]

In the area of Dąbrowa Tarnowska the *Judenjagd* occurred in two stages: the actions of Germans helped by Poles in the liquidation of the ghetto and its aftermath, followed by later activities. In the first stage the Germans were actively involved, whilst in the second stage those involved were local Poles and the blue police.[73] After the ghetto was cleared the Germans needed to locate the remaining Jews, which required assistance from the native population.[74] The circumstances of the death of Jews in hiding in the area of Dąbrowa Tarnowska County are significant. The vast majority were killed directly by Poles or after being denounced to the Germans by the local population. Of 286 Jews killed, 105 were killed by Germans – of which 98 had been denounced by locals; the remaining 181 were killed by locals and blue police, or, in the case of fifty-nine, the circumstances of death are unknown.[75] These figures are cited by Grabowski of just one area of Poland, but are probably a fair reflection of activities elsewhere. Hunts for Jews were organized using previous self-defence structures involving many locals. They were particularly effective in rural areas where Jewish refugees were hiding and involved peasants and official groups. In one incident in Dąbrowa Tarnowska County at least forty-seven Jews were killed in a single hunt.[76]

It is known that firefighters would conduct drills as a premise to search for Jews.[77] An example cited in literature is of an incident at the village of

Racławice in which firemen searched a farm looking for a family of Jews. Once located the family were handed over to local peasants and taken to a blue police station where they were killed.[78] Although not all firemen were antisemitic it is probable that sufficient numbers were, who could then influence colleagues to conform.[79]

The activities of the Polish blue police in hunts for Jews are cited widely, both in cooperation with the Germans and committing crimes independently. The role of the Polish police changed. In the pre-war years of the 1930s they understood that part of their role was to prevent anti-Jewish pogroms, irrespective of their own prejudices.[80] However, when the Polish state ceased to exist following the occupation, the police became subservient to the Germans, and changed into the Polish Order Police, or blue police, with ultimate subordination to Himmler.[81] The blue police became part of German racial activities.[82] It has been observed that much less historical attention has been paid to the smaller ghettos where most Jews lived. It is in these areas – often with minimal German presence – that the role of the Polish blue police grew.[83] It was the blue police, for example, who enforced the wearing of identifying armbands for Jews.[84]

On 15 October 1941, a proclamation was issued for 'the 3rd Regulation Concerning the Limitations of the Right of Residence' in the General Government.[85] This included the death penalty for Jews found outside of ghettos without official authorization. The blue police were tasked with enforcing this regulation.[86] In early November 1941 the blue police were given orders to shoot men, women and children attempting to cross the boundary of the Warsaw ghetto.[87] By 17 November 1941, in Warsaw's Gęsia Street prison the blue police performed two mass executions.[88] By autumn and winter of 1941, the role of the blue police, on orders from the Germans, included the shooting of Jews. This included executions.[89] Furthermore, prior to the implementation of the 'Final Solution' in early 1942, the blue police were involved in moving Jews into the larger ghettos.[90] The liquidation of the smaller ghettos involved not just the blue police, but also firefighters and members of the Polish community.[91] Zygmunt Klukowski described a massacre during the Zamość action and noted how Poles helped the Germans search for Jews, and laughed during the killings.[92] Additionally, Klukowski observed how, after the destruction of the community of Szczebrzeszyn, the Polish police and the gendarmerie actively hunted for Jews.[93] Describing a mass murder in the town of Węgrów in September 1942, Grabowski details how Germans and the Polish blue police formed a cordon around the town. Once most Jews from the ghetto had been rounded up in the square, they were killed.[94]

Following the suppression of the Warsaw ghetto uprising in 1943, SS-Brigadeführer Jürgen Stroop wrote in his report: 'The Polish Police received permission to seize one-third of all goods seized upon the persons of Jews apprehended and arrested on the Aryan side of the city. This measure was very successful.'[95] The Polish historian Emanuel Ringelblum opined that the deaths of hundreds of thousands of Polish Jews were attributable to the Polish police.[96] Grabowski cites Christopher Browning who observed that for the Germans killing Jews was a matter of duty, whereas for Polish police and firefighters the killings originated from a deeper hatred which had been 'enriched and cultivated by centuries of the teachings of the Church'.[97] The role of the Church will be discussed further.

There are mixed reasons for the actions and inactions of the Catholic Church in Poland with regards to the Holocaust. The prevailing Catholic opinion held Jews to be responsible for the death of Jesus.[98] Furthermore – and this fitted neatly with the propaganda of the Nazis – the Church also linked the Jews to communism.[99] Survivor accounts describe how Poles would torment and attack Jews during key Christian festivals such as Christmas and Easter, with reference being made to the presumed blood libel associated with Judaism.[100] Gross notes that Easter was a time when Catholic priests evoked the idea that Jews were God-killers, which would then lead to antisemitic violence.[101] Similarly, the belief in the blood libel, or ritual murder, remained a strongly held idea for many Polish Catholics.[102] Among the survivors cited by Grabowski, Freda Walzman and Morris Suss both offered the opinion that the Catholic clergy was responsible for the hostility towards Jews.[103] It has been asserted that antisemitic hatred was inspired in the 1930s by elements of the Catholic press, including, in Kraków, *Dzwon Niedzielny* and *Gosc Niedzielny*, whilst in Tarnow the weekly journal *Nasza Sprawa* often demanded the 'de-Judaification' of Polish culture and the economy.[104] Snyder suggests that pre-war antisemitism from both the Catholic Church and the political secular right also resulted in fear of Poles from Poles when it came to assisting Jews.[105]

It is apparent that there were no clear directives from the Vatican, which allowed lower clergy to form their own opinions. This led to a mixed response of principled assistance of Jews, or fearful prejudice.[106] There are multiple conflicting examples. The priest from Radomysl Wielski incited peasant hostility against Jews and then refused to return Jewish property.[107] Conversely there were those Catholic priests who helped. Kitty Hart-Moxon describes how her father hid in the coal shed of Father Krasowski in Lublin, near the Gestapo headquarters. The priest was asked for help and provided Kitty and her parents with false birth certificates, identity cards and passports.[108] Furthermore, he encouraged Kitty and her mother to flee to Germany as he believed that they would be safer there, where most Jews had already been caught, rather than in Poland where Jews were being hunted.[109]

It has been suggested that those Catholics – and indeed Protestants – that helped Jews did so out of individualism, their own interpretation of Christian teachings, and in conflict with predominant religious doctrine.[110] It has been asserted that a clearer picture of the role of the Catholic Church in Poland during the Holocaust will only become apparent when Church archives are made available for independent scrutiny.[111] A further issue for Jews – in the ghettos, or in hiding – were the risks of denouncement and bribery by the Polish population. This too needs to be examined.

A derivative of the Polish word for the 'scum' or 'grease' who blackmailed Jews is *szmalcownicy*. It has been implied that such individuals operated on the margins of society and were therefore not representative of the whole.[112] By adopting a readily acceptable narrative that bribery, blackmail and extortion were crimes of the few rather than the many, it has been easier to exculpate those who may also have participated. Furthermore, as it is understood that such individuals were dealt with by underground courts, which allows the matter to be closed to further contemplation by the wider Polish society, with a casual assertion that there are wrongdoers in every community.[113]

In the rural areas the motivation for crimes against Jews occurred partly due to a belief that they had hidden wealth, and that those hiding Jews were getting rich in the process. This contributed to the distorted rationale for torture before murder, and also a belief that as Jews were already destined to die, they would not be needing their belongings.[114]

In cities and urban areas Poles would use the threat of denouncement as leverage over Jews in order to ensure a steady stream of income.[115]

It is possible that the impact of occupation – and indeed double occupation – with the violence it involved, affected the moral standards of those who were willing to denounce friends, neighbours, family members, and of course, Jews.[116] In a somewhat controversial editorial piece in 2009, *Der Spiegel* observed:

> Denunciation was so common in Poland that there was a special term for paid informants '*Szmalcowniki*' (previously a term for a fence). In many cases, the denouncers knew their victims. And while the French, Dutch or Belgians could submit to the illusion that the Jews deported to the east from Paris, Rotterdam or Brussels would be all right in the end, the people in Eastern Europe learned through the grapevine what lay in store for the Jews in Auschwitz or Treblinka.[117]

Denunciation, the fear of being denounced, bribery, threats, danger from locals, danger from the blue police and fire service, danger from Polish officialdom, entrenched antisemitism, and of course, the threat of being found and killed by Germans, all made life perilous to Jews throughout occupied Poland. As has been shown so far, at its extreme, the risks to Jews from Poles ultimately included violence, beatings, sexual assaults, robbery, extortion, blackmail, loss of homes, murder, mass executions and pogroms. These are realities of history verified from multiple contemporaneous sources and cross-checked by historians with other data including Polish and German court records, witness testimony and evaluation of the changing Polish historiographical narrative as it has evolved since the Second World War.

It is known that antisemitism – sometimes with violent and fatal consequences – existed in Poland before the German occupation, manifested in pogroms after the war, and may still be a problem in the modern Polish state. Although this book is primarily focused on the period of the Holocaust, it is necessary to examine pre- and post-war antisemitism in Poland. Antisemitism – politically, culturally and religiously fuelled – existed in Poland before the war, during the period of German occupation, and has manifested since that time. Poland had one of the oldest, and certainly the largest, Jewish populations in Europe prior to the German and the Soviet invasions of September 1939. Of course, antisemitism on its own does not presuppose violence towards Jews, but it is indicative of hostility and mistrust, which, when combined with other factors, can lead to harm.

Poland had been a multi-ethnic society for over nine centuries prior to the Second World War, with Jews making up 10 per cent of the population.[118] It is notable that in 1935, of the 425,566 Jewish school-aged children, only 19 per cent attended Jewish schools.[119] Most Jews in Poland were seen as being socially Polish.[120] But, nonetheless, antisemitism had been apparent since the late nineteenth century, and following Poland's independence in 1918, it had on occasion manifested in pogroms.[121] Indeed, during the interwar period, nationalist parties actively encouraged the population to boycott Jewish businesses.[122] Survivors speak of this. As Esther Brunstein observed: 'Life in pre-war Poland was difficult, and even as a child I was acutely aware of antisemitism and experienced many jibes in my direction.'[123] Daniel Falkner described how, after moving to Warsaw in 1936: 'Anti-Jewish propaganda was increasing every day. Radio from Germany was broadcasting stories about "evil" Jews and this propaganda fell on eager ears in Poland.'[124] Furthermore, Tony Biber stated that: 'For Jews in Poland, however, life was never really comfortable; the Poles were and are antisemitic.'[125] Noted survivor and Holocaust educator Kitty Hart-Moxon wrote about how, in 1939, she won a bronze medal for Poland in a swimming competition against Hungary. She was the youngest member of the team, aged only 12 or 13, and justly proud of what she had done but stated: 'At the same time I was disturbed by the way Jewish members of our team were jeered at by our fellow Poles. This was my first encounter with antisemitism and it made no sense.'[126] Many years after the war – when is not specified in her book – Kitty travelled to Lublin and visited the Jewish cemetery with a group of people. The group was stoned by young Poles as their parents looked on and laughed. The caretaker of the cemetery suggested that this occurred often and that he had received threats because he worked with Jews.[127]

It has been noted that attitudes against Jews, particularly cultural, religious or linked to the myth of ritual murder, continued from the pre-war period into the time of occupation.[128] The myth of blood libel and ritual murder attributed to Jews was adopted by Polish nationalists during the interwar period, and will appear again in discussions about post-war pogroms.[129] It was a literal and metaphorical belief that Jews were involved in vampirism and also that they were sucking the blood of the Polish nation.[130]

Other factors contributed to the hostility directed at Jews in post-war Poland. Some Poles considered the Jews to be ungrateful to those who had provided refuge during the war.[131] This was despite the earlier mentioned multiple incidents of Polish involvement in crimes against Jews. Furthermore, the Poles had anticipated independence from external powers after the war, and yet the Soviet-backed Communist regime took control of the state.[132] Poles alleged that this was supported by the Jews and reinforced the concept of *Zydokomuna*, or Jewish Communists.[133] Jews were also alleged to have collaborated with the Soviets, particularly in the East, during the war.[134] Additionally, there was a common perception that Jews were disproportionately represented in the various machinations of the new ruling regime.[135] Notably, it was alleged that Jews were abundant in the ranks of the security services, and yet, in February 1946, in the Lublin region as an example, Jews made up only 19 members of the 1,122 people employed by the Provincial Public Security Office.[136] It is asserted by Kopciowski that Jews became convenient scapegoats to whom anger and disenchantment could be directed.[137]

The period following liberation from German occupation was marred by instances of significant violence by Poles against Jews. The period 1945–6 in the Lublin and Radon districts resulted in the killing of more than 300 Jews.[138] As will be shown, other figures have been offered for the total number killed, but these may vary due to the detail of the region being referred to. It has been observed that nationalists attributed such pogroms to the *Zydokomuna* allegation proposed by Poles, but it is also likely that some of the violence was specifically directed against Jews returning home from exile in the Soviet Union, from the Nazi camps, or after being in hiding.[139] An example found in the literature is that of Faiga Himelblau, who returned to the Lublin district in June 1945, and was murdered when she attempted to take back her sewing machine.[140]

At the end of the Second World War there were 4,791 Jews residing in Lublin Province. A further 1,130 Jews arrived from the Soviet Union and by May 1946 the population of Jews in the area had increased to over 6,100.[141] Citing David Engel, Kopciowski notes that between December 1944 and February 1946, 69 Jews were murdered in the region, which accounted for over 20 per cent of all murders of Jews in Poland during that period.[142] However, when the period is extended from summer 1944 to December 1946, the total increased to 118 Jews killed in the Lublin region, with 79 of those being between January and June 1945.[143] Kopciowski observes that the killings gradually stopped throughout the country in autumn 1946 and ceased altogether the next year.[144] However, it is estimated that the total number of Jews killed in the period 1944–6 is anything from 600 to 3,000.[145] Gross suggests the total murders of Jews in this period was between 500 and 1,500.[146]

There were a number of bloody and significant pogroms in the immediate post-war period. They varied in severity, but some common factors are apparent. On 12 June 1945 the pogrom at Rzeszów was probably the first indicator of the violence that was going to be unleashed elsewhere.[147] It does not appear to be a widely documented pogrom, which in part may be because no one was killed and fewer people were injured than in other incidents.[148]

The upsurge of post-war anti-Jewish violence really commenced in Kraków on 11 August 1945, and, as in other pogroms, it appears to have begun following a rumour of Jews being involved in ritual murder.[149] In her research into mob behaviour and language during three post-war pogroms Joanna Tokarska-Bakir noted how they all followed a similar conspiracy pattern of a rumour about a child being murdered for blood, an aggressive mob seeking vengeance, attempted control by the security services, and failure of those security services to assert authority.[150] Furthermore, she observes that the mob behaviour occurred within the structure of the post-war Polish state and hostility between Communists of Jewish and also of non-Jewish backgrounds.[151]

The initial violence in Kraków was directed against a synagogue where it was rumoured that a child had been killed, following which Jews were pursued through the streets.[152] The police and some of the military were involved in the attacks, with six militiamen and five soldiers being among the twenty-five individuals named in the indictment against those who took part in the pogrom.[153] It is suggested that a 13-year-old boy fled the synagogue on Miodowa Street whilst shouting: 'Help people, the Jews were trying to murder me.'[154] In one of the responses the wife of a judge is alleged to have said, 'We did not raise our children to have them murdered by the Jews.'[155] Further mob shouting asserted that a Jewish woman had murdered two Polish children, and that she had committed the crime in the prayer house.[156] In a mix of vocalized hostility and the rationale behind the pogrom, the caretaker of a shelter is alleged to have suggested that Jews were on Polish soil and murdered Polish children, before adding: 'If Hitler couldn't finish you off, we will.'[157] The same man described how soldiers asked him to help find Jews, and during that exercise, whilst armed with an axe and a gun, he stole a pair of boots from one of his victims.[158] Further mob language associated Jews with Communism and Bolshevism, whilst making threats to cut heads off, to stone Jews, and of course to kill.[159] In one of the final gestures, in an act similar to the pogroms that occurred during the German occupation, a synagogue was burned and the Torah scrolls were set on fire in the street.[160]

The danger to Jews during the Kraków pogrom did not stop in what should have been the safety of a hospital. An account of one woman describes an escorting soldier and nurse discussing Jews as 'scum' and opining that they should not have to save them as they had murdered children.[161] The same woman described how, after surgery, a soldier suggested Jews should be taken to prison. The same soldier assaulted Jews in the waiting area, and holding a loaded gun, refused to allow them to drink water. Some Jews were assaulted by fellow patients, whilst nurses and others issued threats to rip them apart.[162] Many Jewish properties – including the synagogue where the pogrom commenced – were plundered, but it is observed by Gross that, unlike other pogroms, the security services and military were able to stop the violence.[163] It is estimated that dozens of Jews were wounded and between one and five were killed.[164]

By far the deadliest post-war pogrom in Poland occurred in Kielce on 4 July 1946. The scenario was similar in many ways to other pogroms in how it commenced and progressed, but the destruction exceeded previous events in the post-war era. On 1 July 1946, an 8-year-old boy named Henryk Błaszczyk went missing from his home after getting a lift to a village twenty-five kilometres away, apparently to pick cherries grown by an old neighbour of his family. He was reported missing to the police that evening, but two days later he returned, with some cherries.[165] That same evening his father went back to the police and reported that his son had escaped from some Jews who had kidnapped him. As his father was drunk, he was told to return the next day.[166]

In the morning of 4 July, the boy, his father and a neighbour went back to the police station. During their journey they passed by 7 Planty Street, which was the Jewish Committee building and home to approximately 180 Jews. The boy claimed that he had been held in the basement of that building.[167] The child identified a Jewish man wearing a green hat as being the individual who had lured him into the property.[168] Orders were issued for the man in the green hat to be brought to the police station for questioning.[169] The boy, his father and the neighbour accompanied the police and told other people what had happened. This led to a crowd gathering.[170] The detained man, Kalman Singer, was taken to the police station and beaten by a police officer.[171]

The head of the Jewish Committee went to the police station and pointed out that the building at 7 Planty Street did not have a basement, and as such the boy's story of being held there could not be true.[172] The police searched the property and confirmed that it did not have a basement. However, they kept Jews in the building during the search and ordered them to surrender their weapons. An angry crowd had gathered outside and did not approve of a police officer publicly reprimanding Henryk Błaszczyk for lying.[173]

The scenario is similar to other pogroms and was predictable in its outcome. A child claimed to have been kidnapped by a Jew. His father believed him and reported it to the police. The police investigated. A man was falsely identified as being implicated in the abduction. The lie about the basement the boy claimed to have been held in was established by the police. When the father and the boy accompanied the police to the property at 7 Planty Street, they agitated those they met into believing the kidnap story. By the time the building was being searched and the Jewish residents were being asked to surrender their weapons, a mob had gathered. It seems probable that whatever the outcome of the police investigation, the mob had made assumptions about the guilt of the Jews in the building.

Some literature suggests that when the boy was aggressively questioned by the police, he was somewhat confused and alluded to knowledge of ritual killings of Christian children.[174] It was then believed that the boy could point out a cellar or basement containing the bodies of children whose bodies had been drained of blood in order to make Passover bread.[175] On the way to the Jewish hostel at 7 Planty Street the police told locals why they were heading there, as a result of which a crowd gathered in the belief that there would be a search for Christian children.[176] This, of course, was reinforcing the old Polish belief in Jewish blood libel and vampirism. It is clear that within the hostel police and soldiers rapidly lost control and disregarded their initial objective of conducting a search. As they entered the building and disarmed the Jews, fighting ensued. It is alleged that soldiers either threw Jews out of windows, or handed them over to the mob outside who killed them.[177] It is apparent that no official order was given to authorize the use of lethal force, but when the soldiers began shooting, it intensified the agitation of the mob outside the building.[178] As the afternoon began the pogrom moved from the building and civilians searched the city looking for Jews.[179] Steelworkers became involved in the attacks, and at the railway station violence was unleashed by police officers, soldiers and railway guards.[180] The railway station attacks involved collaboration with passengers and boy scouts in identifying suspected Jews.[181] Skulls were crushed with heavy pieces of railway equipment.[182] As in previous pogroms the language of the mob made reference to beliefs that Jews were kidnapping Polish children to kill them and drink their blood.[183] The mob also had some form of allegiance with the police and soldiers and openly encouraged the violence of their actions.[184] In total, forty-two Jews are known to have been killed during the Kielce pogrom.[185]

Kielce was the most destructive post-war pogrom. The similarities in all those thus-far mentioned are clear to be seen. Most notably it is the initial belief in the wrongdoing of Jews, the added conviction that some form of blood libel crime has occurred, the agitation and aggression of the civilian population, the shared involvement of civilians and security services in acts of violence, and the eventual control of the mob by the police and military. The language used during the pogroms shares many common features.

By 1946, the number of Jews living in Poland was about 216,000, or less than 1 per cent of the total Polish population.[186] During the ensuing period until the early 1970s most of those who identified as being in some way Jewish had left Poland.[187] Reasons given for this outward migration are the Kielce pogrom, the blaming of Jews for communism, allegations that they collaborated with the Soviets and the state police, and the anti-Zionist campaign of the Polish authorities in 1967/8.[188] It is estimated in some literature that after the war 30,000 Jews survived in Poland either after being liberated from the camps or from living in hiding.[189] The post-war minority population of Poland had reduced from a third in the interwar period to about 1.5 per cent.[190] Three waves of emigration are identified: in the later 1940s following the Kielce pogrom, in the period 1956–9, and in 1968, because of the antisemitic campaign by the Polish authorities, a further 15,000 Jews left.[191]

During the 1960s, the Polish Communist Party became more nationalistic, with increased antisemitism and hostility towards Germany. This led to the antisemitic and anti-Zionist campaign of 1967/8.[192] Further influencing the antisemitic and anti-Zionist policies of the Polish state was the Six-Day War between Israel and its Arab neighbours that commenced on 5 June 1967. The Arab forces were trained and armed by the Soviet Union which had implications for countries, including Poland, in the wider Soviet sphere of influence.[193] On 7 June 1967, the Warsaw Treaty Organization signed a declaration which condemned Israel, and on 12 June 1967, Poland joined the other partner nations in breaking off diplomatic relations with Israel.[194] The Arab–Israeli war demonstrated a split between the population and the ruling party in Poland. Large numbers of Poles were sympathetic to the Israelis (but not to Jews) due to the fact that the Arab nations were being supported by the Soviets.[195] On 27 June 1967, preparations were made for 'anti-Zionist purges' by the Ministry of Internal Affairs. A list was produced by the security police of 382 writers, state officials, journalists and economic managers who were presumed to be supportive of Israel. Further instructions were given to gather information on those of Jewish origin working in the government, mass media and scientific institutions.[196] Although the initial purge of Jews was selective and impacted mainly on local party organizations and the military, it caused concern and uncertainty among liberal intellectuals and students.[197] There was also a sense that it would take little to initiate a significant political crisis in Poland.[198]

There are mixed figures regarding the current Jewish population of Poland, which in part are based upon how individuals identify themselves. In 2010 it was suggested that the Jewish population of Poland was between 1,000 and 50,000.[199] Research published in 2011 suggests that 2,000 individuals identified themselves in the census of that year as being Jewish and 5,000 as Polish and Jewish.[200] Research in 2000 suggested that there were 20,000–25,000 Polonized Jews.[201] Estimates cited in 2014 suggest that some Jewish organizations believe there are 30,000–40,000 Jews living in Poland who are connected to the religion and culture, and as many as 70,000–100,000 who identify as having Jewish heritage.[202]

It is has been suggested that a majority of Poles do not know or are not interested in how many Jews live in the country, but that 12 per cent of Poles believe that there are many Jews in Poland.[203] Jolanta Ambrosewicz-Jacobs cites an unspecified American report on antisemitism from 1995 in which Poland was positively evaluated.[204] In a more contemporaneous study from 2015, the Anti-Defamation League suggested that 14 million or 45 per cent of Poles harbour antisemitic attitudes. That assessment is based on telephone interviews with 500 individuals. By comparison, the same study suggested that 8 per cent of the UK population harbour antisemitic attitudes.[205]

Antisemitism on its own does not necessarily imply harmful intent towards Jews, but in the wider political, religious and cultural history of Poland, combined with the impact of Nazi and Soviet occupation, it has manifested in pre-war, wartime, and post-war violence, significant pogroms, and ultimately the decimation of the Jewish population that survived the Second World War. It is of relevance to the significance of the Holocaust Law and the insistence that any suggestion of Polish collaboration with, participation in, or initiating of events associated with, the Holocaust is wrong and deserving of punishment. There were crimes committed against the Jews by the indigenous populations of all countries occupied by the Nazis, and, in Poland, where most of the Holocaust took place, it is possible that these crimes were part of a wider and more established social, cultural and political history of antisemitism.

This chapter has sought to consider the evidence against some of the Polish population that implicates them in the crimes of the Holocaust during the German occupation of Poland. Multiple historians since the end of the war have accessed abundant primary and secondary sources showing anti-Jewish activities by Poles. Despite having the largest Jewish population in Europe, much of which was socially Polish and assimilated, Poland had a history of antisemitism before the war that had on occasion manifested in pogroms – particularly after independence was gained in 1918. The antisemitism of Poland prior to, during, and following the war, had a mix of religious, cultural, social and political influences.

It must be concluded that evidence exists of criminality by some Poles during the period of German occupation. Such criminality occurred in most of the countries that were occupied by German forces during the war. Asserting that Poland, even as a subjugated nation, was unique and not involved with the crimes of the Holocaust is to distort history and deny evidence.

Conclusion

Historians may disagree on exact – or approximate – figures of the numbers killed during the Holocaust and the period of the Nazi regime. It is generally accepted that approximately six million Jews died: many through the deliberate acts of gassing, poisoning, shooting, hanging, beating, torture and other means of murder. Many died through overwork, starvation, deprivation, cruelty, disease and the unsustainable conditions for life encountered in ghettos, camps and wider society. Others died too because, for various inexplicable reasons; they were deemed to be unworthy of life: Roma, Sinti, Slavs, political opponents, prisoners of war, homosexuals, Jehovah Witnesses, elderly, young, disabled, mentally ill and mentally impaired and other minorities or 'undesirable' human beings.

Most of the perpetrators of those crimes are dead. Some may still be with us, but age will ensure that their existence will soon end. Most of those who supported the cruelty and murder are no longer here. Those people alive today, whatever their nationality or heritage, do not bear responsibility for crimes that were committed before they were born. And that is a key point of this book. Criticism of nation states, and the people that identify with those nations, is necessary, if those nations and peoples committed wrongs. But the criticisms are of the nations, people and societies of the past, not the nations, people and societies of the present.

The countries discussed in this book all have a noble history of resistance or of fighting the oppressive, brutal, cruel and murderous regime of Nazi Germany. Elements of those same societies were at fault too, and those faults need to be owned and accepted. Failure to do so fails history and the truth of the past. Those same nations have also contributed much to the understanding of history and the education of newer generations to the realities of how hatred and intolerance can have deadly consequences. Whether it is the United States, Great Britain, France, the Netherlands, Ukraine, Hungary or Poland, the history is there. We need to be able to honestly accept the evidential proof – even if it's uncomfortable – because if we do not, we let down all of those who lived, suffered and died during more uncomfortable periods of the past. We also fail the present and the future. Failing to learn from history risks repeating the same mistakes; so, however we may wish to reinterpret or change perspectives, we need to acknowledge, own, accept and talk about known truths. There is always the potential to enter into futile arguments and discussions of false equivalence or 'whataboutism' in discussing the Holocaust and other genocides. Such arguments and discussions can diminish the acceptance of the harm caused and the role of individuals and societies involved.

This book has its origins in considering the Polish government's decision to enact the Holocaust law in 2018. Many of the pages herein are critical of that law, and seek to show that in Poland, as elsewhere in occupied Europe, there was antisemitism, open hostility to Jews, apathy, indifference, antipathy, collusion and collaboration in regard to crimes against Jews. Poland suffered terribly during the period of occupation. It had the misfortune of being chosen as the site for the mass slaughter. Three million Jews lived in Poland when the Germans invaded – most would die. Two and a half million non-Jewish Poles would also die. In 1939 Poland was occupied by Germans in the west, and by Soviet Russia in the east. In 1941 the whole of Poland was occupied by the Nazis, and then, in 1944, the Soviets advanced westward to liberate that territory, only to replace it with another authoritarian regime and ideology. Polish society, as it had been, was torn asunder by these invasive regimes. Many other nations were invaded and occupied, but few suffered – comparatively – as much as Poland did. That ultimately Poland has emerged to be the country that it is, should be admired.

It is said that the narrative of history belongs to the victor. There is some truth in that. One would hope that those nations that claim to be democracies would also be willing to admit to errors, mistakes, faults and even crimes of the past. That hope may be optimistic. Authoritarian nations are more controlling about how history is discussed and taught. Formerly authoritarian nations may still have that sensitivity and need to ensure that the country and its people are portrayed in an acceptable and positive manner. Perhaps that is a factor in Poland's Holocaust law. It may also influence those nations that had been under the Soviet sphere of influence and control. But westernized democracies such as the

United States, United Kingdom, France and the Netherlands also have a perspective on history that may be seen as selective and unduly positive. This book has tried to bring an honest perspective based on survivor and witness testimony, contemporary reports, and the work of multiple credible historians.

Throughout these pages it has been attempted to honestly consider primary- and secondary-source information, combined with acknowledged academic opinion, to discuss with fairness the wider guilt of the Holocaust. The focus has not been on Nazi Germany as it has been accepted throughout this work that it was the main perpetrator nation. As was mentioned earlier, the Holocaust occurred more widely than the gas chambers, execution pits, ghettos and places of mass slaughter in Poland and elsewhere in Europe. Of course, Poland – due to a combination of the contempt the Germans held for the people and the geographical benefits of isolated territory with rail links – was chosen as the main regional site of the Holocaust. It was to that subjugated country that most of the Jews of Europe were sent for slave labour and extermination. For European Jews in the various regions of conquest and occupation, the Nazi policies of antisemitism, and ultimately of the Final Solution, sealed their fate. The dangers from the Nazi regime were immense, and, even without assistance, would have caused an obscene amount of harm. But the Germans entered countries where their anti-Jewish ideas and policies were welcomed.

One can argue about whether the Holocaust was *intentional* – Hitler's plan all along – or *functional* – it developed as Nazi forces in Eastern Europe found that they had more Jews than they could cope with. One can argue that the Nazis initially *merely* wanted to expel Jews from Germany and Europe rather than kill them – ethnic cleansing in modern parlance. One can debate rationally, and based on genuine research, the number of lives lost, but the consensus among honest academic historians is that between 5.1 and 6.5 million Jews were killed during the Holocaust. The negationists will quibble over details, but they do not produce evidence to truly support their politically motivated, pseudo-scientific and pseudo-academic agenda which is invariably associated with far-right, far-left or religiously, culturally and nationally motivated antisemitism.

The crimes associated with the Holocaust were also committed by citizens of countries such as France, the Netherlands, Hungary, Ukraine and Poland; they are a stain on the history of Europe. In France and the Netherlands officials, citizens, civil servants, the police and others helped to isolate, round up, ghettoize and deport Jews. This was done unquestioningly in many instances, and while intelligence reports reached western nations that detailed what was happening to the Jews, deportations continued. Many in Ukraine welcomed the Nazi invaders and readily associated their Jewish fellow citizens with the horrors of Soviet communism. Ukraine is where the Holocaust truly began. Most of the killing, as elsewhere, was perpetrated by the Germans, but the evidence is that many Ukrainians were also involved. In Hungary there was anti-Jewish legislation long before the Nazis came to power in Germany and long before any allegiance with the Germans. Hungarians were active and enthusiastic participants in the programmes that isolated and removed Jews from their country. When the deportations to Auschwitz ceased in July 1944, the Hungarians continued to send Jews to the Reich for forced labour, ghettoized the Jews of Budapest, and, even with the Red Army knocking on the door, the Arrow Cross militias continued to murder Budapest Jews in their thousands.

Some efforts have been made – often belatedly – to acknowledge these crimes and make amends. Apologies and requests for forgiveness have also been made. Victim communities have been compensated. Memorials have been erected. Laws against Holocaust denial have been enacted. Museums have been opened, and efforts have been made to honour those who suffered within living memory. Historians and sites of Holocaust memory in Poland have been at the forefront in education and a determination to ensure the lessons from history are learned. The United States was not occupied; Great Britain experienced occupation of the Crown Dependency Channel Islands and the threat of a mainland invasion. Both countries were among the Allied nations that eventually prevailed in the war against Nazi Germany. They helped to lead the quest for post-war justice, and also contributed to the denazification and rebuilding of Germany, which led, ultimately, to the democratic country it is today.

The Polish Holocaust law has led to generalized condemnation from a broad spectrum of interested parties within and outside Poland. Some commentators rationalize the objections to the 2018 Holocaust bill as being due to Jews – mainly from Israel – seeking some form of financial recompense for losses during the Second World War. The research conducted during the compilation of this book has not found evidence to justify such claims. The criticism of the Holocaust law is due to its interpretation of recorded history and the potential for imposing punishments upon those who write or express opinions that contradict some form of preordained or politically prescribed narrative.

The historiography and narrative of how history is interpreted or taught can be heavily influenced by authoritarian regimes. Following liberation in 1945, Poland was under the control of the Communist Party and came under the Soviet sphere of influence until the early 1990s. It is possible that some of that old influence has had a bearing on the more nationalistic political outlook of the current government. Poland is seeking to reassert its identity, particularly as a nation that suffered during Nazi occupation, which of course it did. The victim status does not leave space for acknowledging criminality by some elements of Polish society during the period from 1939 to 1945. The nationalistic outlook also increases the sensitivity of the state to accusations of wrongdoing. Certainly, Poles were victims, and millions of non-Jewish Poles died. Polish Jews were also victims, and that community was almost annihilated. Many Poles helped Jews, as has been acknowledged by Yad Vashem and as witnessed by the numbers awarded the status of Righteous Among Nations.

Poland ceased to be an independent, self-governing state during the period of occupation, and normal offices of nationhood were eliminated, or were very much under the control of the Germans. Some Poles, either working alongside the Germans, or acting independently, committed crimes and atrocities against Jews. Abundant evidence supports this observation and identifies police officers, firefighters, civic leaders and civilians as being involved. This would concur with crimes committed by similar individuals across the occupied territories of Europe. Where Poland differs is that it was the location chosen by the Germans as the main site of the Final Solution; it was the territory in which the extermination camps were based, and to where the Jews of Europe were transported. Additionally, Poland had the largest Jewish population in Europe, and that population was nearly eradicated. It is can be argued that the Holocaust law relates to criticism of Poland as a nation and state which ceased to function as a traditionally independent and autonomous country during the occupation. However, as has been shown, elements of the offices and structures of the state were maintained even if, strictly, they were under

German control. Those offices and structures worked with the Germans, and at times independently of the occupying regime, in causing harm to Jews. Similarly, some civilians actively and enthusiastically participated in hunting, harming and killing their Jewish neighbours. The independent nation state of Poland may have been occupied, but the nationhood and national identity of Poles continued with all of its historical and cultural influences, including antisemitism. Acknowledging these factors is essential to a healthy study of the Holocaust in the territorial and cultural landmass of Poland.

Furthermore, in the post-war period a series of violent and murderous pogroms took place, which cannot be blamed on Germans, and must solely be attributed to Poles against their Jewish neighbours. The attitudes and influences that contributed to those pogroms – including up to 1968 and even modern-day antisemitism – may have political, cultural and religious roots, but they are destructive acts that were perpetrated by Poles.

The sensitivity of some in Poland to the description of 'Polish camps' rather than 'German Nazi camps' is understandable. Whether punishment by fines or imprisonment for such language is appropriate is questionable. Of course, some will deliberately make the allusion to Polish camps, but it is likely that in many, if not most instances, this is erroneous, misguided and an unintended mistake. It is asserted herein that the most constructive approach is by consistency in language amongst politicians, journalists, historians, educators and remembrance organizations. Obviously, there are occasions when societies feel it necessary to punish false historical claims; Holocaust denial is one such example. However, unlike Holocaust denial, which has clear political and antisemitic motivations, the reference to camps in Poland as being Polish rather than in the occupied territory of Poland, does not seem to have the same motivating factors. It must be questioned whether the imposition of punishment for any suggestion of wrongdoing by Poles – or more specifically the Polish nation – during the Holocaust is an unreasonable and disproportionate response that hinders the integrity of legitimate historical research, debate, discussion and opinion. It risks politically controlling the narrative of history in a way that is unfitting in a modern democracy. Furthermore, it risks accusations against Poland of state-enforced denial of evidence, revisionism, or negationism, which would be unfortunate in a nation that has contributed so much to Holocaust research and education. It is asserted in this book that the Polish Holocaust law is an excessive and unnecessary response that empowers the jurisprudence system to punish those who would better benefit from education and informed discourse.

Poland suffered extreme harm during the years of Nazi occupation. The concentration and extermination camps were German facilities in occupied Polish territory, and Poland cannot be held responsible for them. However, crimes against Jews, including murder, were committed by Poles. That reality is confirmed by multiple sources and is an issue on which there is much agreement within the historical community. It is a part of Poland's history that needs to be acknowledged and accepted for the benefit of future research and exploration of the events of the German occupation.

The fluidity, rather than the static nature of historical research and knowledge, requires flexibility and openness in analysis and interpretation. The imposition of criminal or civil court sanctions is at best unhelpful and more importantly it is counterproductive. Education rather than punishment is needed, and that should be the role of scholars, academics, historians, educators, politicians and Holocaust remembrance organizations within and outside Poland.

The other nations discussed in this book, particularly those that experienced German occupation and the realities of the Holocaust, must also consider how history is viewed and the nature of national memory. As has been shown, efforts have been made to acknowledge the past, but there are also examples where the victim status of the nation – which is of course valid – prevails over the acknowledgement of wrongdoing, collusion, collaboration and criminality during the Holocaust. Honest self-critical discourse is needed along with constructive programmes of education. Any efforts to limit or legislate against open analysis and discussion of history should be challenged and contested. Germany – the country that initiated the Holocaust and perpetrated most of the crimes of that period – has acknowledge and accepted its past. Some in German society may be uncomfortable with national guilt from so long ago, but there appears to be a recognition that such guilt is part of German history. It is the guilt from another time and of different German citizens, but it must be accepted to ensure that lessons are learned. That would seem to be a reasonable example for other nations to follow.

Epilogue: Lessons for Today

Whilst the Holocaust may be one of many genocides in history, it is, helpfully, also the most researched and analysed. In Europe particularly, but also on other continents, it stands as the ultimate lesson of where hatred and contempt can lead. It provides us with evidence – not just of the crimes committed, the perpetrators and societies involved, the propaganda of hate, and the power of a message of intolerance reaching popular appeal – it also teaches us of the dangers involved with saying nothing or standing by as harm is promoted and inflicted upon others.

The hatred that led to the Holocaust originated and was engineered in Nazi Germany, but it found willing co-conspirators in occupied territories. The pre-war German Jewish population was 525,000, and included 100,000 recent immigrants from the east; the latter group faced hostility from sections of German society, including Jews. Most of the Jewish population was long established in Germany and fully integrated. The majority lived in major urban centres and large cities; indeed, 144,000 lived in Berlin. As a people, by and large, they were not discernibly different from the majority population. Furthermore, half of Germans lived in rural villages and small towns, and as such would rarely, if ever, have had contact with, or have had personal reasons to be hostile to, Jews they had not met.[1]

Yet, amid the social upheaval and economic collapse of post-First World War Germany, Hitler and the NSDAP managed to scapegoat Jews as being responsible for everything from the surrender in the First World War, to the Treaty of Versailles, to the post-war sanctions and financial reparations that helped to cripple the economy, and were associated with mass unemployment, hyperinflation and the financial crash, the loss of territory, the *Dolchstoßlegende* (stab-in-the-back myth) and through to the rise of Bolshevism. Jews were portrayed as a danger to Germany and Europe, and referred to in the dehumanizing language so often heard directed at minority racial, religious, ethnic and cultural communities today. Nazism stands as a stark warning of what can happen when charismatic rabble-rousing populist nationalists are given a platform, and are not opposed by united voices of reason. The political classes believed that once the NSDAP achieved electoral success, they could accommodate them and rein them in. The French and British used the established diplomatic tools of appeasement – quite probably to buy time – but found that Hitler rearmed Germany and his territorial ambitions went far beyond Germanic communities in the Rhineland, Austria and the Sudetenland. By the time the true scale of Hitler's territorial aims was known, it was too late. There were warnings about harmful intentions towards Jews. These manifested most clearly with the Reich citizenship laws of 1935 and the pogrom of 9/10 November 1938.

Hindsight provides perfect vision, but the dangers that Nazi Germany posed to its own citizens and the citizens of Europe seem obvious now. Indeed, when the mass killings began in Poland, they were reported. The horrors of the concentration and extermination camps were known about long before they were seen when liberated.

Antisemitism still exists. There are still people with high levels of power and influence who suggest that Jewish conspiracies are afoot. Sometimes the antisemitic theories are dressed differently. The language used to describe the philanthropist George Soros is rooted in this most ancient of hatreds. The reluctance of politicians, political parties, institutions and organizations to address antisemitism merely gives it legitimacy – a criticism levelled at the Labour Party in the UK. When such politicians are challenged, a glance at social media sites reveals the intensity of the hatred and contempt some people have for Jews.

Other minority faiths are targeted, most notably Muslims. Casual racism and disdain for foreigners have been normalized in some quarters. Antipathy towards Muslims is not confined to western countries. It is found in countries such as India and Myanmar – in the latter case leading to allegations of genocide by the government against the Rohingya Muslim minority. The Uighurs of China are held in concentration and 're-education' camps with little in the way of protest from the wider word. Elsewhere, such as in the Middle East, Christians are targeted, as indeed, are the followers of many faiths. It is a reasonable observation to suggest that the antisemitic writings and speeches of senior Nazis could transfer easily to contemporary language, rhetoric, attitudes and intolerance merely by changing 'Jew' to Muslim, refugee, asylum seeker, immigrant or foreigner. One simply has to look back to the passionate opposition to the Wagner-Rogers Bill in the United States, or the hesitance and concerns about anti-Jewish public opinion that influenced the British government when considering offering refuge to German Jewish children. When the MS *St. Louis* was unable to disembark its passengers in Cuba, the governments of Britain, France, Belgium and the Netherlands only agreed to accept them *temporarily*, on the understanding that they would eventually settle in the United States. The scenarios have a startling similarity to the contemporary world.

Influential and successful politicians, activists, broadcasters and social media agitators thrive on promoting fear, distrust, hatred and contempt. They repeat messages consistently with no effort made to provide proof. Dehumanizing language is used with casual ease. They have a willing and receptive audience who do not wish to hear alternative narratives, and dismiss evidence and facts as fake. The independence of the judiciary and the press is at risk and yet, this is seen not only as acceptable, but necessary. Those who oppose them are described as 'woke' – out-of-touch liberal elites. Crimes, misdemeanours and allegations that would previously have ended political careers and led to governments falling now seem to occur with barely a critical comment passed. The normality of previous times seems to be in a distant and unrecognizable past.

The world is in a potentially dangerous place. Populist nationalist far-right politicians are gaining electoral success in Europe, South America, the United States and Australia. The Russia of Vladimir Putin is regularly accused of interfering in democratic elections to ensure that favourable or preferred candidates succeed. It does not take much thought to see why a destabilized European Union and a fractured North Atlantic alliance may be desirable to a former superpower seeking to flex its economic, military and political muscles to gain greater influence.

Societies that purport to be democracies have the ultimate weaponry against the proponents of hate – the ballot box. The parties on the political extremes have a populist appeal that often only has the support of a minority of the electorate. Those who oppose them can be complacent and fail to vote. That complacency empowers and encourages the proponents of intolerance, ultra-nationalism, and nativism. If tolerant people, who value democracy, vote en masse, the haters lose their platform and their voice. Failure to vote gives their voices volume and range.

We can use hindsight to see the warnings of danger that preceded the crimes of Nazi Germany and the crimes of every genocide before and since. We must use foresight to be alert to current and future dangers. From dehumanizing language, the scapegoating of minority communities as convenient enemies to blame for the wrongs and ills of society, through to ostracizing, isolating, disenfranchising, and ultimately to legislation, forced migration or deportation, violence and murder. Hindsight also shows – as has been demonstrated in these pages – that the perpetrators and enablers of harm can be the supposedly normal members of society who turn a blind eye, casually support, or actively empower and help the wrongdoers. Multiple ingredients create the perfect storm found at such times. When democratic norms are suspended and lost, when politicians and influencers compete to sound more radical, or established rules of checks and balances fail, then the risks increase.

And that perfect storm can hit democratic societies as easily as it hits autocratic ones. We must use the template of history as our guide, and we must try to ensure that we learn its lessons and act when the danger signals flash their warning lights.

Notes

Introduction
1. Jan Grabowski, The Holocaust and Poland's "History Policy", *Israel Journal of Foreign Affairs*, 10 (3) (2016) p. 485
2. *ibid*, p. 485
3. *ibid*, p. 485
4. *ibid*, p. 485
5. Deborah Lipstadt, *Denial: Holocaust History on Trial* (Harper Collins; 2016) pp. 24–5
6. Robert Jan van Pelt, *The Case for Auschwitz: Evidence from the Irving Trial* (Indiana University Press: 2016) p. 2.
7. Grabowski, The Holocaust and Poland's "History Policy", p. 484
8. Viktor E. Frankl, *Man's Search for Meaning* (London: 2004) p. 17

Chapter 1: Legislation: The Polish Holocaust Law
1. Associated Press, Obama Offends Poles in Death Camp Slip Up, *Times of Israel* (30 May 2012)
2. *ibid*
3. *ibid*
4. *ibid*
5. Benjamin Frommer, Postscript: The Holocaust in Occupied Poland, Then and Now, *East European Politics and Societies*, 25 (3) (August 2011) p. 576
6. Radio Free Europe, Poland's President Signs Holocaust Bill, *Radio Free Liberty*, 6 February 2018, www.rferl.org/a/poland-president-sign-holocaust-bill-controversy-israel-us-ukraine/29023222.html (Accessed 21 March 2018)
7. Martha Vazquez, Poland, the Holocaust, and Free Speech, *The German Law Journal*, March 2018, www.germanlawjournal.com/special-issue-contl-id-in-migration-1/ (Accessed 21 March 2018)
8. *ibid*
9. Grabowski, The Holocaust and Poland's "History Policy", p. 483
10. *ibid*, p. 483
11. Names of Righteous by Country, Yad Vashem, www.yadvashem.org/righteous/statistics.html (Accessed 19 August 2018)
12. Grabowski, The Holocaust and Poland's "History Policy", p. 484
13. Anna Azari, AP & TOI Staff, Top Polish official accuses Jews of 'passivity' in Holocaust, *Times of Israel*, 21 March 2018, www.timesofisrael.com/top-polish-official-accuses-jews-of-passivity-in-holocaust/ (Accessed 21 March 2018)
14. *ibid*
15. Orrin Hatch, Statement on Poland's Controversial Holocaust Bill, Press Release 6 February 2018, Orrin Hatch, United States Senator for Utah, www.hatch.

senate.gov/public/index.cfm/2018/2/hatch-statement-on-poland-s-controversial-holocaust-bill (Accessed 21 March 2018)

16. Yad Vashem Response to the Law Passed in Poland Yesterday, Press Release, 27 January 2018, www.yadvashem.org/press-release/27-january-2018-18-43.html (Accessed 21 march 2018)

17. *ibid*

18. Yad Vashem response to the Law Passed in the Polish Senate, Press Release, 1 February 2018, www.yadvashem.org/press-release/01-february-2018-10-04.html (Accessed 21 March 2018)

19. *ibid*

20. *ibid*

21. Yad Vashem Response Regarding Act of National Remembrance by Poland's President, 6 February 2018, www.yadvashem.org/press-release/06-february-2018-16-02.html (Accessed 21 March 2018)

22. *ibid*

23. Karen Pollock, *Karen Pollock MBE's response to Holocaust legislation in Poland, Holocaust Educational Trust,* www.het.org.uk/news-and-events/697-karen-pollock-mbe-s-response-to-holocaust-legislation-in-poland *(Accessed 21 March 2018)*

24. Museum Statement on Holocaust Legislation in Poland, 28 January 2018, United States Holocaust Memorial Museum, www.ushmm.org/information/press/press-releases/museum-statement-on-holocaust-legislation-in-poland (Accessed 21 March 2018)

25. *ibid*

26. *ibid*

27. Stephen Smith, Poland's Holocaust law defies history – and embodies a troubling trend, USC Shoah Foundation, 9 February 2018, https://sfi.usc.edu/blog/stephen-smith/polands-holocaust-law-defies-history-and-embodies-troubling-trend (Accessed 21 March 2018)

28. *ibid*

29. Wiener Library Blog, 8 February 2018, www.wienerlibrary.co.uk/Blog?item=292&returnoffset=0 (Accessed 22 March 2018)

30. Professor Yehuda Bauer, Honorary Chairman to the IHRA. IHRA Honorary Chairman Statement on Polish Legislation, 1 February 2018 www.holocaustremembrance.com/statements/ihra-honorary-chairman-statement-polish-legislation (Accessed 25 March 2018)

31. *ibid*

32. *ibid*

33. *ibid*

34. *ibid*

35. Vanessa Gera, Polish TV riposte to Holocaust bill criticism: 'Auschwitz was Jewish death camp', *Times of Israel,* 31 January 2018, www.timesofisrael.com/israeli-criticism-of-holocaust-bill-sparks-antisemitic-backlash-in-poland/ (Accessed 21 March 2018)

36. Justyna Pawlak & Lidia Kelly, Polish Lawmakers back Holocaust bill, drawing Israeli outrage, U.S. concern, Reuters, 31 January 2018, https://uk.reuters.com/article/uk-israel-poland-usa/polish-lawmakers-back-holocaust-bill-drawing-israeli-outrage-u-s-concern-idUKKBN1FK3ER (Accessed 21 March 2018)

37. *Financial Times*, Poland's Holocaust law has worrying echoes, 9 February 2018, www.ft.com/content/ccaf3370-0da7-11e8-8eb7-42f857ea9f09 (Accessed 22 August 2018)

38. *ibid*

39. *ibid*

40. Jonathan Freedland, Poland can't lay its Holocaust ghosts to rest by censoring free speech, *The Guardian* (2 February 2018) www.theguardian.com/commentisfree/2018/feb/02/poland-holocaust-free-speech-nazi (Accessed 22 August 2018)

41. *ibid*

42. *ibid*

43. Jan T. Gross, Poland's death camp law is designed to falsify history, *Financial Times* (6 February 2018)

44. *ibid*

45. *ibid*

46. Vincent Boland, Poland's Holocaust Law is a licence to whitewash history, *Irish Times (*8 February 2018) www.irishtimes.com/opinion/poland-s-holocaust-law-is-a-licence-to-whitewash-history-1.3383516

47. Frommer, Postscript, p. 580

Chapter 2: Holocaust Denial

1. Paolo Lobba, Punishing Denialism Beyond Holocaust Denial: EU Framework Decision 2008/913/JHA and Other Expansive Trends, *New Journal of European Criminal Law*, 5 (1) (2014) p. 59

2. Lipstadt, *Denial: Holocaust History on Trial,* p. 23

3. Peter R. Teachout, Making "Holocaust Denial" a Crime: Reflections on European Anti-Negationism Laws from the Perspective of U.S. Constitutional Experience, *Vermont Law Review*, 30 (2006) p. 663

4. Dan Stone, *Concentration Camps: A Short History* (Oxford: 2017) p. 38

5. Deborah Lipstadt, *Denying the Holocaust: The Growing Assault on Truth and Memory* (London: 1993) p. 27

6. Van Pelt, *The Case for Auschwitz*, p. 12

7. *ibid*, p. 6

8. Nikolaus Wachsmann, *KL: A History of the Nazi Concentration Camps* (London: 2013) p. 6

9. *ibid*, p. 6

10. Lobba, Punishing Denialism Beyond Holocaust Denial, p. 58

11. *ibid*, p. 59

12. *ibid*, p. 59

13. *Ibid*, p. 59

14. *Ibid*, p. 62

15. *ibid*, p. 61

16. *ibid*, pp. 64–5

17. Sean Gorton, The Uncertain Future of Genocide Denial Laws in the European Union, *The George Washington International Law Review*, 47 (2) (2015) p. 425

18. Paul Behrens, Genocide Denial and the Law: A Critical Appraisal, *Buffalo Human Rights Law Review*, 21 (2014–2015) p. 31

19. Gorton, The Uncertain Future of Genocide Denial Laws in the European Union, pp. 423–4

20. *ibid*, pp. 425–6
21. *ibid*, pp. 425–6
22. Behrens, Genocide Denial and the Law, p. 27
23. *ibid*, p. 30
24. *ibid*, p. 27
25. *ibid*, p. 27
26. Lawrence Mcnamara, History, Memory and Judgement: Holocaust Denial, the History Wars and Law's Problems with the past, *Sydney Law Review*, 26 (2004) pp. 369–70
27. Mcnamara, History, Memory and Judgement, p. 370
28. Behrens, Genocide Denial and the Law, pp. 27–8
29. Richard J. Evans, *Telling Lies About Hitler: The Holocaust, History and the David Irving Trial* (London: 2002) p. 16
30. Evans, *Telling Lies About Hitler*, p. 16
31. Lipstadt, *Denying the Holocaust*, p. 5
32. *ibid*, p. 7
33. *ibid*, p. 7
34. Evans, *Telling Lies About Hitler*, p. 116
35. *ibid*, p. 116
36. *ibid*, p. 115
37. Teachout, Making "Holocaust Denial" a Crime, p. 661
38. *ibid*, pp. 661–2
39. Evans, *Telling Lies About Hitler*, p. 115
40. *ibid*, pp. 115–16
41. *ibid*, pp. 131–2
42. Dan Cohn-Sherbok, Neo-Nazism, Holocaust Denial and UK Law, *European Judaism*, 43 (1) (Spring 2010) pp. 111–12
43. Van Pelt, *The Case for Auschwitz*, pp. 51–3
44. Evans, *Telling Lies About Hitler*, p. 132
45. Lipstadt, *Denying the Holocaust*, p. 5
46. Teachout, Making "Holocaust Denial" a Crime, p. 662
47. *ibid*, p. 662
48. Lipstadt, *Denying the Holocaust*, pp. 5–6
49. *ibid*, p. 12
50. Sophie Tatum, CNN Politics, Holocaust Denier is Officially the GOP Nominee in Chicago Area House Race, 21 March 2018, https://edition.cnn.com/2018/03/20/politics/holocaust-denier-gop-illinois-third-district/index.html, Accessed 30 April 2019
51. Google search 'Holohoax', 30 April 2019
52. Gorton, The Uncertain Future of Genocide Denial Laws in the European Union, p. 428
53. *ibid*, p. 428
54. Behrens, Genocide Denial and the Law, p. 31
55. *ibid*, p. 31
56. *ibid*, p. 32
57. *ibid*, p. 33
58. *ibid*, p. 33
59. *ibid*, p. 34

60. Gorton, The Uncertain Future of Genocide Denial Laws in the European Union, p. 422
61. *ibid*, pp. 422–3
62. *ibid*, p. 426
63. Jennifer M. Allen & George H. Norris, Is Genocide Different? Dealing with Hate Speech in a Post-Genocide Society, *Journal of International Law & International Relations*, 7 (2011) p. 160
64. *ibid*, p. 159
65. *ibid*, p. 159
66. Gorton, The Uncertain Future of Genocide Denial Laws in the European Union, pp. 427
67. Allen & Norris, Is Genocide Different?, p. 160
68. Gorton, The Uncertain Future of Genocide Denial Laws in the European Union, pp. 426–7
69. *ibid*, pp. 426–7
70. *ibid*, p. 427
71. Abenaa Owusu-Bempah, Prosecuting Hate Crime: Procedural Issues and the Future of the Aggravated Offences, *Legal Studies*, 35 (3) (2015) p. 446
72. *ibid*, p. 446
73. *ibid*, p. 447
74. CPS, Hate Crime, www.cps.gov.uk/hate-crime (Accessed 6 May 2019)
75. Allen & Norris, Is Genocide Different?, p. 165
76. *ibid*, p. 165
77. Teachout, Making "Holocaust Denial" a Crime, p. 674
78. *ibid*, p. 674
79. *ibid*, p. 687

Chapter 3: The United States

1. Frank W. Brecher, David Wyman and the Historiography of America's Response to the Holocaust: Counter Considerations, *Holocaust and Genocide Studies*, 5 (4) (1990) p. 423
2. *ibid*, p. 423
3. Robert Slayton, 'Children in Europe Are Europe's Problem!' When the United States turned its back on the Jewish youth of Nazi Germany, *Commentary*, 138 (3) (October 2014) p. 45
4. *ibid*, p. 45
5. James Q. Whitman, *Hitler's American Model: The United States and the Making of Nazi Race Law* (Woodstock, Oxfordshire: 2017) p. 12
6. Slayton, 'Children in Europe Are Europe's Problem!', pp. 45–6
7. *ibid*, pp. 45–6
8. *ibid*, pp. 45–6
9. *ibid*, p. 46
10. Brecher, Wyman and the Historiography of America's Response to the Holocaust, p. 424
11. Slayton, 'Children in Europe Are Europe's Problem!', p. 46
12. *ibid*, p. 46
13. *ibid*, p. 46
14. *ibid*, p. 46

15. *ibid*, p. 46
16. *ibid*, p. 47
17. *ibid*, p. 47
18. *ibid*, p. 47
19. Amanda J. Rothschild, Rousing a Response: When the United States Changes Policy Toward Mass Killing, *International Security*, 42 (2) (Fall 2017) p. 139
20. *ibid*, p. 139
21. *ibid*, p. 140
22. C. Paul Vincent, The Voyage of the *St. Louis* revisited, *Holocaust and Genocide Studies*, 25 (2) (Fall 2011) p. 255
23. *ibid*, p. 255
24. Barry J. Konovitch, The Fiftieth Anniversary of the *St. Louis*: What Really Happened, *American Jewish History*, 79 (2) (Winter 1989/1990) p. 209
25. Vincent, The Voyage of the *St. Louis* revisited, p. 274
26. *ibid*, p. 273
27. Konovitch, The Fiftieth Anniversary of the *St. Louis*, p. 203
28. ibid, p. 203
29. *ibid*, pp. 203–4
30. *ibid*, p. 205
31. *ibid*, pp. 205–6
32. *ibid*, p. 206
33. *ibid*, p. 206
34. *ibid*, p. 204
35. *ibid*, p. 206
36. *ibid*, p. 208
37. *ibid*, pp. 208–9
38. *ibid*, p. 204
39. *ibid*, pp. 208–9
40. *ibid*, p. 204
41. A. T. Williams, *A Passing Fury: Searching for Justice at the End of World War II* (London: 2016) p. 32
42. *ibid*, p. 35
43. *ibid*, pp. 35–6
44. *ibid*, p. 36
45. David Cesarani, *Final Solution: The Fate of the Jews 1939-49* (London: 2016) p. 289
46. Malvina Halberstam, Framing the Issues, *Cardozo Law Review*, 20 (1998) pp. 449–50
47. *ibid*, p. 450
48. Cesarani, *Final Solution*, pp. 576–7
49. Williams, *A Passing Fury*, p. 36
50. *ibid*, p. 36
51. Kevin A. Mahoney, An American Operational Response to a Request to Bomb Rail Lines to Auschwitz, *Holocaust and Genocide Studies*, 25 (3) (Winter 2011) p. 438
52. *ibid*, pp. 438–9
53. *ibid*, pp. 438–9
54. *ibid*, p. 439

55. *ibid*, p. 439
56. *ibid*, p. 439
57. *ibid*, pp. 439–40
58. *ibid*, pp. 439–40
59. *ibid*, p. 440
60. *ibid*, p. 440
61. *ibid*, p. 440
62. *ibid*, p. 440
63. *ibid*, pp. 440–1
64. *ibid*, p. 441
65. Richard Overy, *The Bombing War: Europe 1939–1945* (London: 2014) pp. 583–4
66. *ibid*, p.584
67. *ibid*, p. 584
68. Noble Frankland, Some Reflections on the Strategic Air Offensive, 1939–1945, *Royal United Services Institution Journal* (11 September 2009) p.98
69. Mark Clodfelter, Aiming to Break Will: America's World War II Bombing of German Morale and its Ramifications, *The Journal of Strategic Studies* 33 (3) (June 2010) p. 410
70. *ibid*, p. 410
71. Frankland, Some Reflections on the Strategic Air Offensive, 1939–1945, p.98
72. Mahoney, An American Operational Response to a Request to Bomb Rail Lines to Auschwitz, pp. 441–2
73. Nicholas P. Weiss, Somebody Else's Problem: How the United States and Canada Violate International Law and Fail to Ensure the Prosecution of War Criminals, *Case Western Reserve Journal of International Law*, 45 (2012) p. 590
74. *ibid*, p. 591
75. *ibid*, pp. 590–1
76. David A. Messenger, Beyond War Crimes: Denazification, 'Obnoxious' Germans and US Policy in Franco's Spain after the Second World War, *Contemporary European History*, 20 (4) (2011) pp. 455–6
77. *ibid*, pp. 455–6
78. *ibid*, p.456
79. *ibid*, p. 456
80. *ibid*, pp. 456–7
81. *ibid*, p. 459
82. *ibid*, pp. 456–7
83. *ibid*, p. 459
84. *ibid*, p. 459
85. *ibid*, p. 459
86. Arthur J. Goldberg, Klaus Barbie and the United States Government, *Harvard Civil Rights–Civil Liberties Law Review*, 19 (1) (1984) p. 1
87. *ibid*, p. 1
88. Christian Delage, The Klaus Barbie Trial: Traces and Temporalities, *Comparative Literature Studies*, 48 (3) (2011) p. 320
89. Delage, The Klaus Barbie Trial, p. 321
90. Goldberg, Klaus Barbie and the United States Government, p. 1
91. *ibid*, pp. 1–2
92. Delage, The Klaus Barbie Trial, p. 330

93. Goldberg, Klaus Barbie and the United States Government, pp. 2-3
94. Allan A. Ryan Jr., Klaus Barbie and the United States Government: A Reply to Mr Justice Goldberg, *Harvard Civil Rights–Civil Liberties Law Review*, 20 (1) (1985) p. 72
95. *ibid*, p. 72
96. Williams, *A Passing Fury*, pp. 270–1
97. Ken Silverstein, Ford: New Documents Reveal the Close Ties Between Dearborn and the Nazis, *The Nation* (24 January 2000) p. 12
98. *ibid*, p. 12
99. *ibid*, p. 12
100. *ibid*, p. 12
101. *ibid*, p. 12
102. Adolf Hitler, *Mein Kampf* (London: 2014) p. 583
103. Silverstein, Ford, p. 12
104. *ibid*, p. 12
105. Patricia Chappine, Delayed Justice: Forced and Slave Labour Restitution After The Holocaust, *Journal of Ecumenical Studies*, 46 (4) (Fall 2011) p. 618
106. *ibid*, p. 618
107. Silverstein, Ford: New Documents Reveal the Close Ties Between Dearborn and the Nazis, p. 11
108. *ibid*, p. 11
109. *ibid*, p. 12
110. Keith Mann, Review of Talbot Imlay and Martin Horn, The Politics of Industrial Collaboration During World War II: Ford France Vichy and Nazi Germany, *American Historical Review*, 120 (3) (June 2015) p. 1129
111. *ibid*, p. 1130
112. *ibid*, p. 1130
113. *ibid*, p. 1130

Chapter 4: Great Britain
1. Norrin M. Ripsman & Jack S. Levy, Wishful Thinking or Buying Time? The Logic of British Appeasement in the 1930s, *International Security*, 33 (2) (Fall 2008) p. 148
2. *ibid*, pp. 148–9
3. *ibid*, pp. 148–9
4. R. Gerald Hughes, The Ghosts of Appeasement: Britain and the Legacy of the Munich Agreement, *Journal of Contemporary History*, 48 (4) (2013) p. 689
5. *ibid*, p. 689
6. *ibid*, p. 689
7. Ripsman & Levy, Wishful Thinking or Buying Time?, pp. 148–9
8. *ibid*, pp. 148–9
9. Keith Neilson, Orme Sargent, Appeasement and British Policy in Europe 1933-39, *Twentieth Century British History*, 21 (1) (2010) p. 1
10. Ripsman & Levy, Wishful Thinking or Buying Time?, p. 149
11. *ibid*, pp. 149–50
12. *ibid*, p. 151
13. Neilson, Orme Sargent, Appeasement and British Policy in Europe 1933–39, p. 4
14. *ibid*, p. 3

15. *ibid*, p. 1
16. *ibid*, p. 4
17. *ibid*, p. 4
18. *ibid*, p. 4
19. *ibid*, p. 4
20. Ripsman & Levy, Wishful Thinking or Buying Time?, p. 151
21. *ibid*, p. 158
22. *ibid*, p. 159
23. *ibid*, p. 159
24. *ibid*, pp. 159–60
25. *ibid*, p. 161
26. *ibid*, pp. 162–3
27. *ibid*, p. 164
28. *ibid*, pp. 169–70
29. *ibid*, p. 176
30. Gilly Carr, Occupation Heritage, Commemoration and Memory in Guernsey and Jersey, *History & Memory*, 24 (1) (Spring/Summer 2012) pp. 87–8
31. *ibid*, p. 88
32. *ibid*, pp. 89–90
33. Paul Sanders, Managing Under Duress: Ethical Leadership, Social Capital and the Civilian Administration of the British Channel Islands During the Nazi Occupation, 1940–1945, *Journal of Business Ethics*, Springer, 93 (1) (2010) p. 116
34. Sanders, Managing Under Duress, p. 117
35. Madeleine Bunting, *The Model Occupation: The Channel Islands Under German Rule 1940–1945* (London:2017) pp. 107–8
36. *ibid*, p. 108
37. *ibid*, p. 108
38. Sanders, Managing Under Duress, p. 118
39. Carr, Occupation Heritage, Commemoration and Memory in Guernsey and Jersey, p. 90
40. *ibid*, pp. 99
41. Sanders, Managing Under Duress, p. 115
42. *ibid*, p. 115
43. Bunting, *The Model Occupation*, p. 305
44. *ibid*, p. 305
45. Sanders, Managing Under Duress, p. 116
46. Bunting, *The Model Occupation*, p. 139
47. *ibid*, p. 318
48. *ibid*, p. 239
49. *Ibid*, p. 76
50. Cesarani, *Final Solution*, p. 213
51. *ibid*, p. 213
52. *ibid*, pp. 213–14
53. *ibid*, p. 214
54. *ibid*, p. 219
55. *ibid*, p. 219
56. J. Angel and D.P Evans, 'Why are we not doing more for them?': Genocide prevention lessons from the Kindertransport, *Public Health*, 153 (2017) pp. 38–9

57. *ibid*, p. 39
58. *ibid*, p. 39
59. *ibid*, p. 40
60. Nedra McCloud, Oswald Mosley and the British Union of Fascists: A Brief Historiographical Inquiry, *History Compass*, 4 (4) (2006) p. 688
61. David Redvaldsen, 'Science Must be the Basis'. Sir Oswald Mosley's Political Parties and their Policies on Health, Science and Scientific Racism 1931–1974, Contemporary British History, 30 (3) (2016) pp. 368–9
62. McCloud, Oswald Mosley and the British Union of Fascists, pp. 687–8
63. *ibid*, p. 688
64. *ibid*, p. 688
65. Matthew Worley, Why Fascism? Sir Oswald Mosley and the Conception of the British Union of Fascists, *History*, 96 (1) (2011) pp. 68–9
66. Redvaldsen, 'Science Must be the Basis', p. 370
67. Worley, Why Fascism?, p. 74
68. *ibid*, p. 79
69. *ibid*, p. 83
70. Redvaldsen, 'Science Must be the Basis', p. 370
71. *ibid*, pp. 370–1
72. McCloud, Oswald Mosley and the British Union of Fascists, p. 691
73. Richard Griffiths, A Note on Mosley, the 'Jewish War' and Conscientious Objection, *Journal of Contemporary History*, 40 (4) (2005) p. 677
74. *ibid*, pp. 677–8
75. *ibid*, p. 678
76. *ibid*, pp. 678–9
77. *ibid*, p. 679

Chapter 5: France
1. Philip Nord, *France 1940: Defending the Republic* (London: 2015) p. 47
2. *ibid*, p. 47
3. Evans, *Telling Lies About Hitler*, pp. 114–15
4. *ibid*, p. 116
5. *ibid*, p. 116
6. Anonymous, Europe: Remembering the Vel d'Hiv; France and Vichy, *The Economist*, 394 (8674) (20 March 2010) p. 1
7. *ibid*, pp. 1–2
8. Henry Rousso, Lucy Golsan & Richard J. Golsan, The Political and Cultural Roots of Negationism in France, *South Central Review*, 23 (1) (Spring 2006) p. 67
9. *ibid*, p. 67
10. *ibid*, p. 67
11. *ibid*, pp. 67–8
12. *ibid*, p. 68
13. *ibid*, p. 68
14. *ibid*, pp. 68–9
15. Victoria Best & Kathryn Robson, Memory and Innovation in Post-Holocaust France, *French Studies*, 59 (1) (2005) pp. 5–6
16. Julian Jackson, *The Fall of France: The Nazi Invasion of 1940* (Oxford: 2003) p. 39
17. *ibid*, p. 181

18. *ibid*, p. 2
19. Jacques Adler, The Jews and Vichy: Reflections on French Historiography, *The Historical Journal*, 44 (4) (2001) p. 1069
20. Nord, France 1940, p. 47
21. Cesarani, *Final Solution*, p. 306
22. *ibid*, p. 307
23. *ibid*, p. 307
24. *ibid*, p. 307
25. Adler, The Jews and Vichy, pp. 1067–8
26. Isabelle Backouche & Sarah Gensburger, Anti-Semitism and Urban Development in France in the Second World War: The Case of *Îlot* 16 in Paris, *Contemporary European History*, 23 (3) (2014) p. 382
27. *ibid*, p. 382
28. *ibid*, p. 384
29. *ibid*, p. 394
30. *ibid*, pp. 394–5
31. *ibid*, pp. 400–1
32. Adler, The Jews and Vichy, p. 1067
33. *ibid*, pp. 1066–7
34. Max Hastings, *All Hell Let Loose: The World at War 1939–1945* (London: 2011) p. 402
35. Cesarani, *Final Solution*, p. 306
36. *ibid*, p. 548
37. *ibid*, p. 548
38. *ibid*, p. 548
39. *ibid*, p. 549
40. *ibid*, pp. 548–9
41. *ibid*, p. 548
42. *ibid*, p. 549
43. Wachsmann, *KL*, p. 305
44. Cesarani, *Final Solution*, pp. 549–50
45. Danuta Czech, *Auschwitz Chronicle 1939–1945: From the Archives of the Auschwitz Memorial and the German Federal Archives* (New York: 1989) p. 207
46. *ibid*, p. 209
47. *ibid*, pp. 211–12
48. *ibid*, p. 213
49. *ibid*, p. 215
50. *ibid*, p. 216
51. Williams, *A Passing Fury*, pp. 155–6
52. Freda Wineman, 'The Red Coated Survivor', in (ed.) *Survival: Holocaust Survivors Tell Their Story* (Laxton: 2003) pp. 391–2
53. *ibid*, p. 392
54. Adler, The Jews and Vichy, p. 1065
55. *ibid*, p. 1066
56. Patrick Henry, The French Catholic Church's Apology, *The French Review*, 72 (6) (1999) p. 1102
57. Adler, The Jews and Vichy, p. 1066

58. Paul Webster, French Catholics Say Sorry for Persecuting Jews, *The Guardian* (11 July 1997)
59. Henry, The French Catholic Church's Apology, p. 1099
60. *ibid*, p. 1100
61. *ibid*, p. 1099
62. *ibid*, p. 1100
63. *ibid*, p. 1100
64. Webster, French Catholics Say Sorry for Persecuting Jews
65. Michael Sutton, Jews and Christians in Vichy France: New and Renewed Perspectives, *French Politics, Culture & Society*, 35 (3) (Winter 2017) p. 107
66. Henry, The French Catholic Church's Apology, p. 1102
67. *ibid*, p. 1102
68. Sutton, Jews and Christians in Vichy France, p. 125
69. *ibid*, p. 125
70. Henry, The French Catholic Church's Apology, p. 1102
71. Names of Righteous by Country, Yad Vashem, www.yadvashem.org/righteous/statistics.html (Accessed 18 May 2019)
72. Henry, The French Catholic Church's Apology, p. 1100
73. *ibid*, p. 1102
74. *ibid*, p. 1101
75. *ibid*, p. 1101
76. *ibid*, p. 1101
77. Hastings, *All Hell Let Loose*, p. 660
78. *ibid*, pp. 660–1

Chapter 6: The Netherlands

1. Yad Vashem, Names of Righteous by Country, Yad Vashem, www.yadvashem.org/righteous/statistics.html (Accessed 24 May 2019)
2. Ben H. Shepherd, *Hitler's Soldiers: The German Army in the Third Reich* (London: 2016) p. 61
3. *ibid*, p. 90
4. Frank Bovenkerk, The Other Side of the Anne Frank Story: The Dutch Role in the Persecution of the Jews in World War Two, *Crime, Law and Social Change*, 34 (2000) pp. 237–8
5. *ibid*, p. 237
6. Anne Frank House, The Netherlands: The greatest number of Jewish victims in Western Europe, www.annefrank.org/en/anne-frank/go-in-depth/netherlands-greatest-number-jewish-victims-western-europe/ (Accessed 8 July 2019)
7. Daniel Boffey, Dutch railway to pay out €50m over role in Holocaust, *The Guardian* (27 June 2019) www.theguardian.com/world/2019/jun/27/dutch-railway-to-pay-out-50m-over-role-in-holocaust (Accessed 27 June 2019
8. Bovenkerk, The Other Side of the Anne Frank Story, p. 255
9. Boffey, Dutch railway to pay out €50m over role in Holocaust
10. *ibid*
11. *ibid*
12. BBC News, Holocaust: Dutch rail firm NS confirms compensation (26 June 2019) www.bbc.co.uk/news/world-europe-48778715 (Accessed 28 June 2019)
13. *ibid*

14. *ibid*
15. Laurence Rees, *The Holocaust: A New History* (London: 2017) p. 183
16. *ibid*, pp. 183–4
17. *ibid*, p. 184
18. *ibid*, p. 184
19. *ibid*, p. 184
20. Pim Griffioen & Ron Zeller, Anti-Jewish Policy and Organization of the Deportations in France and the Netherlands, 1940–1944: A Comparative Study, *Holocaust and Genocide Studies*, 20 (3) (Winter 2006) p. 438
21. Rees, *The Holocaust: A New History*, pp. 184–5
22. Griffioen & Zeller, Anti-Jewish Policy and Organization of the Deportations, p. 438
23. Rees, *The Holocaust: A New History*, p. 282
24. Marnix Croes, Holocaust Survival Differentials in the Netherlands, 1942–1945: The Role of Wealth and Nationality, *Journal of Interdisciplinary History* (15 (1) (Summer 2014) p. 1
25. *ibid*, pp. 3–4
26. Eva Schloss, *After Auschwitz* (London: 2013) p. 69
27. Bovenkerk, The Other Side of the Anne Frank Story, p. 242
28. *ibid*, p. 243
29. *ibid*, p. 238
30. Griffioen & Zeller, Anti-Jewish Policy and Organization of the Deportations, p. 447
31. *ibid*, p. 447
32. *ibid*, p. 447
33. *ibid*, p. 447
34. Bovenkerk, The Other Side of the Anne Frank Story, pp. 238–9
35. Peter Tammes, Jewish Immigrants in the Netherlands During the Occupation, *Journal of Interdisciplinary History*, 37 (4) (Spring 2007) pp. 547–8
36. *ibid*, pp. 551–3
37. *ibid*, pp. 543–4
38. *ibid*, p. 544
39. *ibid*, p. 546
40. *ibid*, pp. 546–7
41. Croes, Holocaust Survival Differentials in the Netherlands, 1942–1945, p. 4
42. *ibid*, p. 5
43. *ibid*, p. 4
44. *ibid*, p. 5
45. *ibid*, p. 5
46. Tammes, Jewish Immigrants in the Netherlands During the Occupation, pp. 546-547
47. *ibid*, p. 547
48. Croes, Holocaust Survival Differentials in the Netherlands, 1942–1945, p. 3
49. *ibid*, pp. 5–6
50. *ibid*, p. 6
51. Wachsmann, *KL*, pp. 305–6
52. *ibid*, p. 306
53. Croes, Holocaust Survival Differentials in the Netherlands, 1942–1945, p. 8

54. Peter Tammes, Surviving the Holocaust: Socio-demographic Differences Among Amsterdam Jews, *European Journal of Population*, 33 (3) (July 2017) p. 296
55. *ibid*, p. 293
56. *ibid*, p. 293
57. Jacob Boas, Yearbooks of the Netherlands State Institute for War Documentation, *Holocaust and Genocide Studies*, 9 (3) (Winter 1995) p. 381
58. Marc L.F. van Berkel, Holocaust representation in Dutch history textbooks 1960-2010, *Studi sulla Formazione*, 2 (2015) pp. 49–50
59. *ibid*, p. 49
60. Bovenkerk, The Other Side of the Anne Frank Story, p. 240
61. *ibid*, p. 240
62. Van Berkel, Holocaust representation in Dutch history textbooks 1960-2010, pp. 47–8
63. Boas, Yearbooks of the Netherlands State Institute for War Documentation, p. 381
64. Bovenkerk, The Other Side of the Anne Frank Story, p. 240
65. *ibid*, p. 240
66. *ibid*, p. 240
67. *ibid*, p. 240
68. Christina Morina, The 'Bystander' in Recent Dutch Historiography, *German History*, 32 (1) (March 2014) p. 103
69. *ibid*, p. 103
70. Bart van der Boom, "The Auschwitz reservation": Dutch Victims and Bystanders and Their Knowledge of the Holocaust, *Holocaust and Genocide Studies*, 31 (3) (Winter 2017) p. 402
71. Van Berkel, Holocaust representation in Dutch history textbooks 1960–2010, p. 48
72. *ibid*, p. 48
73. Eva Schloss, *Eva's Story* (Peterborough: 2014) p. 38
74. Van Berkel, Holocaust representation in Dutch history textbooks 1960–2010, pp. 48–9
75. Griffioen & Zeller, Anti-Jewish Policy and Organization of the Deportations, p. 454
76. Van Berkel, Holocaust representation and Organisation of the Deportations, p. 49
77. *ibid*, p. 49
78. Anne Frank: *The Diary of a Young Girl* (London: 2012) pp. 301–2
79. Van der Boom, "The Auschwitz reservation", p. 402
80. *ibid*, p. 389
81. *ibid*, pp. 385–6
82. *ibid*, p. 386
83. Rees, *The Holocaust: A New History*, p. 282
84. *ibid*, p. 282
85. *ibid*, p. 283
86. Van der Boom, "The Auschwitz reservation", p. 386
87. Van Berkel, Holocaust representation in Dutch history textbooks 1960–2010, p. 47
88. *ibid*, p. 52
89. *ibid*, p. 50

90. *ibid*, p. 50
91. *ibid*, p. 51
92. *ibid*, p. 53

Chapter 7: Ukraine
1. Carl Gershman, Ukraine is where the Holocaust began. It should properly memorialize the victims, *The Washington Post* (27 May 2019) www.washingtonpost.com/opinions/ukraine-is-where-the-holocaust-began-it-should-properly-memorialize-the-victims/2019/05/27/38e283e2-7e42-11e9-8bb7-0fc796cf2ec0_story.html (Accessed 18 January 2020)
2. Gershman, Ukraine is where the Holocaust began.
3. Christoph Mick, Incompatible Experiences: Poles, Ukrainians and Jews in Lviv under Soviet and German Occupation, 1939-44, *Journal of Contemporary History*, 46 (2) (April 2011) p. 337
4. Vladimir Melamed, Organised and Unsolicited Collaboration in the Holocaust: The Multifaceted Ukrainian Context, *East European Jewish Affairs*, 37 (2) (August 2007) p. 237
5. Mick, Incompatible Experiences, p. 345
6. *ibid*, p. 346
7. Simone A. Bellezza, The Discourse over the Nationality Question in Nazi-occupied Ukraine: The Generalbezirk Dnjepropetrowsk, 1941-3, *Journal of Contemporary History*, 43 (4) (October 2008) p. 579
8. Anne Applebaum, *Red Famine: Stalin's War on Ukraine* (London: 2018) pp. 327–8
9. *ibid*, p. 328
10. Bellezza, The Discourse over the Nationality Question in Nazi-occupied Ukraine, p. 578
11. Rebekah Moore, "A Crime Against Humanity Arguably Without Parallel in European History": Genocide and the "Politics" of Victimhood in Western Narratives of the Ukrainian *Holodomor*, *Australian Journal of Politics and History*, 58 (3) (2012) p. 368
12. *ibid*, p. 368
13. Applebaum, *Red Famine*, pp. 284–5
14. David R. Marples, Ethnic Issues in the Famine of 1932–1933 in Ukraine, *Europe-Asia Studies*, 61 (3) (May 2009) p. 506
15. *ibid*, p. 506
16. Horoaki Kuromiya, The Soviet Famine of 1932–1933 Reconsidered, *Europe-Asia Studies*, 60 (4) (June 2008) p. 668
17. Applebaum, Red Famine, p. 331
18. *ibid*, p. 331
19. *ibid*, p. 331
20. *ibid*, p. 332
21. *ibid*, p. 270
22. *ibid*, p. 285
23. USHMM, The Holocaust in Ukraine, www.ushmm.org/information/exhibitions/online-exhibitions/special-focus/ukraine (Accessed 14 November 2019)
24. USHMM, The Holocaust in Ukraine
25. Yad Vashem, Names of Righteous by Country, www.yadvashem.org/righteous/statistics.html (Accessed 14 November 2019)

26. Markus Eikel & Valentina Sivaieva, City Mayors, Raion Chiefs and Village Elders in Ukraine, 1941–4: How Local Administrators Cooperated with the German Occupation Authorities, *Contemporary European History*, 23 (3) (2014) p. 411
27. *ibid*, p. 408
28. Mick, Incompatible Experiences, p. 350
29. *ibid*, p. 347
30. Eikel & Sivaieva, City Mayors, Raion Chiefs and Village Elders in Ukraine, 1941–4, p. 425
31. Yuri Radchenko, Accomplices to Extermination: Municipal Government and the Holocaust in Kharkiv, 1941–1942, *Holocaust and Genocide Studies*, 27 (3) (Winter 2013) p. 443
32. *ibid*, p. 444
33. *ibid*, pp. 444–5
34. *ibid*, p. 444
35. *ibid*, p. 444
36. Applebaum, *Red Famine*, p. 329
37. *ibid*, p. 329
38. *ibid*, p. 329
39. Bellezza, The Discourse over the Nationality Question in Nazi-occupied Ukraine, pp. 573-574
40. Mick, Incompatible Experiences, p.337
41. *ibid*, pp. 337–8
42. Philippe Sands, *East West Street: On the Origins of Genocide and Crimes Against Humanity*. (London: 2016) p. 182
43. Eikel & Sivaieva, City Mayors, Raion Chiefs and Village Elders in Ukraine, 1941–4, p. 410
44. *ibid*, p. 410
45. Bellezza, The Discourse over the Nationality Question in Nazi-occupied Ukraine, p. 576
46. *ibid*, p. 576
47. Timothy Snyder, *Black Earth: The Holocaust as History and Warning* (London, Vintage, 2016) pp. 134–5
48. Cesarani, *Final Solution*, p. 372
49. Melamed, Organised and Unsolicited Collaboration in the Holocaust, p. 229
50. *ibid*, p. 229
51. *ibid*, p. 229
52. Cesarani, *Final Solution*, pp. 648–9
53. Radchenko, Accomplices to Extermination, p. 445
54. Melamed, Organised and Unsolicited Collaboration in the Holocaust, p. 231
55. Mick, Incompatible Experiences, p. 344
56. *ibid*, p. 344
57. Melamed, Organised and Unsolicited Collaboration in the Holocaust, pp. 220–1
58. Eikel & Sivaieva, City Mayors, Raion Chiefs and Village Elders in Ukraine, 1941–4, p. 427
59. *ibid*, p. 412
60. *ibid*, p. 413
61. *ibid*, p. 413

62. *ibid*, pp. 414–5
63. *ibid*, p. 416
64. *ibid*, p. 425
65. Agnes Grunwald-Spier, *Who Betrayed the Jews? The Realities of Nazi Persecution in the Holocaust* (Stroud: 2017) p. 544
66. Melamed, Organised and Unsolicited Collaboration in the Holocaust, p. 227
67. *ibid*, pp. 227–8
68. Louise O. Vasvári, The Yellow Star and Everyday Life under Exceptional Circumstances: Diaries of 1944–1945 Budapest, *Hungarian Cultural Studies*, 9 (2016) p. 44
69. Melamed, Organised and Unsolicited Collaboration in the Holocaust, p. 232
70. *ibid*, p. 232
71. *ibid*, pp. 234–5
72. Mick, Incompatible Experiences, p. 348
73. *ibid*, p. 349
74. Cesarani, *Final Solution*, p. 401
75. Mick, Incompatible Experiences, pp. 351–2
76. *ibid*, p. 351
77. *ibid*, p. 351
78. *ibid*, p. 351
79. *ibid*, p. 353
80. *ibid*, p. 349
81. Milka Levine, "Look After the Children", in (ed.) *Survival: Holocaust Survivors Tell Their Story* (Laxton: 2003) p. 266
82. Eikel & Sivaieva, City Mayors, Raion Chiefs and Village Elders in Ukraine, 1941–4, p. 426
83. Rees, *The Holocaust: A New History*, P. 218
84. Cesarani, *Final Solution*, p. 386
85. *ibid*, p. 387
86. Dmitry Shlapentokh, Babi Yar, *Modern Age* (Winter/Spring 2013) p. 124
87. Joan Peterson, Iterations of Babi Yar, *Journal of Ecumenical Studies*, 46 (4) (Fall 2011) p. 586
88. *ibid*, p. 586
89. Cesarani, *Final Solution*, pp. 407–8
90. Grunwald-Spier, *Who Betrayed the Jews?*, p. 466
91. United States Holocaust Memorial Museum, Kiev and Babi Yar, https://encyclopedia. ushmm.org/content/en/article/kiev-and-babi-yar (Accessed 14 November 2019)
92. United States Holocaust Memorial Museum, Kiev and Babi Yar,
93. Cesarani, *Final Solution*, p. 404
94. *ibid*, p. 404
95. United States Holocaust Memorial Museum, Kiev and Babi Yar,
96. *ibid*
97. Peterson, Iterations of Babi Yar, pp. 586–7
98. Shepherd, *Hitler's Soldiers*, p. 172
99. Yad Vashem, Shoah Resource Centre, www.yadvashem.org/untoldstories/ documents/Perpetrators/Paul_Blobel.pdf (Accessed 8 May 2021)
100. Mick, Incompatible Experiences, p. 352
101. Rees, *The Holocaust: A New History*, P. 218

102. Cesarani, *Final Solution*, p. 401
103. Radchenko, Accomplices to Extermination, pp. 457–8
104. *ibid*, p. 458
105. *ibid*, p. 452
106. *ibid*, p. 453
107. Eikel & Sivaieva, City Mayors, Raion Chiefs and Village Elders in Ukraine, 1941–4, p. 416
108. *ibid*, pp. 416-417
109. Cesarani, Final Solution, p. 402
110. Radchenko, Accomplices to Extermination, p. 453
111. *ibid*, pp. 454–5
112. Eikel & Sivaieva, City Mayors, Raion Chiefs and Village Elders in Ukraine, 1941-4, pp. 417–18
113. Melamed, Organised and Unsolicited Collaboration in the Holocaust, p. 226
114. *ibid*, p. 226
115. Eikel & Sivaieva, City Mayors, Raion Chiefs and Village Elders in Ukraine, 1941–4, p. 407
116. Gershman, Ukraine is where the Holocaust began

Chapter 8: Hungary
1. Rees, *The Holocaust: A New History*, p. 379
2. Vera Ranki, Goulash-fascism: a socio-legal analysis of Hungarian fascism in the 30s, *Australian Journal of Law and Society*, 6 (1990) p. 147
3. *ibid*, p. 147
4. *ibid*, p. 147
5. *ibid*, p. 147
6. Raz Segal, Beyond Holocaust Studies: rethinking the Holocaust in Hungary, *Journal of Genocide Research*, 16 (1) (2014) p. 4
7. Ranki, Goulash-fascism, p. 147
8. *ibid*, pp. 147–8
9. Norman Stone, *Hungary: A Short History* (London: 2020) p. 115
10. *ibid*, p. 115
11. *ibid*, p. 115
12. Segal, Beyond Holocaust Studies, p. 4
13. *ibid*, p. 4
14. Ranki, Goulash-fascism, p. 145
15. *ibid*, p. 146
16. Grunwald-Spier, *Who Betrayed the Jews?*, p. 277
17. Tsvi Erez, Hungary – Six Days in July 1944, *Holocaust and Genocide Studies*, 3 (1) (1988) p. 40
18. *ibid*, p. 40
19. Cesarani, *Final Solution*, p. 703
20. Grunwald-Spier, *Who Betrayed the Jews?*, pp. 277–8
21. *ibid*, p. 282
22. Ranki, Goulash-fascism, p. 152
23. *ibid*, p. 152
24. *ibid*, p. 152
25. *ibid*, p. 153

26. Cesarani, *Final Solution*, p. 702
27. Segal, Beyond Holocaust Studies, p. 4
28. *ibid*, p. 5
29. *ibid*, p. 5
30. Stone, *Hungary: A Short History*, pp. 136–7
31. *ibid*, p. 137
32. Cesarani, *Final Solution*, p. 704
33. *ibid*, p. 704
34. Rees, *The Holocaust; A New History*, p. 292
35. Cesarani, *Final Solution*, p. 703
36. Segal, Beyond Holocaust Studies, p. 6
37. *ibid*, p. 7
38. *ibid*, p. 8
39. *ibid*, p. 9
40. Rees, p. 292
41. *ibid*, p. 292
42. Segal, Beyond Holocaust Studies, p. 13
43. Rees, *The Holocaust: A New History*, p. 318
44. Michael Fleming, British Narratives of the Holocaust in Hungary, *Twentieth Century British History*, 27 (4) (2016) pp. 561–2
45. Cesarani, *Final Solution*, p. 701
46. *ibid*, p. 701
47. Rees, *The Holocaust: A New History*, p. 377
48. Cesarani, *Final Solution*, p. 701
49. Rees, *The Holocaust: A New History*, pp. 318–19
50. Trude Levi, "'She isn't Worth a Bullet'", in (ed.) *Survival: Holocaust Survivors Tell Their Story* (Laxton: 2003) p. 257
51. *ibid*, p. 257
52. Yad Vashem, Names of Righteous by Country, www.yadvashem.org/righteous/statistics.html?gclid=EAIaIQobChMI9rf5wIbM5wIVRrTtCh2Jego9EAAYASA CEgLKqPD_BwE (Accessed 12 February 2020)
53. Ibi Ginsburg, I Shall Never Forget, in (ed.) *Survival: Holocaust Survivors Tell Their Story* (Laxton: 2003) p. 137
54. John Chillag, Memories of a Lost Youth, in (ed.) *Survival: Holocaust Survivors Tell Their Story* (Laxton: 2003) p. 35
55. *ibid*, p. 35
56. *ibid*, p. 36
57. Cesarani, *Final Solution*, p. 706
58. *ibid*, p. 707
59. Stone, *Hungary: A Short History*, p. 142
60. Cesarani, *Final Solution*, p. 707
61. Peter Longerich, *Goebbels* (London: 2015) p. 626
62. USHMM, Deportation of Hungarian Jews, www.ushmm.org/learn/timeline-of-events/1942-1945/deportation-of-hungarian-jews (Accessed 12 February 2020)
63. Czech, *Auschwitz Chronicle 1939–1945*, p. 633
64. Cesarani, *Final Solution*, p. 710
65. *ibid*, p. 710
66. *ibid*, pp.721–2

67. Erez, Hungary – Six Days in July 1944, p. 42
68. *ibid*, p. 42
69. Henriett Kovács & Ursula K. Mindler-Steiner, Hungary and the Distortion of Holocaust History: the Hungarian Holocaust Memorial year 2014, *Politics in Central Europe*, 11 (2) (2015) pp. 53–4
70. Erez, Hungary – Six Days in July 1944, pp. 37–8
71. *ibid*, p. 38
72. *ibid*, p. 38
73. Rees, *The Holocaust: A New History*, p. 397
74. *ibid*, p. 398
75. *ibid*, pp. 398–9
76. *ibid*, pp. 399–400
77. Fleming, British Narratives of the Holocaust in Hungary, p. 571
78. Rees, *The Holocaust: A New History*, p. 400
79. Stone, *Hungary: A Short History*, p. 142
80. *ibid*, p. 143
81. *ibid*, p. 144
82. USHMM, Budapest, https://encyclopedia.ushmm.org/content/en/article/budapest (Accessed 12 February 2020)
83. Rees, *The Holocaust: A New History*, p. 408
84. USHMM, Budapest
85. Rees, *The Holocaust: A New History*, p. 409
86. *ibid*, p. 409
87. *ibid*, p. 409
88. USHMM, Budapest
89. Grunwald-Spier, *Who Betrayed the Jews?*, p. 113
90. *ibid*, p. 113
91. *ibid*, p. 112
92. *ibid*, p. 525
93. Rees, *The Holocaust: A New History*, p. 409
94. *Hastings, All Hell Let Loose, p. 603*
95. *ibid, p. 601*
96. Stone, *Hungary: A Short History*, p. 147
97. *Hastings, All Hell Let Loose, p. 601*
98. Yad Vashem, Murder of Hungarian Jewry, www.yadvashem.org/holocaust/about/fate-of-jews/hungary.html#narrative_info (Accessed 12 February 2020)
99. Kovács & Mindler-Steiner, Hungary and the Distortion of Holocaust History, p. 50
100. Gilad Hirschberger, Anna Kende & Shoshana Weinstein, Defensive representations of an uncomfortable history: The case of Hungary and the Holocaust, *International Journal of Intercultural Relations*, 55 (2016) p. 41
101. *ibid*, p. 41
102. *ibid*, p. 39
103. Kovács & Mindler-Steiner, Hungary and the Distortion of Holocaust History, p. 50
104. *ibid*, p. 50
105. *ibid*, p. 50
106. Hirschberger et al, Defensive representations of an uncomfortable history, p. 41

107. *ibid*, p. 41
108. *ibid*, p. 41
109. Segal, Beyond Holocaust Studies, p. 2
110. *ibid*, p. 2
111. *ibid*, p. 16
112. Hirschberger et al, Defensive representations of an uncomfortable history, p. 32
113. *ibid*, p. 33
114. *ibid*, p. 33
115. *ibid*, p. 33
116. Laleh Ispahani & Sarah R. Knight, Shoring Up a Democracy Under Siege, *Journal of International Affairs*, 71 (1) (Fall/Winter 2017) p. 51
117. *ibid*, p. 53
118. *ibid*, p. 59
119. Rees, *The Holocaust: A New History*, p. 379
120. USHMM, The Holocaust in Hungary, www.ushmm.org/information/exhibitions/online-exhibitions/special-focus/the-holocaust-in-hungary (Accessed 12 February 2020)
121. William A. Galston, Hungary: Canary in the Illiberal Coal Mine; An alarming rise in antisemitism and attacks on press and academic freedom, *Wall Street Journal* (19 December 2018) www.wsj.com/articles/hungary-canary-in-the-illiberal-coal-mine-11545179625 (Accessed 6 February 2020)
122. *ibid*
123. *ibid*
124. *ibid*
125. *Ibid*

Chapter 9: Poland

1. Grabowski, The Holocaust and Poland's "History Policy", p. 482
2. *ibid*, p. 482
3. Grabowski, The Holocaust and Poland's "History Policy", p. 482
4. Natalia Aleksiun, Polish Historiography of the Holocaust – Between Silence and Public Debate, *German History*, 22 (3) (2004) p. 406
5. *ibid*, p. 406
6. *ibid*, p. 406
7. *ibid*, p. 406
8. Jan Grabowski, *Hunt for the Jews: Betrayal and Murder in German-Occupied Poland* (Bloomington, Indiana: 2013) p. 11
9. *ibid*, p. 11
10. *ibid*, p. 12
11. *ibid*, p. 13
12. Nechama Tec, Diaries and Oral History: Some Methodological Considerations, *Religion and the Arts*, 4 (1) (2000) p. 90
13. *ibid*, p. 90
14. Beate Müller, Trauma, Historiography and Polyphony. Adult Voices in the CJHC's Early Post-war Child Holocaust Testimonies, *History & Memory*, 24 (2) (2012) p. 158
15. Tec, Diaries and Oral History, p. 88
16. Müller, Trauma, Historiography and Polyphony, p.159

17. *ibid*, p. 159
18. Tec, Diaries and Oral History, pp. 87–8
19. Grabowski, *Hunt for the Jews*, p. 11
20. Jan T. Gross, *Neighbours: The Destruction of the Jewish Community of Jedwabne, Poland, 1941* (Princeton: 2003) p. 7
21. *ibid*, p. 57
22. *ibid*, p. 57
23. Snyder, *Black Earth*, p. 158
24. *ibid*, p. 158
25. *ibid*, p. 158
26. *ibid*, p. 161
27. Krzysztof Persak, Jedwabne before the Court: Poland's Justice and the Jedwabne Massacre – Investigations and Court Proceedings, 1947–1974, *East European Politics and Societies*, 25 (3) (August 2011) p. 411
28. *ibid*, p. 411
29. Snyder, *Black Earth*, pp. 160–1
30. Persak, Jedwabne before the Court, p. 412
31. *ibid*, p. 412
32. *ibid*, p. 412
33. *ibid*, p. 412
34. Gross, *Neighbours*, p. 73
35. *ibid*, p. 75
36. *ibid*, pp. 169-170
37. Persak, Jedwabne before the Court, p. 410
38. *ibid*, p. 410
39. *ibid*, p. 410
40. *ibid*, p. 417
41. *ibid*, p. 420
42. *ibid*, pp. 420–1
43. *Ibid*, p. 428
44. *ibid*, p. 421
45. Aleksiun, Polish Historiography of the Holocaust, pp. 407–8
46. Gross, *Neighbours*, pp. 176–7
47. *ibid*, pp. 176–7
48. *ibid*, pp. 176–7
49. *ibid*, pp. 176–7
50. Martin Winstone, *The Dark Heart of Hitler's Europe* (New York: 2015) p. 177
51. Persak, Jedwabne before the Court, p. 413
52. *ibid*, p. 414
53. Snyder, *Black Earth*, p. 151
54. *ibid*, p. 206
55. *ibid*, p. 206
56. *ibid*, p. 206
57. Cesarani, *Final Solution*, p. 646
58. *ibid*, p. 649
59. Grabowski, *Hunt for the Jews*, p. 172
60. Cesarani, *Final Solution*, p. 647
61. *ibid*, p. 647

62. *ibid*, p. 647
63. Kitty Hart-Moxon, *Return to Auschwitz* (Newark: 2007) p. 31
64. Cesarani, *Final Solution*, p. 647
65. *ibid*, p. 647
66. Winstone, *The Dark Heart of Hitler's Europe*, p. 177
67. Cesarani, *Final Solution*, p. 647
68. *ibid*, pp. 647-648
69. Winstone, *The Dark Heart of Hitler's Europe*, pp. 177–8
70. *ibid*, p. 178
71. Grabowski, *Hunt for the Jews*, p. 5
72. Winstone, *The Dark Heart of Hitler's Europe*, p. 183
73. Grabowski, *Hunt for the Jews*, p. 52
74. *ibid*, p. 55
75. *ibid*, p. 61
76. *ibid*, pp. 75–6
77. *ibid*, p. 73
78. *ibid*, p. 73
79. *ibid*, pp. 73–4
80. Snyder, *Black Earth*, p. 112
81. *ibid*, p. 112
82. *ibid*, p. 112
83. Jan Grabowski, The Polish Police Collaboration in the Holocaust, Ina Levine Annual Lecture, The United States Holocaust Memorial Museum, 17 November 2016 (April 2017) p. 3
84. *ibid*, p. 4
85. *ibid*, p. 5
86. *ibid*, p. 5
87. *ibid*, p. 5
88. *ibid*, p. 5
89. *ibid*, p. 7
90. *ibid*, p. 6
91. *ibid*, p. 10
92. Cesarani, *Final Solution*, p. 648
93. *ibid*, p. 648
94. Grabowski, The Polish Police Collaboration in the Holocaust, p. 9
95. *ibid*, p. 19
96. *ibid*, p. 25
97. Grabowski, The Polish Police Collaboration in the Holocaust, p. 28
98. Snyder, *Black Earth*, p. 291
99. *ibid*, p. 291
100. Grabowski, *Hunt for the Jews*, p. 20
101. Gross, *Neighbours*, p. 38
102. Marek Kucia, Marta Duch-Dyngosz & Mateusz Magierowski, Anti-Semitism in Poland: survey results and a qualitative study of Catholic communities, *Nationalities Papers*, 42 (1) (2014) p. 9
103. Grabowski, *Hunt for the Jews*, p. 20
104. *ibid*, p. 20
105. Snyder, *Black Earth*, p. 205

106. Grabowski, *Hunt for the Jews*, p. 83
107. *ibid*, p. 83
108. Hart-Moxon, *Return to Auschwitz*, p. 46
109. *ibid*, p. 47
110. Snyder, *Black Earth*, p. 276
111. Grabowski, *Hunt for the Jews*, p. 83
112. Gross, *Neighbours*, p. 8
113. *ibid*, pp. 138-139
114. Winstone, *The Dark Heart of Hitler's Europe*, p. 179
115. *ibid*, p. 179
116. *ibid*, p. 184
117. Spiegel Staff, The Dark Continent: Hitler's European Holocaust Helpers, *Der Spiegel* (20 May 2009), www.spiegel.de/international/europe/the-dark-continent-hitler-s-european-holocaust-helpers-a-625824.html (Accessed 8 October 2018)
118. Jolanta Ambrosewicz-Jacobs, Attitudes of Young Poles Toward Jews in Post-1989 Poland, *East European Politics and Societies*, 14 (3) (2000) p. 565
119. Cesarani, *Final Solution*, p. 247
120. *ibid*, p. 247
121. *ibid*, p. 247
122. *ibid*, p. 247
123. Esther Brunstein, 'But Not Without Scars', in (ed.) *Survival: Holocaust Survivors Tell Their Story* (Laxton, Notts: 2003) p. 27
124. Daniel Falkner, 'Surviving the Warsaw Ghetto', in (ed.) *Survival: Holocaust Survivors Tell Their Story* (Laxton, Notts: 2003) p. 79
125. Toby Biber, 'Life Would Never Be The Same Again', in (ed.) *Survival: Holocaust Survivors Tell Their Story* (Laxton, Notts: 2003) p. 13
126. Hart-Moxon, *Return to Auschwitz*, p. 23
127. *ibid*, pp. 234-235
128. Adam Kopciowski, Anti-Jewish Incidents in the Lublin Region in the Early Years After World War II, *Holocaust. Studies and Materials*, 1 (2008) p. 179
129. Joanna Tokarska-Bakir, Cries of the Mob in the Pogroms in Rzeszów (June 1945) Cracow (August 1945) and Kielce (July 1946) as a Source for the State of Mind of the Participants, *East European Politics and Societies*, 25 (3) (August 2011) p. 563
130. *ibid*, p. 563
131. Kopciowski, Anti-Jewish Incidents in the Lublin Region, p. 182
132. *ibid*, p. 182
133. *ibid*, p. 182
134. *ibid*, p. 181
135. *ibid*, p. 182
136. *ibid*, pp. 182–3
137. *ibid*, p. 183
138. Winstone, *The Dark Heart of Hitler's Europe*, p. 247
139. *ibid*, p. 247
140. *ibid*, p. 247
141. *ibid*, pp. 177–8
142. *ibid*, pp. 177–8
143. *ibid*, p. 203
144. *ibid*, p. 203

145. *ibid*, p. 203
146. Jan T. Gross, *Fear: Anti-Semitism in Poland After Auschwitz* (Princeton: 2006) p. 35
147. *ibid*, p. 73
148. *ibid*, p. 73
149. *ibid*, p. 81
150. Tokarska-Bakir, Cries of the Mob, p. 563
151. *ibid*, p. 563
152. Gross, *Fear: Anti-Semitism in Poland After Auschwitz*, p. 81
153. *ibid*, p. 35
154. Tokarska-Bakir, Cries of the Mob, p. 556
155. *ibid*, p. 556
156. *ibid*, p. 556
157. *ibid*, p. 558
158. *ibid*, p. 558
159. *ibid*, p. 559
160. *ibid*, p. 558
161. Gross, *Neighbours*, p. 150
162. *ibid*, p. 150
163. Gross, *Fear: Anti-Semitism in Poland After Auschwitz*, p. 82
164. *ibid*, p. 81
165. *ibid*, p. 83
166. *ibid*, p. 83
167. *ibid*, p. 83
168. *ibid*, p. 83
169. *ibid*, pp. 83–4
170. *ibid*, p. 84
171. *ibid*, p. 84
172. *ibid*, p. 84
173. *ibid*, p. 84
174. Anita J. Prazmowska, The Kielce Pogrom 1946 and the Emergence of Communist Power in Poland, *Cold War History*, 2 (2) (2010) pp. 113–14
175. *ibid*, pp. 113–14
176. *ibid*, pp. 113–14
177. *ibid*, p. 114
178. Gross, *Fear: Anti-Semitism in Poland After Auschwitz*, p. 87
179. *ibid*, p. 99
180. Prazmowska, The Kielce Pogrom 1946, p. 115
181. Gross, *Fear: Anti-Semitism in Poland After Auschwitz*, p. 110
182. *ibid*, p. 110
183. Tokarska-Bakir, Cries of the Mob, pp. 555–6
184. *ibid*, p. 559
185. Jan T. Gross, *Neighbours*, p. 148
186. Kucia *et al*, Anti-Semitism in Poland, p. 10
187. *ibid*, p. 10
188. *ibid*, p. 11
189. Ambrosewicz-Jacobs, Attitudes of Young Poles Toward Jews in Post-1989 Poland, p. 571

190. *ibid*, p. 571
191. *ibid*, pp. 571–2
192. Mikolaj Kunicki, The Red and the Brown: Bolesaw Piasecki, the Polish Communists, and the Anti-Zionist Campaign in Poland, 1967–68, *East European Politics and Societies*, 19 (2) (2005) p. 186
193. *ibid*, pp. 206–7
194. *ibid*, pp. 206–7
195. *ibid*, p. 207
196. *ibid*, pp. 208
197. *ibid*, pp. 209
198. *ibid*, pp. 209
199. Michal Bilewicz, Anti-Semitism in Poland and Ukraine: The Belief in Jewish Control as a Mechanism of Scapegoating, *International Journal of Conflict and Violence*, 4 (2) (2010) p. 236
200. Kucia *et al*, Anti-Semitism in Poland, p. 11
201. Ambrosewicz-Jacobs, Attitudes of Young Poles Toward Jews in Post-1989 Poland, p. 572
202. Kucia *et al*, Anti-Semitism in Poland, p. 11
203. *ibid*, p. 11
204. Ambrosewicz-Jacobs, Attitudes of Young Poles Toward Jews in Post-1989 Poland, p. 580
205. ADL Global Index of Anti-Semitism. http://global100.adl.org/#country/poland/2014 (Accessed 30 October 2018)

Epilogue: Lessons for Today

1. Cesarani, Final Solution, p. 7

Bibliography

Adler, Jacques, 'The Jews and Vichy: Reflections on French Historiography', *The Historical Journal*, 44 (4) (2001)

Aleksiun, Natalia, 'Polish Historiography of the Holocaust – Between Silence and Public Debate', *German History*, 22 (3) (2004)

Allen, Jennifer M. & Norris, George H., 'Is Genocide Different? Dealing with Hate Speech in a Post-Genocide Society', *Journal of International Law & International Relations*, 7 (2011)

Ambrosewicz-Jacobs, Jolanta, 'Attitudes of Young Poles Toward Jews in Post-1989 Poland', *East European Politics and Societies*, 14 (3) (2000)

Angel, J, Evans, D. P, '"Why are we not doing more for them?": Genocide prevention lessons from the Kindertransport', *Public Health*, 153 (2017)

Anne Frank House, The Netherlands: 'The greatest number of Jewish victims in Western Europe', www.annefrank.org/en/anne-frank/go-in-depth/netherlands-greatest-number-jewish-victims-western-europe/

Anonymous, 'Europe: Remembering the Vel d'Hiv; France and Vichy', *The Economist*, 394 (8674) (20 March 2010)

Anti-Defamation League, ADL Global Index of Anti-Semitism, http://global100.adl.org/#country/poland/2014

Applebaum, Anne, *Red Famine: Stalin's War on Ukraine* (London, Penguin, 2018)

Associated Press, 'Obama Offends Poles in Death Camp Slip Up', *Times of Israel* (30 May 2012)

Azari, Anna, AP & TOI Staff, 'Top Polish official accuses Jews of "passivity" in Holocaust', *Times of Israel* (21 March 2018) www.timesofisrael.com/top-polish-official-accuses-jews-of-passivity-in-holocaust/

Backouche, Isabelle & Gensburger, Sarah, 'Anti-Semitism and Urban Development in France in the Second World War: The Case of *Îlot* 16 in Paris', *Contemporary European History*, 23 (3) (2014)

Bauer, Professor Yehuda, Honorary Chairman to the IHRA. IHRA Honorary Chairman Statement on Polish Legislation, 1 February 2018, www.holocaustremembrance.com/statements/ihra-honorary-chairman-statement-polish-legislation

BBC News, 'Holocaust: Dutch rail firm NS confirms compensation' (26 June 2019) www.bbc.co.uk/news/world-europe-48778715

Behrens, Paul, 'Genocide Denial and the Law: A Critical Appraisal', *Buffalo Human Rights Law Review*, 21 (2014/5)

Bellezza, Simone A., 'The Discourse over the Nationality Question in Nazi-occupied Ukraine: The Generalbezirk Dnjepropetrowsk, 1941–3', *Journal of Contemporary History*, 43 (4) (October 2008)

Best, Victoria & Robson, Kathryn, 'Memory and Innovation in Post-Holocaust France', *French Studies*, 59 (1) (2005)

Biber, Tony, 'Life Would Never Be the Same Again', in (ed.) *Survival: Holocaust Survivors Tell Their Story* (Laxton, Quill Press, 2003)

Bilewicz, Michal, 'Anti-Semitism in Poland and Ukraine: The Belief in Jewish Control as a Mechanism of Scapegoating', *International Journal of Conflict and Violence*, 4 (2) (2010)

Boas, Jacob, Yearbooks of the Netherlands State Institute for War Documentation, *Holocaust and Genocide Studies*, 9 (3) (Winter 1995)

Boland, Vincent, 'Poland's Holocaust Law is a licence to whitewash history', *Irish Times* (8 February 2018) www.irishtimes.com/opinion/poland-s-holocaust-law-is-a-licence-to-whitewash-history-1.3383516

Boffey, Daniel, 'Dutch railway to pay out €50m over role in Holocaust', *The Guardian* (27 June 2019) www.theguardian.com/world/2019/jun/27/dutch-railway-to-pay-out-50m-over-role-in-holocaust

Bovenkerk, Frank, 'The Other Side of the Anne Frank Story: The Dutch Role in the Persecution of the Jews in World War Two', *Crime, Law and Social Change*, 34 (2000)

Brecher, Frank W., David Wyman and the Historiography of America's Response to the Holocaust: Counter Considerations', *Holocaust and Genocide Studies*, 5 (4) (1990)

Brunstein, Esther, 'But Not Without Scars', in (ed.) *Survival: Holocaust Survivors Tell Their Story* (Laxton, Quill Press, 2003)

Bunting, Madeleine, *The Model Occupation: The Channel Islands Under German Rule 1940–1945*, (Penguin Random House, London, 2017)

Carr, Gilly, 'Occupation Heritage, Commemoration and Memory in Guernsey and Jersey', *History & Memory*, 24, (1) (Spring/Summer 2012)

Cesarani, David, *Final Solution, The Fate of the Jews 1933–49* (London, Macmillan, 2016)

Chappine, Patrice, 'Delayed Justice: Forced and Slave Labour Restitution After the Holocaust', *Journal of Ecumenical Studies*, 46 (4) (Fall 2011)

Chillag, John, 'Memories of a Lost Youth', in (ed.) *Survival: Holocaust Survivors Tell Their Story* (Laxton, Quill Press, 2003)

Clodfelter, Mark, 'Aiming to Break Will: America's World War II Bombing of German Morale and its Ramifications', *The Journal of Strategic Studies* 33 (3) (June 2010)

Cohn-Sherbok, Dan, 'Neo-Nazism, Holocaust Denial and UK Law', *European Judaism*, 43 (1) (Spring 2010)

CPS, 'Hate Crime', www.cps.gov.uk/hate-crime

Croes, Marnix, 'Holocaust Survival Differentials in the Netherlands, 1942–1945: The Role of Wealth and Nationality', *Journal of Interdisciplinary History*, (15 (1) (Summer 2014)

Czech, Danuta, *Auschwitz Chronicle 1939–1945: From the Archives of the Auschwitz Memorial and the German Federal Archives* (Holt, New York, 1989)

Delage, Christian, 'The Klaus Barbie Trial: Traces and Temporalities', *Comparative Literature Studies*, 48 (3) (2011)

Eikel, Markus & Sivaieva, Valentina, 'City Mayors, Raion Chiefs and Village Elders in Ukraine, 1941–4: How Local Administrators Cooperated with the German Occupation Authorities', *Contemporary European History*, 23 (3) (2014)

Erez, Tsvi, 'Hungary – Six Days in July 1944', *Holocaust and Genocide Studies*, 3 (1) (1988)

Evans Richard J., *Telling Lies About Hitler: The Holocaust, History and the David Irving Trial*, (London, Verso, 2002)

Falkner, Daniel, 'Surviving the Warsaw Ghetto', in (ed.) *Survival: Holocaust Survivors Tell Their Story* (Laxton, Quill Press, 2003)

Financial Times, 'Poland's Holocaust law has worrying echoes' (9 February 2018) www.ft.com/content/ccaf3370-0da7-11e8-8eb7-42f857ea9f09

Fleming, Michael, 'British Narratives of the Holocaust in Hungary', *Twentieth Century British History*, 27 (4) (2016)

Frank, Anne, *The Diary of a Young Girl* (London, Penguin, 2012)

Frankl, Viktor E., *Man's Search for Meaning* (London, Random House, 2004)

Frankland, Noble,' Some Reflections on the Strategic Air Offensive, 1939–1945', *Royal United Services Institution Journal* (11 September 2009)

Freedland, Jonathan, 'Poland can't lay its Holocaust ghosts to rest by censoring free speech', *The Guardian* (2 February 2018) www.theguardian.com/commentisfree/2018/feb/02/poland-holocaust-free-speech-nazi

Frommer, Benjamin, 'Postscript: The Holocaust in Occupied Poland, Then and Now', *East European Politics and Societies*, 25 (3) (August 2011)

Galston, William A., Hungary, 'Canary in the Illiberal Coal Mine; An alarming rise in antisemitism and attacks on press and academic freedom', *Wall Street Journal* (19 December 2018) www.wsj.com/articles/hungary-canary-in-the-illiberal-coal-mine-11545179625

Gera, Vanessa, 'Polish TV riposte to Holocaust bill criticism: "Auschwitz was Jewish death camp"', *Times of Israel* (31 January 2018) www.timesofisrael.com/israeli-criticism-of-holocaust-bill-sparks-antisemitic-backlash-in-poland/

Gershman, Carl, 'Ukraine is where the Holocaust began. It should properly memorialize the victims', *The Washington Post* (27 May 2019) www.washingtonpost.com/opinions/ukraine-is-where-the-holocaust-began-it-should-properly-memorialize-the-victims/2019/05/27/38e283e2-7e42-11e9-8bb7-0fc796cf2ec0_story.html

Ginsburg, Ibi,' I Shall Never Forget', in (ed.) *Survival: Holocaust Survivors Tell Their Story* (Laxton, Quill Press, 2003)

Goldberg, Arthur J., 'Klaus Barbie and the United States Government', *Harvard Civil Rights–Civil Liberties Law Review*, 19 (1) (1984)

Google search 'Holohoax' (30 April 2019)

Gorton, Sean, 'The Uncertain Future of Genocide Denial Laws in the European Union', *The George Washington International Law Review*, 47 (2) (2015)

Grabowski, Jan, *Hunt for the Jews: Betrayal and Murder in German-Occupied Poland* (Bloomington, Indiana, Indiana University Press, 2013)

Grabowski, Jan, 'The Holocaust and Poland's "History Policy"', *Israel Journal of Foreign Affairs*, 10 (3) (2016)

Grabowski, Jan,' The Polish Police Collaboration in the Holocaust', Ina Levine Annual Lecture, The United States Holocaust Memorial Museum, 17 November 2016 (April 2017)

Griffioen, Pim & Zeller, Ron, 'Anti-Jewish Policy and Organization of the Deportations in France and the Netherlands, 1940–1944: A Comparative Study', *Holocaust and Genocide Studies*, 20 (3) (Winter 2006)

Griffiths, Richard, 'A Note on Mosley, the "Jewish War" and Conscientious Objection', *Journal of Contemporary History*, 40 (4) (2005)

Gross, Jan T., *Fear: Anti-Semitism in Poland After Auschwitz* (Princeton, Princeton, 2006)

Gross, Jan T. *Neighbours: The Destruction of the Jewish Community of Jedwabne, Poland, 1941* (Princeton, Princeton, 2003)

Gross, Jan T.,' Poland's death camp law is designed to falsify history', *Financial Times* (6 February 2018)

Grunwald-Spier, Agnes, *Who Betrayed the Jews? The Realities of Nazi Persecution in the Holocaust* (Stroud, Amberley, 2017)

Halberstam, Malvina, 'Framing the Issues', *Cardozo Law Review*, 20 (1998)

Hart-Moxon, Kitty, *Return to Auschwitz* (Newark, Quill Press, 2007)

Hastings, Max, *All Hell Let Loose: The World at War 1939–1945* (London, William Collins, 2011)

Hatch, Orrin, Statement on Poland's Controversial Holocaust Bill, Press Release 6 February 2018, Orrin Hatch, United States Senator for Utah, www.hatch.senate.gov/public/index.cfm/2018/2/hatch-statement-on-poland-s-controversial-holocaust-bill

Henry, Patrick, 'The French Catholic Church's Apology', *The French Review*, 72 (6) (1999)

Hirschberger, Gilad, Kende, Anna & Weinstein, Shoshona, 'Defensive representations of an uncomfortable history: The case of Hungary and the Holocaust', *International Journal of Intercultural Relations*, 55 (2016)

Hitler, Adolf, *Mein Kampf* (London, Pimlico, 2014)

Hughes, R. Gerald, 'The Ghosts of Appeasement: Britain and the Legacy of the Munich Agreement', *Journal of Contemporary History*, 48 (4) (2013)

Ispahani, Laleh & Knight, Sarah R., 'Shoring Up a Democracy Under Siege', *Journal of International Affairs*, 71 (1) (Fall/Winter 2017)

Julian Jackson, *The Fall of France: The Nazi Invasion of 1940* (Oxford, Oxford University Press, 2003)

Konovitch, Barry J., 'The Fiftieth Anniversary of the *St. Louis*: What Really Happened', *American Jewish History*, 79 (2) (Winter 1989/1990)

Kopciowski, Adam, 'Anti-Jewish Incidents in the Lublin Region in the Early Years After World War II', *Holocaust. Studies and Materials*, 1 (2008)

Kovács, Henriett & Mindler-Steiner, Ursula K., 'Hungary and the Distortion of Holocaust History: The Hungarian Holocaust Memorial Year 2014', *Politics in Central Europe*, 11 (2) (2015)

Kucia, Marek, Duch-Dyngosz, Marta & Magierowski, Mateusz, 'Anti-Semitism in Poland: survey results and a qualitative study of Catholic communities', *Nationalities Papers*, 42 (1) (2014)

Kunicki, Mikolaj, 'The Red and the Brown: Bolesaw Piasecki, the Polish Communists, and the Anti-Zionist Campaign in Poland, 1967–68', *East European Politics and Societies*, 19 (2) (2005)

Kuromiya, Horoaki, 'The Soviet Famine of 1932–1933 Reconsidered', *Europe-Asia Studies*, 60 (4) (June 2008)

Levi, Trude, 'She isn't Worth a Bullet', in (ed.) *Survival: Holocaust Survivors Tell Their Story* (Laxton, Quill Press, 2003)

Levine, Milka, 'Look After the Children', in (ed.) *Survival: Holocaust Survivors Tell Their Story* (Laxton, Quill Press, 2003)

Lipstadt, Deborah, *Denial: Holocaust History of Trial* (New York, Harper Collins, 2016)

Lipstadt, Deborah, *Denying the Holocaust: The Growing Assault on Truth and Memory* (London, Penguin, 1993)

Lobba, Paolo,' Punishing Denialism Beyond Holocaust Denial: EU Framework Decision 2008/913/JHA and Other Expansive Trends', *New Journal of European Criminal Law*, 5 (1) (2014)

Longerich, Peter, *Goebbels* (London, Bodley Head, 2015)

Mahoney, Kevin A., 'An American Operational Response to a Request to Bomb Rail Lines to Auschwitz', *Holocaust and Genocide Studies*, 25 (3) (Winter 2011)

Mann, Keith, 'Review of Talbot Imlay and Martin Horn, The Politics of Industrial Collaboration During World War II: Ford France Vichy and Nazi Germany', *American Historical Review*, 120 (3) (June 2015)

Marples, David R., 'Ethnic Issues in the Famine of 1932–1933 in Ukraine', *Europe-Asia Studies*, 61 (3) (May 2009)

McCloud, Nedra, 'Oswald Mosley and the British Union of Fascists: A Brief Historiographical Inquiry', *History Compass*, 4 (4) (2006)

Mcnamara, Lawrence, 'History, Memory and Judgement: Holocaust Denial, the History Wars and Law's Problems with the past', *Sydney Law Review*, 26 (2004)

Melamed, Vladimir, 'Organised and Unsolicited Collaboration in the Holocaust: The Multifaceted Ukrainian Context', *East European Jewish Affairs*, 37 (2) (August 2007)

Messenger, David A.,' Beyond War Crimes: Denazification, "Obnoxious" Germans and US Policy in Franco's Spain after the Second World War', *Contemporary European History*, 20 (4) (2011)

Mick, Christoph, 'Incompatible Experiences: Poles, Ukrainians and Jews in Lviv under Soviet and German Occupation, 1939–44', *Journal of Contemporary History*, 46 (2) (April 2011)

Moore, Rebekah, "'A Crime Against Humanity Arguably Without Parallel in European History": Genocide and the "Politics" of Victimhood in Western Narratives of the Ukrainian *Holodomor*', *Australian Journal of Politics and History*, 58 (3) (2012)

Morina, Christina, 'The "Bystander" in Recent Dutch Historiography', *German History*, 32 (1) (March 2014)

Müller, Beate, Trauma, 'Historiography and Polyphony. Adult Voices in the CJHC's Early Post-war Child Holocaust Testimonies', *History & Memory*, 24 (2) (2012)

Neilson, Keith, Orme Sargent, 'Appeasement and British Policy in Europe 1933–39', *Twentieth Century British History*, 21 (1) (2010)

Nord, Philip, *France 1940: Defending the Republic* (London, Yale University Press, 2015),

Overy, Richard, *The Bombing War: Europe 1939–1945* (London, Penguin, 2014)

Owusu-Bempah, Abenaa, 'Prosecuting Hate Crime: Procedural Issues and the Future of the Aggravated Offences', *Legal Studies*, 35 (3) (2015)

Pawlak, Justyna & Kelly, Lidia, 'Polish Lawmakers back Holocaust bill, drawing Israeli outrage, U.S. concern, Reuters (31 January 2018) https://uk.reuters.com/article/uk-israel-poland-usa/polish-lawmakers-back-holocaust-bill-drawing-israeli-outrage-u-s-concern-idUKKBN1FK3ER

Persak, Krzysztof, 'Jedwabne before the Court: Poland's Justice and the Jedwabne Massacre – Investigations and Court Proceedings', 1947–1974, *East European Politics and Societies*, 25 (3) (August 2011)

Peterson, Joan, 'Iterations of Babi Yar', *Journal of Ecumenical Studies*, 46 (4) (Fall 2011)

Pollock, Karen, 'Karen Pollock MBE's response to Holocaust legislation in Poland, Holocaust Educational Trust', www.het.org.uk/news-and-events/697-karen-pollock-mbe-s-response-to-holocaust-legislation-in-poland

Prazmowska, Anita J., 'The Kielce Pogrom 1946 and the Emergence of Communist Power in Poland', *Cold War History*, 2 (2) (2010)

Radchenko, Yuri, 'Accomplices to Extermination: Municipal Government and the Holocaust in Kharkiv, 1941–1942', *Holocaust and Genocide Studies*, 27 (3) (Winter 2013)

Radio Free Europe, 'Poland's President Signs Holocaust Bill', *Radio Free Liberty* (6 February 2018) www.rferl.org/a/poland-president-sign-holocaust-bill-controversy-israel-us-ukraine/29023222.html

Ranki, Vera, 'Goulash-fascism: a socio-legal analysis of Hungarian fascism in the 30s', *Australian Journal of Law and Society*, 6 (1990)

Redvaldsen, David, 'Science Must be the Basis: Sir Oswald Mosley's Political Parties and their Policies on Health, Science and Scientific Racism 1931–1974', *Contemporary British History*, 30 (3) (2016)

Rees, Laurence, *The Holocaust: A New History* (London, Penguin Viking, 2017)

Ripsman, Norrin M. & Levy, Jack L., 'Wishful Thinking or Buying Time? The Logic of British Appeasement in the 1930s', *International Security*, 33 (2) (Fall 2008)

Rothschild, Amanda J., 'Rousing a Response: When the United States Changes Policy Toward Mass Killing', *International Security*, 42 (2) (Fall 2017)

Rousso, Henry, Golsan, Lucy & Golsan, Richard J., 'The Political and Cultural Roots of Negationism in France', *South Central Review*, 23 (1) (Spring 2006)

Ryan Jr., Allan A., 'Klaus Barbie and the United States Government: A Reply to Mr Justice Goldberg', *Harvard Civil Rights–Civil Liberties Law Review*, 20 (1) (1985)

Sanders, Paul, 'Managing Under Duress: Ethical Leadership, Social Capital and the Civilian Administration of the British Channel Islands During the Nazi Occupation, 1940–1945', *Journal of Business Ethics*, Springer, 93 (1) (2010)

Sands, Philippe, *East West Street: On the Origins of Genocide and Crimes Against Humanity* (London, Weidenfield & Nicholson, 2016)

Schloss, Eva, *After Auschwitz* (London, Hodder & Stoughton, 2013)

Schloss, Eva, *Eva's Story* (Peterborough, Castle-Kent, 2014)

Segal, Raz, 'Beyond Holocaust Studies: Rethinking the Holocaust in Hungary', *Journal of Genocide Research*, 16 (1) (2014)

Shepherd, Ben H., *Hitler's Soldiers: The German Army in the Third Reich* (London, Yale University Press, 2016)

Shlapentokh, Dmitry, 'Babi Yar', *Modern Age* (Winter/Spring 2013)

Silverstein, Ken, 'Ford: New Documents Reveal the Close Ties Between Dearborn and the Nazis', *The Nation*, (24 January 2000)

Slayton, Robert, '"Children in Europe Are Europe's Problem!" When the United States turned its back on the Jewish youth of Nazi Germany', *Commentary*, 138 (3) (October 2014)

Smith, Stephen, 'Poland's Holocaust law defies history – and embodies a troubling trend', USC Shoah Foundation (9 February 2018) https://sfi.usc.edu/blog/stephen-smith/polands-holocaust-law-defies-history-and-embodies-troubling-trend

Snyder, Timothy, *Black Earth: The Holocaust as History and Warning* (London, Vintage, 2016)

Spiegel Staff, 'The Dark Continent: Hitler's European Holocaust Helpers', *Der Spiegel* (20 May 2009) www.spiegel.de/international/europe/the-dark-continent-hitler-s-european-holocaust-helpers-a-625824.html

Stone, Dan, *Concentration Camps: A Short History* (Oxford, Oxford University Press: 2017)

Norman Stone, *Hungary: A Short History* (London, Profile Books, 2020)

Sutton, Michael, 'Jews and Christians in Vichy France: New and Renewed Perspectives', *French Politics, Culture & Society*, 35 (3) (Winter 2017)

Tammes, Peter, 'Jewish Immigrants in the Netherlands During the Occupation', *Journal of Interdisciplinary History*, 37 (4) (Spring 2007)

Tammes, Peter, 'Surviving the Holocaust: Socio-demographic Differences Among Amsterdam Jews', *European Journal of Population*, 33 (3) (July 2017)

Tatum, Sophie, CNN Politics, 'Holocaust Denier is Officially the GOP Nominee in Chicago Area House Race' (21 March 2018) https://edition.cnn.com/2018/03/20/politics/holocaust-denier-gop-illinois-third-district/index.html

Teachout, Peter R., 'Making "Holocaust Denial" a Crime: Reflections on European Anti-Negationism Laws from the Perspective of U.S. Constitutional Experience', *Vermont Law Review*, 30 (2006)

Tec, Nechama, 'Diaries and Oral History: Some Methodological Considerations', *Religion and the Arts*, 4 (1) (2000)

Tokarska-Bakir, Joanne, 'Cries of the Mob in the Pogroms in Rzeszów (June 1945), Cracow (August 1945), and Kielce (July 1946) as a Source for the State of Mind of the Participants', *East European Politics and Societies*, 25 (3) (August 2011)

United States Holocaust Memorial Museum, Budapest, https://encyclopedia.ushmm.org/content/en/article/budapest

United States Holocaust Memorial Museum, Deportation of Hungarian Jews, www.ushmm.org/learn/timeline-of-events/1942-1945/deportation-of-hungarian-jews

United States Holocaust Memorial Museum, Kiev and Babi Yar, https://encyclopedia.ushmm.org/content/en/article/kiev-and-babi-yar

United States Holocaust Memorial Museum, Museum Statement on Holocaust Legislation in Poland, 28 January 2018, United States Holocaust Memorial Museum, www.ushmm.org/information/press/press-releases/museum-statement-on-holocaust-legislation-in-poland

United States Holocaust Memorial Museum, The Holocaust in Hungary, www.ushmm.org/information/exhibitions/online-exhibitions/special-focus/the-holocaust-in-hungary

United States Holocaust Memorial Museum, The Holocaust in Ukraine, www.ushmm.org/information/exhibitions/online-exhibitions/special-focus/ukraine

Van Berkel, Marc L. F, 'Holocaust representation in Dutch history textbooks 1960–2010', *Studi sulla Formazione*, 2 (2015)

Van der Boom, Marc, '"The Auschwitz Reservation": Dutch Victims and Bystanders and Their Knowledge of the Holocaust', *Holocaust and Genocide Studies*, 31 (3) (Winter 2017)

Van Pelt, Robert Jan, *The Case for Auschwitz: Evidence from the Irving Trial* (Indiana, Indiana University Press, 2016)

Vasvári, Louise O., 'The Yellow Star and Everyday Life under Exceptional Circumstances: Diaries of 1944–1945 Budapest', *Hungarian Cultural Studies*, 9 (2016)

Vazquez, Martha, 'Poland, the Holocaust, and Free Speech', *The German Law Journal* (March 2018) www.germanlawjournal.com/special-issue-contl-id-in-migration-1/

Vincent, C. Paul, 'The Voyage of the *St. Louis* revisited', *Holocaust and Genocide Studies*, 25 (2) (Fall 2011)

Wachsmann, Nikolaus, *KL: A History of the Nazi Concentration Camps* (London, Little Brown, 2013)

Webster, Paul, 'French Catholics Say Sorry for Persecuting Jews', *The Guardian*, (11 July 1997)

Weiss, Nicholas P., 'Somebody Else's Problem: How the United States and Canada Violate International Law and Fail to Ensure the Prosecution of War Criminals', *Case Western Reserve Journal of International Law*, 45 (2012)

Whitman, James Q., *Hitler's American Model: The United States and the Making of Nazi Race Law* (Woodstock, Oxfordshire, Princeton University Press, 2017),

Wiener Library Blog (8 February 2018) www.wienerlibrary.co.uk/Blog?item=292&returnoffset=0

Williams, A. T., *A Passing Fury: Searching for Justice at the End of World War II* (London, Penguin Random House, 2016)

Wineman, Freda, 'The Red Coated Survivor', in (ed.) *Survival: Holocaust Survivors Tell Their Story* (Laxton, Quill Press, 2003)

Winstone, Martin, *The Dark Heart of Hitler's Europe* (New York, I. B. Tauris, 2015)

Worley, Matthew, 'Why Fascism? Sir Oswald Mosley and the Conception of the British Union of Fascists', *History*, 96 (1) (2011)

Yad Vashem, 'Murder of Hungarian Jewry', www.yadvashem.org/holocaust/about/fate-of-jews/hungary.html#narrative_info

Yad Vashem, 'Names of Righteous by Country', www.yadvashem.org/righteous/statistics.html

Yad Vashem, 'Response to the Law Passed in Poland Yesterday', Press Release (27 January 2018) www.yadvashem.org/press-release/27-january-2018-18-43.html

Yad Vashem, 'Response to the Law Passed in the Polish Senate', Press Release (1 February 2018) www.yadvashem.org/press-release/01-february-2018-10-04.html

Yad Vashem, 'Response Regarding Act of National Remembrance by Poland's President' (6 February 2018) www.yadvashem.org/press-release/06-february-2018-16-02.html

Yad Vashem, Shoah Resource Centre, www.yadvashem.org/untoldstories/documents/Perpetrators/Paul_Blobel.pdf

Index